Political Science: Looking to the Future

Volume Three

Political Science: Looking to the Future

William Crotty, General Editor

Political Science: Looking to the Future

Edited by William Crotty

Volume Three
Political Behavior

Northwestern University Press

Evanston, Illinois

Northwestern University Press
Evanston, Illinois 60201

Copyright © 1991 by Northwestern University Press
All rights reserved. Published 1991
Printed in the United States of America

First printing, 1991

ISBN: 0-8101-0951-4 (cloth)
      0-8101-0952-2 (paper)

Library of Congress Cataloging-in-Publication Data

Political science : looking to the future / edited by William Crotty.
    p.   cm.
    Includes bibliographical references.
    Contents: v. 1. The theory and practice of political science — v.
2. Comparative politics, policy, and international relations — v.
3. Political behavior — v. 4. American institutions.
    ISBN 0-8101-0922-0 (v. 1 : alk. paper). — ISBN 0-8101-0923-9 (v.
1 : pbk. : alk. paper)
    1. Political science.   2. International relations.   3. United
States—Politics and government.   I. Crotty, William J.
JA37.P75   1991
320—dc20   91-7988
                                                               CIP

The paper used in this publication meets the minimum requirements of American
National Standard for Information Sciences—Permanence of Paper for Printed Library
Materials, ANSI Z39.48-1984.

Contents

Acknowledgments

A project of this magnitude involves the efforts of a large number of people. Among those contributing in significant ways to the publication of these volumes have been Alan D. Monroe, Richard P. Farkas, Ruth S. Jones, Catherine E. Rudder, Molly Crotty, Dale D. Vasiliauskas, M. L. Hauch, Lucille Mayer, Laura Olson, and Ada W. Finifter, whose advice in the preliminary stages of the undertaking was of great assistance. The evaluations of the entire manuscript by Jonathan D. Caspar, Leon D. Epstein, and Joseph M. Schwartz were deeply appreciated.

Those at Northwestern University Press who were particularly helpful include: Jonathan Brent, the press's director; Susan Harris, Managing Editor, who oversaw the editorial process; Nan Crotty, Jill Shimabukuro, Amy Schroeder, Rina Ranalli, and Rachel Inger.

To all, we are grateful.

Introduction: Setting the Stage

William Crotty

Political science, like much of academia, is at a crossroads.[1] The causes are many.

First is the problem of generational change. Estimates vary, but one-half or more of the practicing political scientists in the United States are expected to retire roughly by the year 2000 (give or take five years or so). A new generation of academicians will take over, with consequences uncertain. The loss of the postwar giants that shaped the modern era of political science will be keenly felt. It is always tricky to select a few names to illustrate a trend, but the legacy of those such as William H. Riker, Robert A. Dahl, Warren E. Miller, Gabriel A. Almond, Harold Guetzkow, Richard F. Fenno, Jr., Donald R. Matthews, Samuel J. Eldersveld, Dwaine Marvick, Philip E. Converse, Donald E. Stokes, Heinz Eulau, David Easton, Joseph LaPalombara, Harry H. Eckstein, and their colleagues is compelling, as the papers published in these volumes make clear. The list of names is obviously incomplete; yet it does illustrate the magnitude—in terms of intellectual force and disciplinary impact—of those for whom replacements must be found.

Where the discipline is to go, who are to be its intellectual patrons, and what concepts, theories, problem areas, or approaches are likely to dominate its collective consciousness—these are some of the questions that led to the explorations contained in these volumes. The aim is not to answer these questions with a degree of certainty: intellectual dogmatism serves no good purpose, and no one point of view (as will become readily apparent) guided these efforts. The idea was to explore options, ask questions, sort through subfields, and attempt to separate that which may be useful and productive from that which may be old, worn-out, or misleading. Each author had license to do this in the manner he

1

or she found most appropriate. There were no preconditions concerning the points to be raised or the intellectual forces to be addressed. The intent was to raise issues and advance ideas, to force people to think. What does the future hold? How should we in political science prepare for it? What is the best we have to offer, and what can most conveniently be left behind?

Generational concerns are also reflected in the balance of authors chosen to write the subfield essays. Most significantly, each was a scholar of stature in his or her subfield. In addition, however, the likelihood is that most of the contributors should be around for the next several decades to help set in broad relief the future directions the discipline will pursue. Thus, there is a heavier reliance than otherwise might be the case on respectable scholars from middle-level age groups who have already made substantial contributions to their particular specialties. Clearly, many who could have qualified have not been included. This is not the point. Those who were chosen must wrestle in the near future with precisely the types of concerns they address in their papers. The selection strategy was intentional.

These essays will be controversial—some more than others. Each, however, represents an author's (or authors') perspective on the broader questions raised as exemplified by his or her subfield. Each author, in turn, is considered an expert in his or her field with something of importance to say concerning its present condition and its likely future course of development. Their ideas are worth considering; they are meant to stimulate, to serve as a basis for discussion and contention, and to force a reexamination, however modest, of a discipline entering a critical phase in its development. If they accomplish these ends, they will have served their purpose.

Social science, like all of academia, has gone through a difficult period. Support for education, funding of original research, and an emphasis on the qualitative development of knowledge have not been priorities in American culture and politics since at least the late 1960s. The predictable result has been a drop-off in the initiation of research and a stabilization, and even decline, in the number of students seeking Ph.D.s. Teaching and research have not been prized career objectives over the last several decades. It is also probable that, with scholarship support decreased and many universities severely restricted in their hiring, graduate schools have not only had fewer applicants, but the quality of those seeking entrance has not been of the caliber it might be. Law, medical, and business and professional schools may be proving more attractive to the abler undergraduates. Little of this can be directly and quantifiably proven. Still, the difficult times faced by the academic community have been real, and the fears expressed about the long-term consequences reflect those heard on campuses throughout the nation.

In more specific relation to political science, there has also been a mood of disenchantment. The unity, cohesiveness, and commonalities of the field seem to be in eclipse; perhaps they have already been abandoned.[2] This is a common theme in many of the essays that follow. Frequently, the approaches or substantive concerns that have held a subfield together and contributed to its distinctiveness are now in doubt. There is change in the redefinition of boundary areas, in what is significant and should continue to be so in contrast to what has been considered important in the past. The subfields are in flux: some are assuming greater importance; the interest in others is declining. Political science is a discipline in transition.

The question of seeking a broader identity for the field is raised in varying contexts by a number of authors. What distinguishes political science as an integrative whole, a bounded and coherent intellectual pursuit? What makes the discipline distinctive? What constitutes its particular problems? What should be the central focus and common bonds among its practitioners? These concerns are addressed in differing contexts and, in particular, served as the basis for those contributing to Volume 1, *The Theory and Practice of Political Science,* arguably the most contentious of the four. These questions are the mega-issues, the ones that concern all of us as practicing academicians. Whether it is preferable to achieve the coherence, stability, and self-assurance that some found in the past, or whether a more eclectic, exploratory, and innovative practice is preferable is debatable. Whether conceptual approaches ("power," "politics," "markets," "representation," "democracy"), subject matter (the study of government, institutions, political behavior), or definitional guides ("the authoritative allocation of values," "who gets what, when, and how") are the best indicators of relevance is also arguable.

Both approaches have their costs: in one, smugness, perhaps, and a hint as to what can or "should" be done, contrasted in the other with a disparate, shotgunlike scattering of interests that raises questions about the interests or bonds that political scientists share. What distinguishes political scientists from sociologists, economists, historians, or anthropologists (or, for that matter, from those who work in professional schools of law, journalism, management, or policy)? Should distinctions among them be made? Can they communicate intellectually with each other? What do they have to share, borrow, or contribute that is distinctive to their respective disciplines? Or, conversely, are those valid concerns? Some believe that each subfield should follow its own road. Eventually, they argue, all—or at least knowledge writ large—should prosper. The role of graduate education—what skills and perspectives are transmitted to future generations of practitioners—in such a scheme is unclear—a further sign of a discipline's indecision. Many believe that this indecision typifies the mood that has been progressively enveloping the discipline over the last generation.

The questions raised in the essays that follow are basic. No effort has been made to supply answers—should they even exist at this point in time—on which the balance of contributors might agree. The purpose is to encourage critical thought at a convenient summing-up point in a discipline's development.

Finally, a note on what the essays that follow are not. They are not intended to be comprehensive reviews of the literature in any given area.[3] In fact, the authors were specifically asked not to do this. These instructions, however, did not exclude the compiling of bibliographies to many of the essays that might provide a reasonable starting point for serious inquiry into the subfield being discussed. Many of these are extensive.

The authors were also asked not to restrict themselves to the need to present a balanced or thorough examination of their respective fields. This type of directive is a little unusual in academia. One result may be the intentional omission of works of stature, the contributions of major scholars. The editor, not the authors, takes full responsibility for such deficiencies. Rather than comprehensiveness, fairness, or balance, we wanted ideas—a freshness of perspective, a personal signature on the observations made. The goal has been to raise issues of significance for discussion and debate. Where are we? Where are we going? What could prove useful to us as we move toward an uncertain future? These are the comments that unite the chapters.

The papers were commissioned for a special series of theme panels held at the 1989 annual meeting of the Midwest Political Science Association. At that time, William Crotty was serving as president of the association and assumed the principal responsibility for organizing these panels. Alan D. Monroe served as program chair for the meeting. In addition, significant support was provided by Richard P. Farkas, then executive director of the Midwest Political Science Association, and Catherine E. Rudder, executive director of the American Political Science Association.

The idea behind the theme panels was to have a distinguished practitioner in a field prepare a paper on his or her specialty written in the context described above. A panel was then built around each paper and included three to four discussants, also individuals of prominence in the subfield, who commented on the paper, challenging its assumptions and often advancing alternative explanations, relevant criteria, or scenarios for future exploration. Most of the individuals who contributed in these ways are acknowledged by the authors in their essays.

The papers were then read before a group presumed to be expert in most cases, or at least interested enough as teachers or researchers in the area under discussion to participate in such a specialized critique. In general, the sessions were well attended. Surprisingly, perhaps, many of the panels had standing-room-only audiences, and in a few cases the meeting rooms were unable to accommodate all those wishing to attend. In most cases, too, the exchanges were lively, perhaps indicating that the issues being addressed and the questions raised reflected generally felt concerns in the discipline.

The authors were asked to incorporate into their essays the points they considered most relevant from the resulting exchanges and, specifically, to address in some fashion any issues that might appear to have been deficiencies in their original presentations. In some cases, the editor also advanced suggestions, but always with the understanding that the author's judgment as to relevance and importance, and the issues and themes that he or she preferred to emphasize, took precedence. No two essayists address the same questions within the same format. Some of the papers are lengthy; others are relatively brief. Some are opinionated; others preferred to mute their approach while allowing their personal preferences to remain clear. Some are cautiously optimistic; others are not. Some attempted to document their arguments extensively; others opted for a simpler thematic presentation. All in all, though, we trust that the essays taken together serve to highlight many of the most significant issues facing the discipline today, and that they provide a starting point for a serious discussion about where we as political scientists now are, what we have to contribute, and where we, as a discipline, may be headed.

IN THIS VOLUME . . .

Norman R. Luttbeg ("Political Attitudes: A Historical Artifact or a Concept of Continuing Importance in Political Science?") begins with a provocative argument, a direct challenge to the current research on political attitudes and the meaning it has for understanding the operation of democratic governments. Luttbeg looks at two disciplines: psychology and political science. He argues that while each has taken separate developmental roads in attitudinal research, neither has been successful in linking attitudinal studies to actual behavior. This failure is more significant for political science, given the nature of the questions it seeks to answer and its concern with the values, motivations, and behavior of both political elites and mass publics. Luttbeg's assessment of the literature is incisive, as would be expected from one who has published extensively in the field; his arguments innovative. He decries the dearth of experimental and exploratory studies in the discipline. The discipline has also shown an increasing willingness to borrow from for-

mal theorizing and economic modeling than from psychological perspectives. Attitudinal analysis often relies on what people say as against
what they actually do; the two are not necessarily equatable in such research.

Luttbeg concludes with several challenging observations that are
likely to prove both discomfiting to practitioners in the field and controversial. His main advice would be to concentrate on the behavior of
individuals, on attitudes directly relevant to and predictive of this behavior, and on the methodologies needed to explore the linkage.
Throughout, Luttbeg keeps his focus on the broader issues that need
exploring and the ties that relate attitudinal research to an understanding of broader-system (i.e., democratic government) values and operations.

M. Margaret Conway ("The Study of Political Participation: Past,
Present, and Future") argues that the study of political participation is
as basic and long-standing as the study of politics. Yet the quality of
knowledge is limited in scope and explanatory power, and thus less useful than one might assume, a fact of life apparent to anyone familiar
with the field. It could be said that a subset of participation—voting—
is far more systematically and comprehensively researched, cumulatively examined, and understood within a social science context than is
the broader conception of participation.

Conway addresses the development of the most significant research
in the field, including some of the more innovative of the recent theorizing and explorations. She examines the problems of measuring participation, which are substantial; contextual influences on levels of
participation; and the "puzzle of nonparticipation," a continuing concern of social scientists. She concludes by offering an agenda for future
research that highlights the need for integrative theorizing and the design of studies specifically intended to test such theorizing. The field
needs a unity, a comparability of research efforts, and a focus on dominant problems that it does not at present possess.

Voting behavior is the one area that is the most cumulatively developed and potentially the most representative in political science of the
best standards of social scientific inquiry. It is also one of the most frequently critiqued. Jack Dennis ("The Study of Electoral Behavior")
traces the intellectual evolution of the subfield. He relates it, in associations often not explicitly examined, both to the other social and political institutions in a society that affect voting decisions and to the
operations of a democracy.

Dennis focuses primarily on the theoretical models, guiding concepts, and most highly developed relationships to sustain his investigation of the field. He explores the contributions sociological,
psychological, and economic approaches have made to explaining vot-

ing behavior, contrasting the differences in perspective and the limits of each, as well as the ways in which they have influenced thinking in the field. He critiques rational actor models and their shortcomings—as he notes, "rationality" can have many meanings—and proposes specific ways in which the approach, recognizing its ambiguities, could be more useful. He also reviews the debate on the party identification-based model put forth by the Michigan School and the performance criteria emphasis for explaining voting favored by some.

Dennis concludes by proposing an opening-up of thinking in this area to take account of electoral contexts, processes, institutions, and leadership influences. Elections serve a variety of functions for a political system; their more general significance can be underestimated. Voting studies appear to have opted for a narrow-gauge approach. Dennis writes, "What this field perhaps lacks . . . are those who, while understanding well the operational problems that data collection and analysis impose in this area, can nonetheless rise above it to pose new modes of thinking about the phenomena of elections at a purely theoretical level."

The study of the consequences that political communication practices and institutions have for political action is, surprisingly, a somewhat new area of political science concern. Doris A. Graber ("Media and Politics") describes the origins of this area of interest and points out its limitations. These include a reliance on overly cautious, limited, and conservative research strategies; the scarcity of courses and programs of study in a subfield uneasily wedded to the discipline; a narrowness of perspective that fails to utilize developments in related disciplines; and an overemphasis on the study of media influence in elections.

Graber explores the themes that political scientists have researched most fully and the quality and significance of the studies executed. The major areas of research concern encompass: what factors determine media content; substantive emphases in the media; how audiences process media information; and the impact of the media on the governmental process. She also evaluates the methodologies employed in the research: this is an area particularly susceptible to an eclecticism of approaches. The analysis indicates where future research efforts might profitably be focused.

The work to date in the problem areas covered is tentative, limited in number or scope, or unrelated to corroborating research on similar questions. Particularly needed, Graber argues, are macro-level investigations of the systemic effects of the media in a society. This is not the type of question usually explored. The field is rich in opportunities. It is a young one and, unlike few others in the social sciences, still open both to integrative and fundamentally transforming work that could set the foundations for future development.

Pamela Johnston Conover ("Political Socialization: Where's the Politics?") reviews the history of a subfield in trouble, one consistently attracting less and less attention, and one in which she notes the critics may outnumber the researchers. It is a sorry state for an area of inquiry that held so much promise for contributing to an understanding of the learning processes that condition democratic acceptance and performance. The subfield is new; most would date it to the 1960s. The early studies were exciting. Unfortunately, both the volume and innovativeness of the research contributions have declined precipitously as the models and assumptions that underlay the most influential of the research efforts have been called into question.

The principal thematic strains in political socialization center on the views and politically relevant learning processes undergone during maturation and presumed to be influential in developing affective political support for a governing system. The schools and the family were the particular targets of research interest. By the 1980s, this thrust had fallen into disfavor.

A second major approach has been to explore the learning processes that individuals undergo in preparation for assuming particular roles within a society. Building on the ideas of sociologist Herbert Hyman, researchers focused on the role of socialization as it impacted on the citizen as voter. Here the emphasis is placed on a developmental learning process that can be studied in adults and is more focused and bounded than the broader efforts to capture the way in which citizenship values are internalized.

Conover sorts through the definitional problems in the subfield, specifying its major concepts and their referent terms. She distinguishes, for example, between "political learning," an inclusive term meant to cover both deliberate and less conscious internalizing processes, and "political socialization," the acquisition of citizen values and roles that help individuals adapt to a society. What she, and others, have found troublesome about the approach is an implicit status-quo bias in favor of a political system's stability and maintenance. She tries to steer around such interpretations by specifying the nature of the ends the research should serve and the questions that should be investigated. A rebirth of interest in socialization/political learning studies (recognizing that the two are not interchangeable) must accept the realities of a political world in which the views of authority figures dominate and where conflict is a normal by-product of social life. Most of all, there is a need to reintroduce a sense of politics into research undertakings.

Political psychology, Betty Glad reports ("Political Psychology: Where Have We Been? Where Are We Going?"), has had its ups and downs. At present, it may be experiencing a creative reinvigoration. Glad reintroduces us to the subfield's early concern in the post–World

War II years with the psychological roots of fascism and totalitarianism. She describes the impact of the monumental *The Authoritarian Personality* (1950), a combination of insight, social science, and psychoanalytic research that asked and attempted to answer questions of fundamental societal importance. A series of significant undertakings followed, using a variety of methodologies employed to assess both macro-level and micro-level concerns. The early research held in common a psychological or psychoanalytic perspective that addressed questions of values, personal needs, or affiliative ties with democratic systems. In addition, a number of psychological biographies began to develop the relationship between personal drives and politically relevant activities.

By the late 1960s, these strains had pretty much exhausted themselves. At this point the turn toward an emphasis on decision-making and the application of rational modeling explicitly and self-consciously excluded emotions, personality, and values in explaining actions. The reason for the deemphasis of psychological influences included: the methodological difficulties involved in measuring such dimensions; the increasing emphasis in the social sciences upon, or the need for, hard data (psychological and especially psychoanalytic research are considered "soft" ventures); and the harsh critical reaction to some of the earlier works. Many social scientists do not feel comfortable with findings based on highly interpretative and personalized insights into human behavior. This may constitute the fundamental problem. As Glad indicates, there are no commonly accepted objective standards against which to measure such analyses. In retrospect, it is curious how unsympathetic many academicians have been to the advances in psychological research.

Nonetheless, the research orientation persevered and by the 1980s was again producing imaginative approaches to problems in a number of substantive areas, from international relations and foreign-policy decision-making to studies of environmental beliefs, postmodern value structures, and the psychological bonds of group movements. Psychological analyses have particular relevance for studying elite behavior in times of crisis (for example, the U.S. response to the Cuban missile crisis).

Glad closes by advocating an increased emphasis on experimental research; a testing of theoretical approaches in field situations where outcomes are uncertain and values are in question; and a renewed interest in psychobiography. The latter might encourage more comparative work (for example, analyses of different leaders assessing the same situation at identical points in time or the performances of different actors in the same situation and confronting much the same type of challenge). There is a need to deal self-consciously with levels of analysis problems and the reductionism inherent in such research. There is a need also for political scientists more generally to accept the complexity of human behavior and the importance that individual and idiosyncratic events have for understanding political phenomena. The bottom line is that political psychology has something of significance to contribute to an understanding of political processes, a point not always appreciated by social scientists.

David C. Leege, Joel A. Lieske, and Kenneth D. Wald ("Toward Cultural Theories of American Political Behavior: Religion, Ethnicity and Race, and Class Outlook") attempt something a little different. They draw on a strain that is gaining favorable attention in the discipline: an emphasis on cultural contexts in explaining political behavior. The authors argue that particular settings condition individual performance. Cultural factors set bounds for behavior, impose meaning upon it, and give birth to the values and motivations that direct actors. The cultural orientation is not new in political science; it has been given varying degrees of weight in the voting studies done between 1940 and 1966. It is the authors' contention, however, that it has not received the attention it should. Economic and rational-actor modeling perspectives, in particular, deemphasize such concerns. This is unfortunate. If properly developed, culture-measurable indicators such as religion, race, ethnic association, class, and region could provide a more inclusive framework for understanding voting behavior and political actions in general. The group and social contexts that predominate in the cultural research tradition contribute much toward explaining political behavior.

The authors examine a broad range of research undertakings in developing their arguments. They point to a series of comparative cross-national and longitudinal empirical investigations to illustrate the influence of cultural considerations in explaining behavior. The quantitative historians, in particular, as well as historians in general, have long recognized ethnocultural dimensions as powerful explanatory tools in accounting for the behavioral patterns they have traced. Political scientists have been slow to draw upon such findings or to develop their own research along compatible lines.

Religion can serve as an example of the relevance of cultural factors for understanding political behavior. The church as a societal agent shapes values and directs the political actions of entire communities of believers, a facet of American life evident in the nation's political movements from the nineteenth century through the civil rights marches of the 1960s. Fundamentalist evangelical Protestantism helped to shape the main currents of political debate during recent decades over such issues as abortion, pornography, family values, morality, and the schoolteaching of creationism. The realization of the kingdom of God on earth, as interpreted by various sects, has provided a vocal political base with which politicians at all levels have chosen to identify. Cultural symbols have political utility. Controversies over cultural values have dominated recent campaigns. These ethnocultural symbols and attachments differ with party (currently to the advantage of the Republicans), group, region, and even locality.

The authors demonstrate that cultural analysis continues to have relevance for explaining American political behavior. The mixture of social groups in this country is in constant transition. The multicultural strains in the society, and assumedly their relevance for understanding political life, if anything, are increasing.

The authors end with a discussion of integrative cultural theories as they relate to the more familiar theorizing on American political behavior. An emphasis on cultural forces in behavioral research is liable to become more pronounced; in effect, a tradition is being reclaimed. This essay reintroduces the concept, reviews works in which it has provided a useful explanatory tool, and discusses questions of conceptualization, operationalization, and measurement. The focus is broader than that often encountered in behavioral analyses. Explicit conceptual and methodological problems are confronted in an attempt to capture cultural dimensions in inquiries. Without them, however, the tale is at best only partly told.

The volume concludes with brief biographical sketches of the authors.

NOTES

1. William G. Boyer and Julie Ann Sosa, *Prospects for Faculty in the Arts and Sciences: A Study of Factors Affecting Demand and Supply, 1987 to 2012* (Princeton, N.J.: Princeton University Press, 1989).

2. Gabriel A. Almond, *A Divided Discipline* (San Mateo, Calif.: Sage Publications, 1989), and idem, "Separate Tables: Schools and Sects in Political Science?" *PS* 21:828–42. See also Kristen Monroe, Gabriel A. Almond, John Gunnell, Ian Shapiro, George Graham, Benjamin Barber, Kenneth Shepsle, and Joseph Cropsey, "The Nature of Contemporary Political Science: A Roundtable Discussion," *PS: Political Science and Politics* 23 (1):34–43.

3. These are needed and welcome. See, as examples, Ada W. Finifter, ed., *Political Science: The State of the Discipline* (Washington, D.C.: American Political Science Association, 1983), and Fred I. Greenstein and Nelson W. Polsby, eds., *Handbook of Political Science,* 4 vols. (Reading, Pa.: Addison-Wesley Publishing Company, 1975). See also Herbert S. Weisberg, *Political Science: The Science of Politics* (New York: Agathon Press, 1986). A guide to the relevant literature critiquing the discipline can be found in Donald M. Freeman's "The Making of a Discipline" in volume 1.

REFERENCES

Almond, Gabriel A. 1989a. *A Divided Discipline*. San Mateo, Calif.: Sage Publications.

———. 1989b. "Separate Tables: Schools and Sects in Political Science?" *PS* 21:828–42.

Boyer, William G., and Julie Ann Sosa. 1989. *Prospects for Faculty in the Arts and Sciences: A Study of Factors Affecting Demand and Supply, 1987 to 2012*. Princeton, N.J.: Princeton University Press.

Finifter, Ada W., ed. 1983. *Political Science: The State of the Discipline*. Washington, D.C.: American Political Science Association.

Greenstein, Fred I., and Nelson W. Polsby, eds. 1975. *Handbook of Political Science*. 8 vols. Reading, Pa.: Addison-Wesley.

Monroe, Kristen, Gabriel A. Almond, John Gunnell, Benjamin Barber, Kenneth Shepsle, Joseph Cropsey, George Graham, and Ian Shapiro. 1990. "The Nature of Contemporary Political Science: A Roundtable Discussion." *PS: Political Science and Politics* 23 (1):34–43.

Weisberg, Herbert F., ed. 1986. *Political Science: The Science of Politics*. New York: Agathon Press.

1

Political Attitudes: A Historical Artifact or a Concept of Continuing Importance in Political Science?

Norman R. Luttbeg

Concern with the concept of attitude began in the 1920s in the field of psychology. It continues to be a concept of great importance both to psychology and political science, as well as other disciplines. In psychology and political science, attitude research has different patterns or histories of development. I will argue that the two disciplines have sought to cope with the major problem in attitude research, that of lack of correspondence between attitudes and behavior, differently but with equal lack of success. In psychology there have apparently been clear periods of development, but there is some justification in saying that the progression from one period to the next has avoided tackling the problem of attitudes not predicting behavior. I do not believe that political science has the luxury psychology does of ignoring the failure to be able to predict behavior, as many of our concerns, derived from democratic theory, necessitate explaining behaviors, such as turnout, civil strife, reelection of incumbents, and so on. Thus, much of the exciting research on attitudes that continues in psychology gives little guidance to our

I would like to thank the discussants of this paper at the meetings, Stanley Feldman, Michael S. Margolis, and Pamela Johnston Conover, for their helpful comments. Several present and former colleagues, Jan Leighly, Patricia Hurley, Michael Gant, and Michael Martinez helped me with early drafts.

use of the concept, especially the concern with predicting behavior. My position in this paper is that we must encourage greater concern with the link between attitudes and behavior, at least when applied to large representative public samples, and that if this fails perhaps we should abandon the concept of attitude.

THE DEVELOPMENT OF ATTITUDE RESEARCH IN PSYCHOLOGY

In the *Handbook of Social Psychology*, McGuire (1985) outlines three periods of social psychological interest in attitudes. They include: (1) attitude measurement, of great concern in the 1920s and 1930s and resulting in the still prevalently used Likert scale, which is supposed to measure both cognitive and affective elements of an attitude; (2) attitude change, of concern in the 1950s and 1960s; and (3) attitude structure or systems, which continues to be of concern since the early 1980s. McGuire sees several causes for these changes in perspective among social psychologists dealing with attitudes. Chief among them are: (1) "as social science topics become more applied to servicing the needs of policymakers, there is an exodus of innovative researchers to fresh (and safer?) topics"; and (2) "premature quantification that progressively smothers a fashionable scientific topic" (237).

Although McGuire does not make such an emphasis, I think there are sociology of knowledge elements here. Focusing on attitude change rather than attitude measurement treats the concept of attitude as a dependent variable, and in turn this has several felicitous implications. For example, the sources of attitude change can be explored, shifting the focus of research either to controlled experiments wherein various stimuli to change attitudes can be introduced, or to time series in which events themselves induce change. Also avoided is the question of precise scalar placement of individuals on an attitude and the associated issues of reliability and validity. One merely need note change between time 1 and time 2 in the attitude as expressed by the individual. And most centrally, I think, the focus on attitude change avoids the lack of correspondence between attitudes and behaviors, which is my central concern here.

Should we expect or do we need any correspondence between what people say and what they do? This question is taken from Deutscher's (1973) book by that name. Contrary to his thesis, is it possible conceptually that some attitudes, perhaps even most attitudes, lack associated behaviors? This may well be true. But, more importantly, I would argue that there are few attitudes of much interest to political science that are unassociated with behavior. Certainly, in a democracy we do not expect that the government will respond to public opinion on an issue, such as handgun registration or abortion, if public dissatisfaction with the actual policy enacted never materializes in terms of some behavior, such as voting against incumbents, supporting them less ardently, failing to vote if incumbents have no viable opponents, or at some point showing lack of support either for office holders or for the institutions themselves.

The most recent concern in social psychology with attitude structure, McGuire argues, assumes bidirectionality, the same attitude being seen both as dependent and independent, and seeks "information rich" if "unwieldly open-ended responses that call for content analysis" (238). It stresses the idiosyncratic structure of attitudes for each individual. This distances the researcher from unresolved issues in attitude measurement and further removes concern with predicting behavior.

ATTITUDES AS SYSTEMS IN PSYCHOLOGY
Miniature Knowledge Structures

It is, of course, in the most recent era of interest in attitudes, focusing on attitude systems or miniature knowledge structures, that the greatest advances are presently being made in psychology. Many names are used for the related if not identical concepts in the new literature of attitude systems. Among them are: "miniature knowledge structures" (McGuire 1985), morsels (Lane 1962, 353), schemata (Barlett 1932), scripts (Abelson 1981), prototypes (Rosch 1977), and initially, a set of inferential assumptions for inductive reasoning (Piaget 1930). Fundamental to these conceptualizations are individuals personally testing hypotheses on the basis of information available to them, with the attitudes systems being the set of confirmed hypotheses for each individual (Kinder 1983).

McGuire focuses on one attitude, ideology, as an example of the troubles in earlier attitude research that resulted in the new perspective of attitude as systems (248–49). Of course, this is an apt choice, given the concern within political science for this concept. McGuire presents eight kinds of evidence supporting the fact that people are nonideological: (1) inability to give correct reasons for attitudinal preferences (Nisbett and Wilson 1977; Wright and Rip 1981) and ignorance of facts (40 percent think Israel is Arab [Hechinger 1979]); (2) prevalent "no opinions" on issues; (3) instability in attitudes expressed (latest, Mischel 1984); (4) the impact on attitudes of trivial changes in the wording of questions (Schuman, Kalton, and Ludwig 1983) and their order (Schuman and Presser 1981); (5) the low correspondence between cognitions and affect (Converse 1964; Lin 1974); (6) the low correlations between attitudes of similar content (Veroff, Douvan, and Kulka 1981); (7) attitudes often being held which are in conflict with self-interest (Converse et al. 1980; Kinder and Sears 1981); and (8) conflict between general and specific positions on issues, such as losing faith in institutions but not in their members (Ladd and Lipset 1980) or favoring capital punishment but not in specific cases (Ellsworth 1982). Of course, most of these findings are not only familiar to political scientists but also have equal application to other political attitudes. Party identification would seem to be the exception.

Naturally there are counterarguments and findings that see more ideological aptitude within the electorate. These include: (1) inadequate measurement (McGuire 1981; Achen 1975; Erikson 1978), in which the opinions of respondents exist but are poorly measured; (2) pressure to give an opinion yielding random responses (Judd, Krosnick, and Milburn 1981); and (3) "miniature knowledge structures," which are most evident in in-depth interviews. We have already noted that within social psychology these concerns have encouraged the movement toward studying attitude systems.

Zaller and Feldman (1988) have completed an interesting study that seeks to resolve whether measurement problems account for unstable public opinions in surveys. They characterize Achen's (1975) initial concern that the questions asked by survey researchers were subject to substantial measurement error as "vague questions." Converse's (1964) alternative explanation, that instability in public opinions is the result of nonopinions that did not exist prior to the individual's being asked, they call "vague opinions." Their experiments find that less vague, longer, and more detailed questions do improve the stability of opinions for many, but that some respondents show just the opposite pattern. They argue that respondents do not reveal preformed preferences to questions but construct responses from the "diverse considerations in their heads" (25). The salience of some of these considerations is seen as resulting in various "effects" on responses. Interestingly, although they do not assess the behavior correspondence between the short, presumably vague, "top-of-the-head" expressed attitudes and the longer, less vague, "stop-and-think" expressed attitudes, they note that Wilson, Dunn, Kraft, and Lisle (forthcoming) find the vague, "top-of-the-head" questions to be substantially better predictors of behavior than the "improved" questions (21). It seems evident that it would be rash to assume that attitude instability is merely measurement error. As with students taking multiple-choice tests, the first response may be better than the considered response. Also see Zaller's (1988 and 1985) further considerations of the "survey response."

Cognitive Psychology

Although cognitive psychology may or may not have separate roots from attitude research, there is little if any conceptual incongruity between the research done now in attitude systems and that done in cognitive psychology. Both stress mentalistic concepts. Since the 1950s, cognitive psychology has seen both exciting new research and another historical explanation for the failure of psychology to deal with the absence of correspondence between attitudes and behaviors. As Knapp (1986) notes, the very act of considering the information-processing of an organism runs counter to Skinner's behaviorism and the assumption that one need only consider stimulus and response. Certainly, one can at least partially understand cognitive psychologists' disinterest in behavior given the long fight that was needed to establish the propriety of even studying cognitions. Political science fortunately has no such dues to pay.

In their introduction to political scientists of this subfield, Lau and Sears (1986) see *The American Voter* as a descendant of cognitive consistency theory and work related to it as frozen in time relative to the evolution of thought in social psychology. They urge political scientists to move on, and there is evidence that some political scientists are using the more current information-processing and schema theories that have currency in social psychology. But, certainly, such ideas have not been fully utilized. Their volume, which gives an excellent introduction to cognitive psychology, continues to ignore the question of dealing with any public behavior other than that of coping with information. And from the beginning of voting research, the public has always been noted to have enormously well-developed and effective psychological processes to cope with information (Berelson, Lazarsfeld, and McPhee 1954, 215–33).

Certainly other concepts in cognitive psychology have important implications for the issue of assessing the true opinions of the general public. Graesser (1985) notes that there is a growing interest across many fields of study in the topic of questioning, or how questions are asked, comprehended, and answered. Most of this research has focused on artificial intelligence and on developing computer programs that can "understand" narratives fed to them and answer questions based on that understanding. Insight into human understanding and answering is thereby gained. It seems excitingly possible to view an answer to our surveys as such an act. This research may guide us to questions that are correctly answered by respondents who understand issues, or to be able to know from answers when opinions are based on understanding. In short, there is exciting promise for political behavior research in cognitive psychology and in the focus on attitude systems. But, to date, it has done little to resolve the lack of correspondence between attitudes and behavior.

IMPLICATIONS OF FOCUSING
ON ATTITUDES AS SYSTEMS

Several implications seem evident in the focus on attitude systems. The intense focus on a limited number of people with in-depth interviews leaves researchers unable to make generalizations concerning the content of the opinions of the general public. This is evident in Lane (1962) and Graber (1984). While it is conceivable that instrumentation improvements in shorter, closed-ended questionnaires might be directed by the knowledge gained with the in-depth interviews, I am unaware of any such efforts. In fact, the more satisfying insight into individuals that is part of in-depth interviewing and the frustrations of survey research on attitudes may make such instrumentation efforts seem retrograde to potential researchers. But to the degree that the focus on attitudes, at least in political science, derives from an interest in characterizing public opinion, the lack of external generalization inherent in the methodology of attitude as systems precludes saying much about the content of public opinion.

Second, and related of course, is the lack of efforts to improve larger sample instrumentation. Because of the preoccupation of academics with attitude systems, criticism of the methods of polling—and indeed even of the most professionally completed survey research—is too often not forthcoming. To be sure, the discomfiting findings of Schuman and Presser (1981) are broadly cited. The lack of certainty as to whether there have been changes in public opinion or merely changes in question wording resulted in this association's journal (May 1978) focusing on two important articles (Bishop, Tuchfarber, and Oldendick 1978; and Sullivan, Pierson, and Marcus 1978). And a two-volume monograph, *Surveying Subjective Phenomena*, has been published, with the editors characterizing it as not the first to deal with questions of the reliability, validity, and relevance of survey research (Turner and Martin 1984). In the meantime, the mass media purchases numerous "polls" from an ever-growing polling industry and broadly reports the results. In the absence of academic criticism, this reifies the poll results in the minds of both the public and its elected representatives as public opinion, which the representative should, if not must, obey to be reelected. All too often we hear that the public has "spoken" in the polls and that the pay raise is dead, assault rifles are to be banned, and drug crime is to be stopped even if it has to be accomplished by declaring martial law.

Third is the issue of behavior. The conative or active aspect of attitudes, the propensity to action, is still conceptualized as the third element in attitudes, although Marcus (1988) suggests that the tripartite conception of attitude is being abandoned. "Why study attitudes at all?" McGuire asks (251), if one is interested in behavior. "Social psychology's long preoccupation with attitudes is surprising since the low correlations between attitudes and behaviors have been the scandal of the field for a half-century," he states (251). True, present attitudes may predict future behaviors better than present behaviors, as attitudes are less subject to changing situations and can be measured more reliably (251). But "only . . . within quite limited circumstances do attitudes account for more than 10 percent of behavioral variance except when they are correlated not with behavior per se but with self-reports of intention to behave (Albrecht and Carpenter 1976; Fishbein and Ajzen 1975 and 1976; Songer-Nocks, 1976)" (252).

While it is not uncommon for the tie between a behavior and an attitude to be taken as validating the attitude (Dawes and Smith 1985), it is possible to argue that the expectation of correspondence is unduly high or that the situations in which both the behavior and the opinion are measured must be substantially the same. Dawes and Smith (1985) give a good discussion of this. This brings to mind the "funnel of causality" concept in *The American Voter* (1960), in which close approximation to the act of voting, such as asking the individual how she was going to vote just prior to entering the voting booth, was seen as yielding the best prediction of her vote. My point is not to dismiss these ideas but to encourage their use in all attitude research, and to suggest that even with such sensitivity, correspondence thus far is not high.

The focus on attitude systems, being what McGuire calls a "mediational" (241) or what others have called a "mentalistic" concept, tends to remove the concern with behavior. A researcher focusing on how individuals process information need not consider behavior as well as attitudes. Similarly, the interest in differentiating between the liberal and the conservative need not consider behavioral differences.

Political scientists have sought to tie this particular attitude, ideology, to one particular act of relevance, voting for president or, to be most correct in expressing my view, to the answers that respondents give as to which presidential candidate they supported. Their success has varied greatly. As my coauthor, Robert Erikson (1988), notes in trying to keep peace between coauthors and his wife: "Reasonable scholars have disagreed on the role of ideology in voting behavior. Compare Luttbeg and Gant (1985), 'The Failure of Liberal-Conservative Ideology as a Cognitive Structure,' Tedin (1987) 'Political Ideology and the Vote,' and Knight (1985) 'Ideology in the 1980 Election: Political Sophistication Matters.' "

Finally and most importantly, to me at least, it is hard to see how an elected representative would give expression to constituent opinions if they were so idiosyncratic and required such thorough consideration to be understood, much less aggregated. It seems unlikely that we could discover how such systems would be aggregated in order to speak of a public attitude system, much less where a representative would gain financial support to pay for the assessment of constituents' attitudes by using expensive, in-depth interviews.

DEVELOPMENTS IN POLITICAL SCIENCE IN ATTITUDE RESEARCH

Certainly it is possible to find counterparts in political science to each of the periods and concerns with attitudes noted by McGuire. Kinder (1983), in fact, urges political science to move into the attitude systems period. But I would suggest that all basically coexist at once, with the predominance of work being somewhere between the attitude measurement and attitude change phases. Certainly the concept of schema is increasingly to be found in our literature (Conover and Feldman 1981; Gant and Davis 1984; and Hagner and Pierce 1982), and probably the most full-blown use of it is in Graber's *Processing the News* (1987). There also is work in attitude change, some of which fails to hold question wording constant, thus meaning that noted differences may well be exclusively the impact of changes in wording (see Nie, Verba, and Petrocik 1979; Bishop, Tuchfarber, and Oldendick 1978; and Sullivan, Piereson, and Marcus 1978). But there is still work on measurement, such as that of Aldrich, Niemi, Rabinowitz, and Rhode (1982), on using branching questions of the political party identification type in assessing public opinion, and Lodge and Tursky (1981), who use magnitude scaling.

It is provocative to consider why, in comparison to social psychology, political science has not shown clear periods of research interest in attitudes. I should clearly note here that I am speculating. Perhaps the tie between attitudes and behavior is too important in political science to move to concepts of attitudes that deemphasize the notion of propensity to action. In the area of mass behavior, few acts are publicly visible. Our studies of participation find that only the act of voting is at all common, and, at the individual level, only the act of voting is publicly visible, not the direction of that vote. It has always seemed curious to me, given the disparity between those claiming to have voted and actual votes cast, that we believe what people say about which party or candidate they supported rather than studying how they actually did vote. Of course, only in the aggregate can we know how people voted. At any rate, we continually see hypothetical action questions such as "If the election were today, would you vote for X or for Y?" or "What would you do were a type of person to approach you in the dark, to move into your neighborhood, etc.?" Such hypothetical behavior is all we have.

Certainly the attitude of party identification has spoiled us, as it is fairly predictive of how people claim to have voted. It persists as the best explanation of which political party's candidate people say they supported for president (DeClercq, Hurley, and Luttbeg 1975; Gant and Luttbeg 1990) and is cited as the best correspondence between attitudes and behavior (Dawes and Smith 1985, citing Abelson 1968). I have always wondered why attitude/behavior correspondences are not studied comparatively, for example, comparing those between religious identification and church attended, or those between sports team supported and games watched on television and games attended.

Perhaps it is a disciplinary bias against controlled or even field experiments that keeps us from moving wholeheartedly into attitudes system or structure research. Although there are exceptions, few experimentally based articles find publication in our journals; it is common to dismiss psychology as the study of college sophomores; and in-depth interviewing such as that by Lane (1962) often elicits derisive comments, such as whether he has brought along one of his subjects in a cage. Since such research is fundamental to the development of the attitudes-as-systems school, our aversion to the method discourages our tagging along.

The continuing success of the Center for Political Studies in obtaining funding for national presidential and congressional election studies may also be responsible for our hesitation to follow psychology. For better or worse, *The American Voter* and the continuing study of presidential elections and now off-year congressional elections have not only absorbed a substantial portion of our available grant funding but has also preoccupied our thinking about elections. Certainly the vast bulk of research on voting derives from these expensive surveys. While the open-ended "likes" and "dislikes" of both political parties and presidential candidates have been continued since the 1950s, they provide insight into the attitude systems of individuals only to a limited degree.

Perhaps we are inclined to think that more factual questions, such as "Did you contribute money to a campaign?" or "Is there anything that would cause you to vote for blank for president?" are *not* in fact attitude questions. As noted earlier relative to whether respondents did indeed cast their votes for the presidential candidate they say they supported, even these questions may assess attitudes that do not correspond to behavior. Is one's stated age necessarily one's age, or rather an attitude toward the desirability of youth?

Because the concept of public opinion predates the development of survey research and the concept of attitude, and because of its role in democratic theory, I am inclined to think that political scientists believe that the public should, and to some degree does, have opinions on the issues of the day and that elected leaders should, and do to some degree, respond to those opinions. No direct behavior is expected of expressed opinions; only if leaders fail to be responsive is the process of opinions shaping actions anticipated. Inaction is seen, not as the lack of correspondence between attitudes and behavior, but rather as overall satisfaction. The success of pollsters in getting news organizations to buy their wares also contributes to what I would call the "reification" of polls as public opinion. A democratic public is believed to have opinions on issues; survey research is a better method for gathering such opinions than is audience response, letters to the editor, or even editorial opinions; and thus poll results are public opinion.

Finally, our discipline's preoccupation with the ideas of pluralism and the preservation of the status quo and stability, I think, contributes to less than enthusiastic further exploration of public electoral capabilities. Since Berelson's (1954) judgment that the voting studies finding that the practice and theory of public involvement in a democracy were different, and that the practice was better than the theory given that the polity's stability was also assured by the practice, pluralists have had little reason to be concerned with a public whose primary role seems to be apathy. Elites and their behavior are more directly relevant and easier to study.

IMPLICATIONS OF OUR NOT FOLLOWING PSYCHOLOGY

I will now turn to the implications of political science holding to its more diverse path in the use of the attitude concept rather than being more fashionable in researching attitude systems. I have labored to suggest that, to use the language of the day, psychologists have "copped out" of the problem of tying attitudes to behavior by saying that they need to deal with the individual in depth. Perhaps the behavior of coping with information is studied, but in general, as stated by McGuire (1985), mediational ideas are the focus. Thus political science, holding to its present course, must continue to endure the question of attitude/behavior correspondence. Perhaps our diversity of approach may lead to some of us being interested in the question of predicting behaviors, such as voting or disobeying the law, from attitude systems.

Kinder (1983), in making a persuasive argument for both following psychology into consideration of schemas (414) and for not treating the public as "accountants," as is the case for public choice theorists (415), suggests that our efforts, without following psychological theory, will not be enriched by the broader efforts at understanding in that discipline. Save for the avoidance of considering behavior that I so regret, I would endorse his position. As noted earlier, I think much is to be gained by looking at political attitudes as a subset of all attitudes.

There is also a focus on the affect side of the tripartite (cognitive, affect, and conative) aspects of attitudes. Kinder (1983) urges this focus, citing Zajonc's (1980) argument that individuals have crude and fast evaluations based on affect and slow, more detailed cognitive reactions that come into play later, perhaps ineffectively. Also Marcus (1988) advanced political science exposure to the usefulness of emotions. His findings centering on NES evaluations of Reagan and Mondale confirm that positive and negative emotions are independent of each other, and that the positive serves the function of judging personal task performance (mastery), while the negative assesses external threats (threat). If issue positions are in the negative realm, which he argues, positive emotions best relate to which candidate people claim they will vote for in the election. To my knowledge, there has been no research on whether cognitively derived propensities to behave predict behavior better than do affective propensities, or whether positive or negative affect yields more accurate predictions of behavior.

Finally, implicit in our following economics rather than psychology I see a continuing loss of enthusiasm about assessing mass behavior. It is easier to attribute motivations to individuals than to assess those motivations; and, of course, this is a basic element in rational choice theory. As noted, Kinder (1983) argues that affect may be more important to how people respond than is cognition. The basic presumption in public choice theory that the cognitive rather than the affective shapes behavior would be seriously shaken were this thoroughly demonstrated.

WHAT IF WE FOLLOWED PSYCHOLOGY?

Of course, chief among my concerns were we to follow psychology rather than continuing on our more diverse course is the perpetuated avoidance of coping with attitude/behavior correspondence. But there are other difficulties. The basic ideas in miniature knowledge structures or schemas, with their emphasis on individuality and learning to understand the individual, would entail abandoning the measurement of the concept, public opinion. It is true that such a thorough understanding of each individual might serve as a criterion variable for developing more close-ended and broadly usable measures. In the long run, measuring public opinion might thereby be improved. In the short run, however, because gathering and aggregating such miniature structures would be prohibitively expensive and if the number of distinct structures were substantial, making aggregation impossible, public opinion would be unavailable as a standard. With it would go our basic standard for assessing the representativeness of elected officials, or at least making such judgments on issues facing society. We could talk about the sharing of schema between representatives and the public, or about which public schema is most common. But how would we say anything about public opinion leading to public policy?

If we were to find a substantial number of distinct miniature structures, what would be expected of the representative of such a constituency? Certainly we could speak of accountability in the sense of standing for reelection in competition with other candidates, but what behaviors on the part of the representative in voting public policy would we expect to improve his or her probabilities of winning reelection?

One could continue to speak of representativeness in terms of demographic variables, however. Many such variables, principally socioeconomic status, have proven to be less related to opinions on issues today than was the case in the past; while others, like married or single status, have increasingly shown distinct opinion differences (Luttbeg and Martinez 1990). Since the days when the attitudes of *The American Voter* replaced the Index of Political Predisposition of *Voting*, direct measurement of attitudes rather than attribution of opinions on the basis of demographic data has been assumed to be more accurate. Notably, public-choice theory attributes attitudes and behaviors by way of utility functions universally to individuals regardless of demographic distinctions; so we are not unfamiliar with attributing rather than directly measuring attitudes. Given the difficulties inherent in direct measurements discussed above, this may be an attractive research strategy. But given the decline of most socioeconomically based opinion differences and failure to replace other demographic determinants of opinion on issues noted by Luttbeg and Martinez (1990), it seems unlikely that behavior predicted from demography would prove to be more accurate than that predicted from attitudes.

Beginning with Converse's (1964) comparison of constraint and ideology between congressmen and the general public, there is the expectation that "Experts in any field (in this case political activists) should have more elaborate, more hierarchically structured, and more easily activated schemata than novices in that field (here read the public)" (Lau and Sears, 1986, 352). While this has been broadly confirmed (Fiske et al. 1983; Lau and Erber 1985), and many implications derived from the findings (Lau and Sears 1986), notably absent is any concern about how a representative might behave accountably given these expert/novice differences in the structure of opinions.

Perhaps we should abandon our concern with public opinion and its measurement by conventional public opinion polls. If certain miniature structures contribute to system stability, to extensive participation in democratic institutions, such as elections and public hearings, or to ready compliance with the policies enacted by governments, identifying them and understanding the process by which they develop could be used to encourage all such behaviors. Certainly, "symbolic representation" (Edelman 1971)—whether viewed positively, as encouragements for public behavior, or negatively, as manipulation of the public—implies that representatives present miniature structures known to please constituents.

CONCLUSION

I am struck by the fact that the interpretation of the American electorate's desire to have Congress and the presidency controlled by different political parties, which incidentally holds for many state governors and legislatures, may evidence a broadly shared public miniature structure. Certainly this structure has always been attributed to the founding fathers of the country in their support for checks and balances and may reflect gradual public acceptance of these ideas. But how should we react to such an event in a democracy; does public satisfaction with divided, and presumably ineffective, government satisfy any theory of democracy? And does the concept of a representative whose sole act of representation is to oppose another representative have any use?

Liberal democracy theory has directed most of our concerns with the public's role. Perhaps we need a better, empirically based, theory which recognizes that it is vital in a democracy only for the public to hold supportive attitude systems that are prevalent in more competitive and enduring democracies. Perhaps ideas such as legitimacy, representative accountability, majority rule, and minority rights only misdirect our efforts. To jettison such theoretical ballast, however, would require most extensive comparative analyses across multiple democracies. We would need first to identify those elements of a political system which are of particular interest rather than speaking of full-blown liberal democracy. Once we had focused on a specific element—such as, perhaps, the speed a government shows in coping with a new problem—then a comparison of the miniature structure in the publics of more and less swiftly acting governments might reveal the important attitude system or systems. In turn, we could explore how better to instill such a system or systems in order to assure swifter public decision-making in our democracy.

Rather than pursuing the question of miniature structures, however, my entreaty is for dealing directly with behavior rather than attitudes that fail to predict behavior. Perhaps we should concentrate on public behaviors that can be observed—patterns of who attends public meetings and why some governments have more acrimonious meetings—or focus on aggregate behaviors, such as the direction of votes, while avoiding the pitfalls of ecological fallacy. Or perhaps behaviors in the laboratory should be the center of our focus. I am not making the argument for phenomenology (Deutscher 1973) here, although I am supportive of some of its arguments, such as in-depth understanding of those studied. Those who study attitudes as systems also share this concern.

I would like to close by stating an extreme position from which I might backtrack in light of further research. It is the position of "radical behavioralists" that attitudes are formed only when the outside world demands (McGuire 249). In application to political science, this would mean that no attitude held by the general public is important to any aspect of government: to ignore any opinion on an issue of the day gathered by survey research would in no way endanger either those holding elected positions in government or the government itself. No expression of unfavorable attitudes toward government or governors has any relevance to the perpetuation of that government or governors. In effect, I am arguing that we doubt the correspondence between attitudes and behavior rather than anticipate it. Certainly, the bulk of the existing research literature suggests that this is the more justified course of action.

REFERENCES

Abelson, Robert P. 1968. "Computers, Polls, and Public Opinion—Some Puzzles and Paradoxes." *Transaction* 5:20–27.

———. 1981. "The Psychological Status of the Script Concept." *American Psychologist* 36:715–29.

Achen, Christopher H. 1975. "Mass Political Attitudes and the Survey Response." *American Political Science Review* 69:1218–31.

Albrecht, S. L., and K. E. Carpenter. 1976. "Attitudes as Predictors of Behavior versus Behavioral Intentions: A Convergence of Research Traditions." *Sociometry* 39:1–10.

Aldrich, John H., Richard G. Niemi, George Rabinowitz, and David W. Rhode. 1982. "The Measurement of Public Opinion about Public Policy: A Report on Some New Issue Question Formats." *American Journal of Political Science* 26:391–414.

Apostle, R. A., C. Y. Piazza, and M. Suelzle. 1983. *The Anatomy of Racial Attitudes*. Berkeley: University of California Press.

Barlett, F. C. 1932. *Remembering*. Cambridge: Cambridge University Press.

Berelson, Bernard R., Paul F. Lazarsfeld, and William N. McPhee. 1954. *Voting:*

A Study of Opinion Formation in a Presidential Campaign. Chicago: University of Chicago Press.

Bishop, George F., Alfred J. Tuchfarber, and Robert W. Oldendick. 1978. "Change in the Structure of American Political Attitudes: The Nagging Question of Question Wording." *American Journal of Political Science* 22: 250–69.

Campbell, Angus, Philip E. Converse, Warren E. Miller, and Donald E. Stokes. 1960. *The American Voter*. New York: Wiley.

Conover, Pamela J., and Stanley Feldman. 1981. "The Origins and Meaning of Liberal/Conservative Self-Identifications." *American Journal of Political Science* 25:617–45.

Converse, Philip E. 1964. "The Nature of Belief Systems in Mass Publics." In *Ideology and Discontent*, ed. David E. Apter. New York: The Free Press.

———, J. D. Dotson, W. J. Hoag, and William H. McGee. 1980. *American Social Attitudes Data Sourcebook 1947–1978*. Cambridge, Mass.: Harvard University Press.

Dawes, Richard M., and Thomas L. Smith. 1985. "Attitude and Opinion Measurement." In *Handbook of Social Psychology*. 3d ed. Vol. 2, ed. Gardner Lindzey and Elliot Aronson. New York: Random House.

DeClercq, Eugene, T. Lane Hurley, and Norman R. Luttbeg. 1975. "Voting in American Presidential Elections." *American Politics Quarterly* 3:222–46.

Deutscher, Irwin. 1973. *What We Say/What We Do: Sentiments and Acts*. Glenview, Ill.: Scott, Foresman.

Edelman, Murray. 1971. *Politics as Symbolic Action: Mass Arousal and Quiescence*. Chicago: Markham.

Ellsworth, P. C. 1982. "Public Attitudes to Capital Punishment in General and in Specific Cases." Personal communication cited in McGuire (1985).

Erikson, Robert S. 1978. "Constituency Opinion and Congressional Behavior: A Reexamination of the Miller-Stokes Representation Data." *American Journal of Political Science* 22:511–35.

———, Norman R. Luttbeg, and Kent L. Tedin. 1988. *American Public Opinion: Its Origins, Content, and Impact*. 3d ed. New York: Macmillan.

Fishbein, Martin, and Icek Ajzen. 1975. *Belief, Attitude, Intention, and Behavior*. Reading, Mass.: Addison-Wesley.

———. 1976. "Misconceptions Revised: A Final Comment." *Journal of Experimental and Social Psychology* 12:591–93.

Gant, Michael M., and Dwight F. Davis. 1984. "Mental Economy and Voter Rationality: The Informed Citizen Problem in Voting Research." *Journal of Politics* 46:132–53.

Gant, Michael M., and Norman R. Luttbeg. 1990. *American Electoral Behavior: 1952–1988*. Itasca, Ill.: Peacock.

Graber, Doris A. 1984. *Processing the News: How People Tame the Information Tide*. New York: Longman.

Graesser, A. C. 1985. "Introduction to the Study of Questioning." In *The Psychology of Questions*, ed. A. C. Graesser and J. B. Black. Hillsdale, N.J.: Erlbaum.

———, and J. B. Black, eds. 1985. *The Psychology of Questions*. Hillsdale, N.J.: Erlbaum.

Hagner, Paul R., and John C. Pierce. 1982. "Correlative Characteristics of Levels of Conceptionalization." *Journal of Politics* 44:779–807.

Hechinger, Fred M. "About Education: Council to Fight U.S. Students' Parochial View." *New York Times*, March 13, 1979, sec. C.

Judd, C. M., J. A. Krosnick, and M. A. Milburn. 1981. "Political Involvement and Attitude Structure in the General Public." *American Sociological Review* 46:660–69.

Kinder, Donald R. 1983. "Diversity and Complexity in American Public Opinion." In *Political Science: The State of the Discipline*, ed. Ada W. Finifter. Washington, D.C.: American Political Science Association.

———, and David O. Sears. 1981. "Prejudice and Politics: Symbolic Racism versus Racial Threats to the Good Life." *Journal of Personality and Social Psychology* 40:414–31.

Knapp, T. J. 1986. "The Emergence of Cognitive Psychology in the Latter Half of the Twentieth Century." In *Approaches to Cognition: Contrasts and Controversies*, ed. T. J. Knapp and L. C. Robertson. Hillsdale, N.J.: Erlbaum.

Knight, Kathleen. 1985. "Ideology in the 1980 Election: Political Sophistication Matters." *Journal of Politics* 47:828–53.

Ladd, Everett C., and Seymour M. Lipset. 1980. "Anatomy of a Decade." *Public Opinion* 3:2–9.

Lane, Robert E. 1962. *Political Ideology*. New York: The Free Press.

Lau, Richard R., and David O. Sears, eds. 1986. *Political Cognition*. Hillsdale, N.J.: Erlbaum.

———, and David O. Sears. 1986. "An Introduction to Political Cognition." In *Political Cognition*, ed. Richard R. Lau and David O. Sears. Hillsdale, N.J.: Erlbaum.

———. 1986. "Social Cognition and Political Cognition: The Past, the Present, and the Future." In *Political Cognition*, ed. Robert R. Lau and David O. Sears. Hillsdale, N.J.: Erlbaum.

Lin, Nan. 1974. "The McIntire March: A Study of Recruitment and Commitment." *Public Opinion Quarterly* 38:562–73.

Lodge, Milton, and Bernard Tursky. 1981. "On the Magnitude Scaling of Political Opinion in Survey Research." *American Journal of Political Science* 25:376–419.

Luttbeg, Norman R., and Michael M. Gant. 1985. "The Failure of Liberal/Conservative Ideology as a Cognitive Structure." *Public Opinion Quarterly* 49:80–93.

————, and Michael Martinez. 1990. "Demographic Differences in Opinion, 1956–1984." *Research in Micropolitics*. New York: JAI Press.

McGuire, William J. 1981. "The Probabilogical Model of Cognitive Structure and Attitude Change." In *Cognitive Responses in Persuasion*, ed. R. E. Petty, T. M. Ostrom, and T. C. Brock. Hillsdale, N.J.: Erlbaum.

————. 1985. "Attitudes and Attitude Change." In *Handbook of Social Psychology*. 3d ed. Vol. 2, ed. Gardner Lindzey and Elliot Aronson. New York: Random House.

Marcus, George E. 1988. "The Structure of Emotional Response: 1984 Presidential Candidates." *American Political Science Review* 82:737–61.

Mischel, W. 1984. "On the Predictability and Consistency of Behavior." In *Personality and the Prediction of Behavior*, ed. R. A. Zucker, J. Aronoff, and A. I. Rabin. New York: Academic Press.

Nie, Norman H., Sidney Verba, and John R. Petrocik. 1979. *The Changing American Voter*. Cambridge, Mass.: Harvard University Press.

Nimmo, Dan, and J. Combs. 1983. *Mediated Political Realities*. New York: Longman.

Nisbett, Richard E., and T. D. Wilson. 1977. "Telling More Than We Can Know: Verbal Report on Mental Processes." *Psychological Review* 84: 231–59.

Piaget, Jean. 1930. *The Child's Conception of Physical Causality*. London: Kegan Paul.

Rosch, E. 1971. "Classification of Real-World Objects: Origins and Representations in Cognition." In *Thinking*, ed. P. N. Johnson-Laird and P. C. Wason. Cambridge: Cambridge University Press.

Schuman, Howard, and Stanley Presser. 1981. *Questions and Answers in Attitude Surveys: Experiments on Question Form Wording and Context*. New York: Academic Press.

————, Graham Kalton, and J. Ludwig. 1983. "Context and Contiguity in Survey Questionnaires." *Public Opinion Quarterly* 47:112–15.

Songer-Nocks, E. 1976. "Situational Factors Affecting the Weighting of Predictor Components in the Fishbein Model." *Journal of Experimental Social Psychology* 122:56–69.

Sullivan, John L., James E. Piereson, and George E. Marcus. 1978. "Ideological Constraint in the Mass Public: A Methodological Critique and Some New Findings." *American Journal of Political Science* 22:233–49.

Tedin, Kent L. 1987. "Political Ideology and the Vote." In *Research in Micro-Politics*. Vol. 2. Greenwich, Conn.: JAI Press.

Turner, Charles F., and Elizabeth Martin, eds. 1984. *Surveying Subjective Phenomena*. New York: Russell Sage.

Veroff, J., E. Douvan, and R. A. Kulka. 1981. *The Inner American: A Self-Portrait from 1957 to 1976*. New York: Basic Books.

Wright, P., and P. D. Rip. 1981. "Retrospective Reports on the Causes of Decisions." *Journal of Personality and Social Psychology* 40:601–14.

Zajonc, R. B. 1980. "Feeling and Thinking: Preferences Need No Inferences." *American Psychologist* 39:151–75.

Zaller, John. 1984. "Toward a Theory of the Survey Response." Presented at the annual meeting of the American Political Science Association, Washington, D.C.

———. 1988. "Vague Questions Get Vague Answers: An Experimental Attempt to Reduce Response Instability." Presented at the annual meeting of the American Political Science Association, Washington, D.C.

———, and Stanley Feldman. 1988. "Answering Questions vs. Revealing Preferences: A Simple Theory of the Survey Response." Presented at the annual meeting of the Political Methodology Society.

2

The Study of Political Participation: Past, Present, and Future

M. Margaret Conway

A concern with the quality, quantity, and consequences of citizens' participation in the polity is as old as the study of politics. Yet the state of our knowledge is not commensurate with the length of time those concerned with politics have focused on participation. This paper examines selected major contributions to the development and institutionalization of research on political participation. The relative utility of various analytic approaches that have been employed in examining patterns of participation and their causes and consequences is assessed. Also addressed are methodological problems in the study of political participation and some alternatives that might be pursued in future research.

ALTERNATIVE DEFINITIONS OF POLITICAL PARTICIPATION

While research has focused on something labeled "political participation," disagreement exists about what that term means and how it should be operationally defined, with consequent implications for the development of theoretical frameworks and the construction of re-

The comments made on an earlier draft by Robert Alperin, Paul Abramson, Stephen Bennett, and Henry Brady are appreciated.

search designs that maximize building on prior research. Verba and Nie (1972) define participation as "those activities by private persons that are more or less directly aimed at influencing the selection of governmental personnel and/or the actions they take" (2). Their research focuses only on activities, not on attitudes, and on activities "within the system" (3). Their research also excludes examination of ceremonial and support activities. In contrast, Milbrath and Goel's definition of political participation as "those actions of private citizens by which they seek to influence or to support governments and politics" extends the focus of research to include largely ceremonial activities and supportive rituals.

Kaase and Marsh (1979) argue that "political participation derives its meaning for the individual and for the political system from the interaction between political authorities and partisans as mediated through political institutions" (28). Political participation is then viewed as "interaction between political authorities and non-authorities" (38). The cross-national study (Barnes and Kaase 1979) in which Kaase and Marsh participated explicitly uses the term "political action" to make clear that the focus includes unconventional activities, both legal and illegal. This conceptualization encompasses the full range of activities by private persons aimed at influencing the choice of government personnel and the activities of government. Individuals are viewed as developing a repertory of political skills that they draw upon as required by the situation as the participant perceives it.

In addition to differences over the range and type of political activities that should be included in the definition of political participation, the goals of political participation research also vary. One is to develop explanatory theory, whether one includes only conventional political acts or broadens the focus of research to cover unconventional acts. The other focus has two components: to consider how institutions contribute to the maximization of citizen participation and the citizen's development in terms of self-actualization (Pateman 1970; Finkel 1985; Finkel 1987; Greenberg 1981); and to explore the potential of various institutional arrangements to contribute to maximizing participation (Scaff 1975; Pateman 1970; Jackman 1987; Powell 1986). However, the instrumental character of participation or participation as a mechanism of exchange in terms of achieving desired governmental personnel and policy outcomes has been the major focus of empirical research. The effects of participation on the individual and participation as a means of developing and sharing a sense of community and acting on the basis of reciprocity in order to promote the "public good" receive far less attention.

THE "SCIENTIFIC STUDY" OF POLITICAL PARTICIPATION

Setting a beginning date for the scientific study of political participation is at best an inexact task, but surely among the first scholars to undertake empirically based studies were Harold F. Gosnell, who examined patterns of participation among political party activists and, together with Charles Merriam, the mass public in Chicago during the 1920s; and Herbert Tingsten, whose *Political Behavior: Studies in Election Statistics* (examining patterns of voting turnout and electoral choice in European nations) was published in 1937. Certainly the study of electoral choice using rigorous survey research methods by scholars at Columbia's Bureau of Applied Social Research, resulting in the publication of Berelson and Lazarsfeld's *The People's Choice* and Berelson, Lazarsfeld, and McPhee's *Voting*, contributed to an increased focus on various forms of campaign-related political action. These two pioneering studies also stimulated a greater interest among scholars in the consequences of low levels of political participation and of electoral choices made by citizens with low levels of interest, information, as well as concern about the consequences of electoral outcomes for the effective functioning of a democratic political system.

Lester Milbrath's *Political Participation*, published in 1965, provides evidence that political participation had been the focus of a substantial amount of empirical research in the two decades after World War II, and this propositional inventory of research findings undoubtedly played a significant role in stimulating further research. In that work Milbrath examines empirical research findings and derives generalizations inductively. The theoretical approaches which guided participation research through that period are evidenced in the chapter headings; participation is examined as a function of stimuli, personal factors, social position, and environmental factors. In the first edition, Milbrath creates a typology of political activism, dividing the public into three types: apathetics, who are withdrawn from politics (estimated to constitute one-third of the citizenry); spectators, who are minimally involved (approximately 60 percent of the electorate); and gladiators, who are active participants (5 to 7 percent of the adult population). In the second edition (1977), Milbrath and his coauthor, M. L. Goel, stimulated by the results of comparative research, viewed participation as multidimensional, with participatory acts being classified according to both the type of behavior involved and its degree of "difficulty" (12). Drawing on the research of Verba, Nie, and Kim (1971) as well as Milbrath's collaborative research with Cataldo, Johnson, Kellstedt, and Somit (Milbrath 1968, 1971a, 1971b), six modes of political participation are identified: voting, working for a party or candidate, community activism, contacting officials, protest behavior, and communications activities. The typology developed specifies both input and "outtake" activities associated with each mode. Milbrath and Goel assert that "it is important to think about these modes of participation as patterns of emphasis and not as discrete or separate behaviors" (20, 1977).

IN SEARCH OF THEORY AND DATA

Much of the research on political participation has used data bases collected for other purposes, such as voting behavior studies. These data, though very useful in studying a restricted set of research questions, limit both the areas of inquiry that may be pursued and the theoretical approaches that can guide the research. Several research projects, however, have collected data solely for the purpose of studying political participation and have therefore examined a broader range of research questions and permitted the testing of hypotheses derived from a number of alternative theoretical formulations. These studies, conducted within several different frameworks, reflect competing views about the utility of various theoretical approaches in developing explanations for participation patterns. Theories drawn from sociology, social psychology, and economics, as well as theories developed within political science, have guided scholarly research on participation. The perceived weaknesses of each theoretical approach result in a continuing search for a more useful theoretical framework for the study of participation.

Guided by psychocultural or culture and personality theories developed in other disciplines, Gabriel Almond and Sidney Verba's *The Civic Culture* (1963) examines the political cultures of five democracies and the social structures and processes that were believed to shape and sustain democracy. *The Civic Culture* considers from a comparative perspective citizens' expectations about what acts of political participation they should perform and the attitudes, beliefs, and values associated with those expectations. The underlying premise of the research design is that citizens' attitudes about and patterns of participation in the political system are very much a function of prior socialization rather than of contemporaneous conditions and their effects on attitudes, beliefs, and behaviors. Through analysis of micro-level data, the research attempts to explain macro-level differences in political systems. The study contributed to an increased focus on political culture in explaining patterns of participation. However, difficulties in measuring hypothetical components of political culture and dissatisfaction with the explanatory power obtained from this conceptual approach eventually resulted in a decreased use of the political culture framework. Nevertheless, attitudinal-based theories continue to play a significant role in political participation research, and a renewed interest in the political culture framework has recently developed (Erikson, McIvor, and Wright 1987; Lieske 1987; Conway 1989; Conway and Dolan 1987).

Sidney Verba and Norman Nie's *Participation in America* (1972) represented a significant advance in empirical research on political participation in the United States. Based on data collected from a national sample for the purpose of studying political participation, seeking to construct topologies of types of political participation and of participants, and examining both the processes of politicization and selected consequences of participation, scholarly knowledge of participation in America was significantly advanced by this study. The basic model guiding the research stresses the importance of socioeconomic resources, with political involvement being partially a product of those resources and also having an independent impact on participation patterns. Once this basic model is established, the effects of racial group membership and group consciousness, point in the life-cycle, membership in voluntary organizations, the community context of participation, and partisan identification on participation patterns all are evaluated. Of course, this research has limitations, as it is time-bound, ignores unconventional forms of participation, suffers from flawed measurement of some key variables (for example, organizational memberships), and includes in its model of the process of politicization only a few of the variables that should be in a fully specified model. The proportion of the variance explained in the limited number of multivariate tests of the politicization model is rather small. Despite these limitations, Verba and Nie's work stands more than twenty years later as a major contribution to the study of participation.

The 1987 General Social Survey, conducted by the National Opinion Research Center (NORC), replicated the Verba and Nie survey and makes possible a comparison of participation patterns in 1967 and 1987. Analysis of the data by Nie, Verba, Brady, Schlozman, and Junn (1988) indicates that a number of changes have occurred which have an impact on participation patterns. These changes are similar to those suggested by other data sets—for example, declining voter turnout, higher rates of monetary contributions, and increased levels of contacting public officials—suggesting that participation is increasingly self-mobilized, or is mobilized through group activity, rather than by political parties. Nie et al. also found an underlying structure to the patterns of participation similar to that found in the 1967 data. As expected, the changing educational composition of the electorate is associated with increased rates of political activity; however, structural changes had occurred over time as a consequence of changes in the relationship of education and race to patterns of participation. Changes also occurred in the patterns of organizational memberships among blacks, with lower rates of organizational membership occurring among blacks with lower levels of educational attainment. In addition, among blacks organizational memberships contributed less to mobilization for political activity in 1987 than in 1967. This longitudinal, cross-sectional study is significant in demonstrating the contribution that such analyses can make to understanding the impact of demographic and structural changes on patterns of participation.

Concurrently with the research design and fieldwork for the data collection that became the basis for *Participation in America*, scholars in six other nations were collaborating with Verba, Nie, and their colleagues in the design and data collection for parallel research on political participation. Although initially formulated as a follow-up to *The Civic Culture*, the focus shifted as the design stage proceeded. The cross-national study placed more emphasis on political action than on attitudes, and on the contemporaneous rather than early antecedent social, psychological, and political contexts of political behavior. The studies conducted within the seven nations produced a number of research reports, a major one being *Participation and Political Equality* (1978) by Sidney Verba, Norman Nie, and Jae-on Kim. Focusing on the differential availability to citizens of various means of influencing the government and differences in the use of those channels, a model of political participation that focuses on both individual and group motivations, resources, and consequent political mobilization processes is specified and tested. The research documents differences in group-based and individual-based inequalities in participation and the differential role of group-based political mobilization processes across nations and for different types of political activity. Although it is an important contribution to our knowledge, the research focus on legal acts, and even more narrowly on conventional political acts, employs an unduly restrictive definition of political participation.

The cross-national research project that resulted in the publication of *Political Action* (1979), edited by Samuel H. Barnes and Max Kaase, addresses this problem by focusing on political action rather than political participation. The scholars involved in this collaborative five-nation project viewed the latter term as more appropriate to their theoretical interest, which is to understand the relationship between what people expect to derive from politics and the political activities in which they take part. These political activities may include participating in violent as well as nonviolent acts of protest. Citizens are viewed as developing a political-action repertory, defined as "the sum of all political skills an individual has acquired through vicarious reinforcement and imitative learning" (1979, 39). This is contrasted with political participation, defined by the authors as "all voluntary activities by individual citizens intended to influence either directly or indirectly political choices at various levels of the political system" (1979, 42). The authors view acquisition of a political-action repertory as necessary for expressing demands on the political system. This contrasts with rational-choice theory, which posits that individuals collect information, assess costs and benefits, and then select their options for action. The action options chosen by citizens in the political-action model are a function not only of learned behavior options but also of the consequences of interactions between authorities and citizens that create a climate of trust or distrust, trust in institutions, perceived success of various action options seeking to influence political outcomes, and authorities' potential for control. As Max Kaase and Alan Marsh explain, "most importantly the concrete nature of the exchange is determined by the responsiveness of the political actors, their chosen means of influence, and the repertory of political resources and activities that partisans command" (1979, 38). The initial model specifies the social location of the actors and the actors' values, ideology, and political satisfaction as independent variables; political efficacy, trust of the system, and trust of the government as intervening variables; and the political action repertory and political participation as dependent variables.

Group-Related Theories of Participation

Group differences in patterns of political participation have been a frequent topic of research. Yet controversy continues about the most appropriate theory to guide such research, construct definition and concept measurement, the operationalization of measures, methods of analysis, and the correct conclusions to be drawn about group differences.

Research on the role of groups in stimulating and structuring participation can be traced to the early empirical work of Gosnell, Merriam, and Tingsten. However, substantial differences exist in the theoretical frameworks within which that work is embedded. Significant questions remain concerning the appropriate theoretical framework for political participation and the role of the concept of group within that framework.

Early research employing the group concept tended to emphasize categoric group membership, groups being classified by such characteristics as age, sex, ethnic group, and place of residence. While these categories have descriptive utility, appropriate and theoretically rich explanatory frameworks are infrequently found in research employing categoric group analysis. In contrast, research that focuses on secondary or primary groups suggests alternative avenues for development of more elaborate theories of political participation. Verba and Nie's

(1972) analysis of the effects of voluntary group membership and of varying levels of activity within voluntary groups illuminates the influence that group membership may have on participation. Of course, controls for prior variables that may impact both on participation and on voluntary group membership and activity are necessary to eliminate the inference of a spurious relationship between group membership and participation patterns. Baumgartner and Walker (1988) provide a further cautionary note on generalizing about the role of voluntary groups in stimulating political participation. The concept of group membership must be broad enough to incorporate patterns of membership that may change over time, multiple memberships within one type of voluntary association, and the development and probably increasing numbers of "checkbook members," who support groups with money but are not formal members of the organization.

Even if individuals are active members of groups in which political discussion occurs, and active members of such groups are more participatory, the question of causality must still be addressed. Is it active membership in voluntary groups in which political discussions occur that stimulates higher levels of participation, or is the relationship spurious? Did those who participate actively in such groups already possess characteristics that impelled them toward both higher levels of political participation and active membership in groups where politically relevant discussions occur?

Other research suggests that a more elaborate approach to the study of group membership would contribute to our understanding of participation patterns (Miller, Gurin, Gurin, and Malarchuk 1981; Gurin, Miller, and Gurin 1979). The focus of that research is on demographic subgroups rather than the voluntary groups studied by Verba and Nie and by Baumgartner and Walker.

Miller, Gurin, Gurin, and Malarchuk argue for the necessity of distinguishing between group identification and group consciousness. In their conceptualization, group identification is a "perceived self-location within a particular social stratum," whereas group consciousness involves both identification with a group and "a political awareness or ideology regarding the group's relative position in society along with a commitment to collective action aimed at realizing the group's interests" (Miller et al. 1981, 495). Group consciousness, as they define it, includes group identification, polar affect, polar power, and individual-versus-system blame. Their definition of group identification includes awareness of similarity of interests and ideas shared with others having the same social characteristics. Components of this shared set of orientations includes polar affect (affective preference for one's own group and a dislike for those outside of it), polar power (satisfaction or dissatisfaction with the group's status, power, or material resources in relation to those of outgroups), and individual-versus-system blame (the belief that the group's status in society can be attributed to either the individual or the system) (Miller et al. 1981, 497). Using this conceptual framework to assess the relationship of group consciousness to turnout, members of subordinate groups (classified on the basis of race, gender, or income) vote at higher rates if they identify with a particular social group, view that group as lacking influence, and blame the system for their ineffectuality. Their research was less conclusive for dominant groups, with a relationship existing between the components of group consciousness for businessmen, but not for whites.

Research by Brody and Sniderman (1977) suggests that group membership would stimulate political activity if the members were committed to the policy-related programmatic concerns of the group above a threshold level and if the individual members were convinced that the policy-related concerns should and could best be resolved by governmental activity. The unexplained variance in the effects of voluntary organization membership on political participation might be reduced if modifications of the concepts of polar affect and system blame were incorporated into the model of voluntary group membership effects.

The theoretical approaches discussed above have drawn on theories developed not only in political science but also in sociology, psychology, and anthropology. Dissatisfaction with inductive theory in general and with the products obtained through use of these approaches has led a number of scholars to try applying formal theories developed in economics to the study of political participation.

Rational Choice Theory and Prospect Theory

Rational choice theory, imported into political science from economics, results in predictions about political action which contradict patterns that actually occur. For example, the costs of voting would appear to exceed the benefits to be derived from doing so, when one takes into account the probability of affecting the outcome. Nonetheless, a substantial, although decreasing, proportion of the American electorate votes. Efforts to account for this anomaly have employed a number of devices. Riker and Ordeshook (1968) posit a long-run participation value derived from the psychological rewards obtained from carrying out one's civic duty through voting. Other suggestions to explain the anomaly include ethical concerns (Goodin and Roberts 1975), minimax regret (Ferejohn and Fiorina 1974, 1975), long-term equilibrium (Ledyard 1985; Palfrey and Rosenthal 1985), altruism and a group-interest-based utility function (Margolis 1982), and group-based effectiveness as opposed to individual effects (Opp 1986).

Efforts by scholars examining participation within the framework of rational choice theory have generally focused on payoffs in terms of individually possessible goods. A promising new approach proposed by Uhlaner (1985, 1989a, 1989b) suggests that payoffs in terms of relational goods, which are obtained through interactions with others, stimulate turnout. The model developed by Uhlaner specifies the conditions under which individuals will participate if they believe others will also participate. The conditions under which mobilization of group members by group leaders will occur are also specified in Uhlaner's model. While developed only with regard to voting participation, elaboration of the model to extend it to other forms of participation would be a contribution to the search for an explanatory theory of patterns of participation.

Others have argued that rational choice theory simply cannot provide an adequate explanation of patterns of participation because the underlying assumptions of this theory are spurious. Certainly rational choice provides a theory that is simple, powerful, and broad in scope. However, it is normative and logical rather than descriptive and empirical. In particular, its assumption of invariance has been shown in experimental studies to be inappropriate. Through a series of experimental studies based on prospect theory and focusing on the framing of choices and the evaluations of outcomes, Kahneman, Tversky, and their associates provide evidence that, contrary to the assumptions underlying rational choice theory, the value function is defined on gains and losses, which generally is concave for gains and convex for losses, and steeper for losses than for gains (Kahneman, Slovic, and Tversky 1982; Quattrone and Kahneman 1988). While rational choice theory predicts that individuals will be risk-averse independent of the reference point, prospect theory predicts that individuals will be risk-averse in the domain of gains and risk-seeking in the domain of losses, and that shifts in reference points induced by the framing of choice alternatives will have predictable effects on risk preferences and subsequent choices made (Quattrone and Tversky 1988; Kahneman and Tversky 1979). Prospect theory provides a theory of choice that could prove very useful in explaining participation decisions. Research designed explicitly to test propositions about political participation derived from prospect theory should have a high priority on the participation research agenda.

A Socialization Theory of Political Participation

What general framework could be used to integrate these various theoretical approaches into a comprehensive theory of political participation? A socialization theory is most appropriate as an integrative theoretical framework. Whether one focuses on political participation or political action, both the frame of reference within which action choices are made and the options for political action—whether to abstain or to act, and if to act, which options to be chosen—are learned. Those variables that are viewed as contributing to patterns of behavior can be interpreted as either additions to the learning process or products of the learning process. For example, education contributes to the learning process in a variety of ways; when we measure educational attainment we are assuming an underlying process of learning skills, attitudes, beliefs, and values that impact in particular ways on participation. When the effects of age or place in the life cycle are examined, an underlying assumption is made about resources and learned methods for using those resources for political action, learned roles and the norms associated with those roles, and acquired wants and the means of gratifying them which are more likely to be associated with particular age groups or places in the life cycle. A socialization theory of political participation makes possible the integration into a comprehensive theory of the diverse theories previously discussed in this paper.

Problems in Measuring Political Participation

Certainly a significant problem in the study of political participation is how to measure it. Unobtrusive measures (Webb, Campbell, Schwartz, and Sechrest 1966) are available for certain types of participation; for example, researchers can use voting turnout records and census data to estimate turnout rates among the eligible voting-age population. The number of contacts with elected officials or bureaucratic agencies; the numbers of persons testifying at public hearings or contributing to parties, candidates, or political action committees; the numbers of letters received by legislators on a particular topic—many forms of participation can be measured unobtrusively. However, measures of variables that would be useful in explaining levels of participation and their associated patterns are generally more difficult to obtain. Scholars have of necessity turned to survey research as the preferred method to obtain measures of both independent and dependent variables, but problems with this data collection method must be kept in mind.

Perhaps more attention has focused on the problem of misreported voting turnout than on any other aspect of measuring dependent variables. Validity checks of self-reported voting turnout contribute to more accurate measurement of dependent variables (Abramson and Claggett 1984; Clausen 1968; Katosh and Traugott 1981; Traugott and Katosh 1979), but controversy remains about the measure to be used in assessing the amount of misreporting. Measures used include: (1) the proportion of those claiming to vote who did not vote; (2) the proportion of those surveyed who misreported their vote; (3) the proportion of nonvoters who claimed that they voted. Each measure may be appropriate, depending on the research question being asked. Using the proportion of those claiming to vote who did not is appropriate if an estimate of the proportion of liars among the respondents sampled is the desired dependent variable. The second is more appropriate if the question being examined is the probability of any respondent's reported behavior not matching actual behavior. The third is the best measure if one is concerned with evaluating the characteristics of nonvoters who are engaging in socially disapproved behavior (Anderson and Silver 1986).

While voter registration and turnout records are available for most states and their subdivisions, thus making possible validity checks for reported participation patterns, such records are either nonexistent or much less accessible for other forms of participation. The validity of other self-reported forms of participation is unknown; one focus for research should be the validity of measures of other self-reported forms of participation. These studies could be conducted in settings where data are available to verify self-reports. For example, validation of self-reported patterns of local community involvement, either as participants in specific groups active in the community or through citizens' contacting specific public officials, could be carried out. Similar validity checks could be made by working backward from campaign contribution records filed by candidates or political-action committees or the political parties, sampling individuals who are known to have made campaign contributions, and inquiring whether they had made any contributions and to what groups they had contributed.

The Political and Social Context of Participation

Comparative research across nations, states, or localities suggests that the context within which political behavior occurs significantly influences patterns of participation (Christy 1987; Jackman 1987; Powell 1984; Powell 1986). Comparisons across time, whether merely comparing between elections held in different years or across political eras, provide evidence that the temporal context of behavior also affects the levels and types of participation that occur among various types of respondents (Beck and Jennings 1979; Beck and Jennings 1984; Conway 1981). Comparative research suggests that without including measures of contextual effects, efforts to explain patterns of participation will be deficient. Contextual analysis should be given a higher priority in research agendas.

Contextual analysis means "cross-level analysis in which both individual-level and contextual-level variables are involved. Contextual variables refer to those generated by summing individual characteristics, by directly characterizing aggregates, or by attributing locational characteristics to individuals" (Books and Prysby 1988, 215). The assumptions underlying contextual analysis are that individuals are significantly influenced by social interactions, social structures, and institutional arrangements.

A variety of types of contextual variables have been used in empirical research on political participation. Most common are social composition measures, such as the proportion of people living in a political or geographic unit who are employed in a particular occupation, fall within a particular income category, or have attained a specified level of education. A second type, social structural indicators of context, measure some aspect of social interaction patterns, such as the amount of campaign activity within an election district. A third type of contextual measure is the global contextual variable, which is an indicator of some property of the social context that is not derived, either directly or indirectly, from characteristics of individuals within the social unit (Books and Prysby 1988). Examples of global contextual effects include the number of parties that are competitive in the election district, the type of legislative-executive system (parliamentary or presidential-congressional), and characteristics of the voter registration system. Contextual research within the United States has tended to focus on compositional variables, although a small number of structural variables, such as the amount of campaign activity or campaign media advertising in a district, have been examined in research on voting. Global measures have been employed more in cross-national research; for example, substantial explanatory power for patterns of voting turnout has been attributed to global contextual variables (Jackman 1987; Powell 1986).

One major focus of contextual research has been on geographic entities, such as neighborhoods, communities, regions, or nations, examining the question of why and how the context influences political participation. The underlying premises in research employing contextual effects are that social contextual variables structure patterns of social interaction, the roles assigned to individuals, and the expectations that accompany those roles and are conveyed by information flows within the social context. A widely shared desire to conform to role expectations results in patterns of political behavior.

Research has inadequately examined the effects of social context on political behavior. The unfortunate tendency has been to focus on the neighborhood; while in an earlier period, in preindustrial societies, that focus would have been appropriate, the high levels of mobility prevalent in most industrial and postindustrial societies make such a focus inappropriate. The social context is individually defined; for example, it may be composed of friends from the workplace, those who share interests or hobbies, members of religious groups, or members of various types of voluntary associations. Research designs should permit the respondents to identify their own social contexts and patterns of interaction within those contexts which impact on political participation. Of course, the types of survey designs necessary to evaluate appropriately the effects of interactive social contexts on individuals' patterns of political behavior are much more complex than those that have generally been employed. A socialization framework for political participation implies that social interaction contributes to learning the expectations associated with social roles, which may include or exclude certain types of political participation. Social interaction also conveys information about political objects, such as political leaders and institutions, and contributes to the formation or modification of attitudes and beliefs about regime structures and performance.

THE PUZZLE OF NONPARTICIPATION

One major focus of participation research has been to explain patterns of political apathy, and particularly the low and declining rate of voting turnout that has occurred in the United States. Several scholars have emphasized structural factors associated with voter registration and election administration (Erikson 1981; Wolfinger and Rosenstone 1980; Piven and Cloward 1988) and the numbers of elections in which Americans are eligible to participate (Boyd 1986). Other factors include the changing sociodemographic characteristics of the electorate, with some changes, such as increasing education, contributing to increased participation rates and others, such as a changed age distribution with more younger citizens eligible to vote, contributing to reduced rates of participation (Boyd 1981; Conway 1991; Teixeira 1987; Wolfinger and Rosenstone 1980). Another explanation focuses on the representational structure of the American political system, which entails competitiveness of districts, disproportionality of translation of votes into seats, degree of party competitiveness, the existence of a variety of political parties, which would result in representation of a variety of class and other interests, and the extent to which political power is dispersed among institutions being credited with contributing significantly to patterns of participation in elections (Burnham 1982a; Burnham 1982b; Jackman 1987; Piven and Cloward 1988). An alternative argument is that the decline in voting turnout that occurred between 1952 and 1980 can be explained as largely a function of lower levels of a sense of external political efficacy and of strength of party identification among the American electorate (Abramson and Aldrich 1982). One would also expect that turnout would be affected by significant levels of political apathy among the citizenry (Bennett 1986).

Several studies have included a variety of sociodemographic, attitudinal, and political variables in their efforts to account for patterns of voting turnout (Brody 1978; Conway 1981; Reiter 1979; Shaffer 1981; Sigelman, Roeder, Jewell, and Baer 1985; Teixeira 1987). Teixeira concludes in his analysis of pooled samples of six American national election study data (1960, 1964, 1968, 1972, 1976, and 1980) that while higher levels of education and occupational status would have increased turnout by 3.9 percent across the twenty-year period, changes in non-SES characteristics (age, marital status, residential mobility, race, religion, and sex) account for approximately two-thirds of the decline in turnout during those two decades, with the remainder being accounted for by declines in feelings about political efficacy, strength of partisan identification, and campaign newspaper reading, with efficacy and newspaper readership declines being more important. Furthermore, the decline in political efficacy was the most important contributor to turnout decline between 1960 and 1968, while the decline in newspaper reading was the most important variable in contributing to turnout decline from 1968 to 1980. Of course, given the controversy over the validity and reliability of political efficacy measures and problems with newspaper reading exposure measures, the conclusions must be considered tentative at best.

CONCLUSIONS

Many questions concerning the causes and consequences of political participation patterns have not been answered; consequently, our research agenda remains quite full. Major elements of that agenda include: (1) developing a coherent, comprehensive theory of political participation to integrate the many fragments of theory already existing; (2) examining the validity of measures of participation, including self-reported forms of participation other than voting turnout; (3) developing research designs and collecting data specifically to test hypotheses derived from a more comprehensive theory of political participation, with the focus of that research extending to engaging or not engaging in a comprehensive set of political acts.

In addition, our research agenda should include a more extensive examination of the influence of primary groups on participation. The social context of participation must be incorporated into research designs. While previous research suggests that a sense of identity with categoric groups may influence participation to a limited degree, primary groups have the potential for a more substantial impact in either promoting or inhibiting participation.

Only a limited amount of research has examined political participation by the same individuals over time (Conway 1991; Sigelman et al.

1985). More extensive research that focuses on patterns of participation over time is needed. For example, what contributes to some individuals dropping out of the electorate? Do those who drop out substitute other forms of participation for voting? A socialization framework suggests that experiences modify attitudes and beliefs or create new ones that result in viewing participation as either futile (for those who had previously perceived participation as having instrumental consequences) or not fulfilling (for those who expected participation to fill expressive needs). Research should focus on what kinds of experiences modify beliefs and attitudes, with consequent effects on patterns of participation.

Much of our research utilizes data collected with a focus on explaining electoral behavior, and particularly electoral behavior in presidential elections. Generalizations developed in the context of presidential elections should be tested for their appropriateness in other political contexts, such as state, local, school board, and special district elections.

Other forms of participation, such as contacting public officials, have received far less research attention than they merit. However, existing research on these nonelectoral participation topics suggests that examining nonelectoral forms of participation is essential in the development of a general theory of political participation (Hero 1986a; Hero 1986b; Jones, Greenberg, Kaufman, and Drew 1977; Sharp 1982; Sharp 1984; Vedlitz, Dyer, and Durand 1980; Verba and Nie 1972).

REFERENCES

Abramson, P., and J. Aldrich. 1982. "The Decline of Electoral Participation in America." *American Political Science Review* 76:502–21.

———, and W. Claggett. 1984. "Race-Related Differences in Self-Reported and Validated Turnout." *Journal of Politics* 46:719–38.

Almond, S., and S. Verba. 1963. *The Civic Culture*. Princeton, N.J.: Princeton University Press.

Anderson, B., and B. Silver. 1986. "Measurement and Mismeasurement of the Validity of Self-Reported Voting." *American Journal of Political Science* 30: 771–85.

Barnes, S., and M. Kaase. 1979. *Political Action*. Beverly Hills, Calif.: Sage Publications.

Baumgartner, F. R., and J. Walker. 1988. "Survey Research and Membership in Voluntary Associations." *American Journal of Political Science* 32:908–28.

Beck, P., and M. K. Jennings. 1979. "Political Periods and Political Participation." *American Political Science Review* 73:737–50.

———. 1984. "Updating Political Periods and Political Participation." *American Political Science Review* 78:198–201.

Bennett, S. E. 1986. *Apathy in America*. Dobbs Ferry, N.Y.: Transnational Publishers.

———, and L. L. M. Bennett. 1986. "Political Participation." In Samuel Long, ed. *Annual Review of Political Science*. Norwood, N.J.: Ablex.

Berelson, B., and H. Lazarsfeld, 1944, 1948. *The People's Choice*. New York: Columbia University Press.

———, H. Lazarsfeld, and W. McPhee. 1954. *Voting*. Chicago: University of Chicago Press.

Books, J., and C. Prysby. 1988. "Studying Contextual Effects on Political Behavior." *American Politics Quarterly* 16:211–38.

Boyd, R. 1981. "Decline of U.S. Voter Turnout." *American Politics Quarterly* 9: 133–59.

———. 1986. "Election Calendars and Voter Turnout." *American Politics Quarterly* 14:89–104.

Brody, R. 1978. "The Puzzle of Political Participation." In *The New American Political System*, ed. A. King, 287–324. Washington, D.C.: American Enterprise Institute for Public Policy Research.

———, and P. Sniderman. 1977. "From Life Space to the Polling Place: The Relevance of Personal Concerns for Voting Behavior." *British Journal of Political Science* 7:337–60.

Burnham, W. D. 1982a. "The Appearance and Disappearance of the American Voter." In W. D. Burnham, *The Current Crisis in American Politics*. Oxford: Oxford University Press.

———. 1982b. "Shifting Patterns of Congressional Voting Participation." In W. D. Burnham, *The Current Crisis in American Politics*. Oxford: Oxford University Press.

Christy, C. 1987. *Sex Differences in Political Participation*. New York: Praeger.

Clausen, A. 1968. "Response Validity: Vote Report." *Public Opinion Quarterly* 32:588–608.

Conway, M. M. 1981. "Political Participation in Midterm Congressional Elections." *American Politics Quarterly* 9:221–44.

———. 1989. "The Political Context of Political Behavior." *Journal of Politics* 51:3–10.

———. 1991. *Political Participation in the United States*. 2d ed. Washington, D.C.: Congressional Quarterly Press.

———, and K. Dolan. 1987. "Explaining Voter Registration." Paper presented at a meeting of the International Society for Political Psychology, San Francisco, July 4–7.

Erikson, R. 1981. "Why Do People Vote? Because They Are Registered." *American Politics Quarterly* 9:259–71.

———, R. McIvor, and G. Wright. 1987. "State Political Culture and Public Opinion." *American Political Science Review* 81:797–813.

Ferejohn, J., and M. Fiorina. 1974. "The Paradox of Non-voting." *American Political Science Review* 68:525–36.

———. 1975. "Closeness Counts Only in Horseshoes and Dancing." *American Political Science Review* 69:920–25.

Finkel, S. 1985. "Reciprocal Effects on Participation and Political Efficacy: A Panel Analysis." *American Journal of Political Science* 29:891–913.

———. 1987. "The Effects of Political Participation on Political Efficacy and Political Support: Evidence from a West German Sample." *Journal of Politics* 49:441–64.

Goodin, R., and K. S. Roberts. 1975. "The Ethical Voter." *American Political Science Review* 69:926–28.

Gosnell, H. 1927. *Getting Out the Vote*. Chicago: University of Chicago Press. Reprinted by Greenwood Press, 1977.

Greenberg, E. 1981. "Industrial Self-Management and Political Attitudes." *American Political Science Review* 75:29–42.

Gurin, P., A. Miller, and G. Gurin. 1979. "Stratum Identification and Consciousness." *Social Psychology Quarterly* 43:30–47.

Hero, R. 1986a. "Citizen Contacting and Bureaucratic Treatment—Response in Urban Government: Some Further Evidence." *Social Science Journal* 22 (1986): 181–87.

———. 1986b. "Explaining Citizen-Initiated Contacting of Government Officials: Socio-Economic Status, Perceived Need, or Something Else?" *Social Science Quarterly* 67:626–36.

Jackman, R. 1987. "Political Institutions and Voter Turnout in the Industrial Democracies." *American Political Science Review* 81:405–23.

Jones, B. D., S. R. Greenberg, C. Kaufman, and J. Drew. 1977. "Bureaucratic Response to Citizen Initiated Contacts: Environmental Enforcement in Detroit." *American Political Science Review* 71:148–65.

Kaase, M., and A. Marsh. 1979. "Political Action: A Theoretical Perspective." In S. Barnes and M. Kaase, *Political Action*. Beverly Hills, Calif.: Sage Publications.

Kahneman, D., and A. Tversky. 1979. "Prospect Theory: An Analysis of Decision under Risk." *Econometrica* 47:264–91.

———, P. Slovic, and A. Tversky. 1982. *Judgment under Uncertainity: Heuristics and Biases*. Cambridge: Cambridge University Press.

Katosh, J., and M. Traugott. 1981. "The Consequences of Validated and Self-reported Voting Measures." *Public Opinion Quarterly* 45:519–35.

Ledyard, J. O. 1985. "The Pure Theory of Large Two Candidate Elections." *Public Choice* 44:7–41.

Lieske, J. 1987. "The Cultural Geography of the American Party System." Paper presented at the annual meeting of the American Political Science Association, Chicago.

Margolis, H. 1982. *Selfishness, Altruism, and Rationality*. Cambridge: Cambridge University Press.

Merriam, C. E., and H. F. Gosnell. 1924. *Non-voting*. Chicago: University of Chicago Press.

Milbrath, L. 1965. *Political Participation*. Chicago: Rand McNally.

———, and M. L. Goel. 1977. *Political Participation*. 2d ed. Chicago: Rand McNally.

Miller, A., P. Gurin, G. Gurin, and O. Malarchuk. 1981. "Group Consciousness and Political Participation." *American Journal of Political Science* 25: 495–511.

Nie, N., S. Verba, H. Brady, K. Schlozman, and J. Junn. 1988. "Participation in America: Continuity and Change." Paper presented at the annual meeting of the Midwest Political Science Association.

Opp, K. D. 1986. "Soft Incentives and Collective Action: Participation in the Anti-nuclear Movement." *British Journal of Political Science* 16:87–112.

Palfrey, T., and H. Rosenthal. 1985. "Voter Participation and Strategic Uncertainty." *American Political Science Review* 79:62–78.

Pateman, Carole. 1970. *Participation and Democratic Theory*. Cambridge: Cambridge University Press.

Piven, F., and R. Cloward. 1988. *Why Americans Don't Vote*. New York: Pantheon.

Powell, G. B. 1984. "Voting Turnout in Thirty Democracies." In R. Niemi and H. Weisberg, *Controversies in Voting Behavior*, 34–53. 2d ed. Washington, D.C.: Congressional Quarterly Press.

———. 1986. "American Voting Turnout in Comparative Perspective." *American Political Science Review* 80:17–43.

Quarttrone, G., and A. Tversky. 1988. "Contrasting Rational and Psychological Analysis of Political Choice." *American Political Science Review* 82: 719–36.

Reiter, H. 1979. "Why Is Turnout Down?" *Public Opinion Quarterly* 43: 297–311.

Riker, W., and P. Ordeshook. 1968. "A Theory of the Calculus of Voting." *American Political Science Review* 63:25–43.

Scaff, L. 1975. "Two Concepts of Political Participation." *Western Political Quarterly* 28:447–62.

Shaffer, S. 1981. "A Multivariate Explanation of Decreasing Turnout in Presidential Elections, 1960–1976." *American Journal of Political Science* 25: 68–95.

Sharp, E. B. 1982. "Citizen-Initiated Contacting of Government Officials and Socio-economic Status: Determining the Relationship and Accounting for It." *American Political Science Review* 76:109–15.

———. 1984. "Citizen Demand in the Urban Context." *American Journal of Political Science* 28:654–70.

Sigelman, L., P. Roeder, M. Jewell, and M. Baer. 1985. "Voting and Non-voting: A Multi-election Perspective." *American Journal of Political Science* 29: 749–65.

Teixeira, R. 1987. *Why Americans Don't Vote*. New York: Greenwood Press.

Tingsten, H. 1937. *Political Behavior: Studies in Election Statistics*. London: P. S. Kind and Son.

Traugott, M., and J. Katosh. 1979. "Response Validity in Surveys of Voting Behavior." *Public Opinion Quarterly* 43:355–77.

Uhlaner, Carole. 1985. "Political Participation, Rational Actors, and Rationality." *Political Psychology* 7:551–73.

———. 1989a. "Rational Turnout: The Neglected Role of Groups." *American Journal of Political Science* 33:390–422.

———. 1989b. " 'Relational Goods' and Participation: Incorporating Sociability into a Theory of Rational Action." *Public Choice*, forthcoming.

Vedlitz, Arnold, James A. Dyer, and Roger Durand. 1980. "Citizen Contacts with Local Government: A Comparative View." *American Journal of Political Science* 24:50–67.

Verba, S., and N. Nie. 1972. *Participation in America*. New York: Harper & Row.

———, N. Nie, and J. Kim. 1978. *Participation and Political Equality*. Cambridge: Cambridge University Press.

Webb, Eugene J., Donald T. Campbell, Richard D. Schwartz, and Lee Sechrest. 1966. *Unobtrusive Measures: Non-Reactive Research in the Social Sciences*. Chicago: Rand McNally.

Wolfinger, R., and S. Rosenstone. 1980. *Who Votes?* New Haven: Yale University Press.

3

The Study of
Electoral Behavior

Jack Dennis

INTRODUCTION

The central institution of democracy as we know it today is that of popular elections. Democracy in Western and a few other, particularly Eng-
lish-speaking nations, had become reasonably well established by the
turn of the twentieth century; and these nations provided natural labo-
ratories for scholars to begin to ask more detailed empirical questions
about the processes of democracy. As democracy's most essential institution, elections attracted attention early; and indeed, the scientific
study of voting dates from just prior to World War I. The study of voting as we know it today thus began within the context of some ongoing
national democratic systems—democracies that included many of the
leading nations of the world by the nineteen-twenties.

The study of democratic institutions that preceded the twentieth
century was largely philosophically normative—or an admixture of normative, definitional, institutional, historical, and legal—which was appropriate to the intellectual style and concerns of political science in the
late nineteenth century (Easton 1953). Prior to World War I, therefore,
the studies on elections had been highly institutional and normative in
focus. The long-standing philosophical questions had been whether democracy, and thus holding elections, is really desirable and whether, in
a regime-stability sense, such institutions are feasible and workable. The

The comments and evaluations of panel members Robert E. Erikson, Charles Franklin,
and James Stimson are appreciated.

latter question had been answered in the affirmative, if broadly and pragmatically, by the historical evidence itself—that is, the existence of a substantial number of established democracies functioning in a successful and stable manner. The wider historical context had thus become ripe, by the time of World War I, for more careful analyses of the causal processes of elections by scholarly investigators.

A second major condition for the development of this field was methodological. In the early phases of this new work, scholars such as Giddings and Siegfried, and their respective students and intellectual descendants, discovered the analytic utility of aggregated, official voting returns. They began to develop more systematic ways to relate official voting records to other comparably aggregated evidence, such as census statistics and information about the demographic composition of particular, comparable geopolitical units. Later work, such as that done by Rice, Tingsten, Gosnell, Titus, Litchfield, Ewing, and Key, carried this methodology forward from a qualitative, cartographic phase to a more statistical, quantitative phase. While in many respects aggregate data analysis of elections has been superseded by the introduction and widescale use of the sample survey in voting studies, the original methodology has never totally disappeared or lost its utility for certain purposes. Indeed, for descriptive and predictive, more than for explanatory purposes, it is still widely used, especially for group, regional, and system-level generalizations. Such evidence is used to describe in sociodemographic terms the results of particular elections and to provide predictions, especially via computer simulations of the electorate, that are based on the electorate's stable aggregative sociogeographical attributes.

What the introduction of increasingly more scientific forms of sample surveys post-1935 allowed this field to do was to move on to a more interesting set of scientific questions, especially explanatory questions about election-relevant intergroup or organizational processes, interpersonal interactions, and intrapsychic processes relevant to voter decision-making. Surveys, with all of their limitations, constitute the most direct, and thus most valid, way of finding answers to explanatory questions about electoral reality. Surveys permit us as observers to get beyond the limits of aggregation and of seeing only the behavioral outcome, because they tell us things that only individual people can—particularly about intrapsychic or interpersonal events that have led to the behavior, and thus to the aggregate outcome. The scientific study of voting thus developed out of a well-established institutional context as well as from the opportunity for improved modes of observation: first were aggregated election returns matched to the social attributes of particular geopolitical units, and then came the rapidly improving methodology of the sample survey.

Less directly but as importantly, election studies also evolved from institutional, cultural, and philosophically normative concerns. Such questions provided the basis for a new scientific discipline once appropriate methods and observations became available. As in the case of most scientific disciplines, this new field grew out of a set of normative and pragmatic concerns that became conjoined to scientific method. Indeed, to be able to conclude that democracy was the best, or a very good, form of governance depends upon a factual premise—namely, that it is a workable form of government. This premise, in turn, is connected to the question of the capacities of ordinary people to participate directly in the public matters that most affect their lives. Whether the general populace is able, through democratic elections, to participate effectively in politics originated as an issue as far back as Plato and Aristotle, both of whom had strong, though opposed, ideas about the capacities of ordinary people to govern, and thus about the workability of a democratic regime. On the positive side was the argument that only legitimate regimes are likely to be successful and thus stable, and that democracy (through elections or other means) is the best way of insuring legitimacy. In addition is the factual hypothesis of Aristotle that the great multitude of people are inherently wiser, and thus more capable of effective government, than any particular subset of individuals in a society—no matter how carefully selected, well-trained, noble, or well-off financially. The countering argument is the Platonic view that only a small, very talented, specially selected, and well-trained subset of persons is likely to be able to govern effectively, and thus to maintain a good society and a stable political regime.

Thus, underlying the present-day efforts of large numbers of political scientists and others who study voting behavior is the very broad substantive question of the workability of democracy, which has become combined with the very extensive application of improved methods of inquiry, particularly sample survey methods. The latter are now backed up by techniques of statistical and psychometric data analysis, computer applications, and even improved ways of employing older methods, such as relating official voting returns to the geography, history, and demography of various political units.

A fourth important ingredient in developing the present-day field of voting studies has been the internal changes within the political science discipline itself. We are apt to forget, in a time in which the political scientists of the world conduct most of the voting studies, that the original impetus to develop the scientific study of voting came from outside our discipline. Sociologists were in general much more prominent in the early days of this field than were political scientists. Such early scholars as Giddings, Ogburn, Peterson, Siegfried, or Rice had little direct connection to what was known at that time as political science. Due to the efforts of later scholars such as Merriam, Gosnell, and Lasswell, however, a "behavioral revolution" began to emerge and to change the intellectual concerns of political scientists by the late 1940s and early 1950s (see Easton 1965; Eulau 1963; and Dahl 1961). This new mood, style, and focus of political inquiry moved quite readily to the study of voting—where the conditions adumbrated above made this political subdiscipline the most susceptible of any to the idea of scientific applications to the study of human behavior.

But one of the ironies left in the wake of the behavioral revolution was that political scientists became not only more open to the application of empirical theories and methods derived from outside our discipline, but that we then tended to become highly dependent upon these "foreign suppliers" of theory from our sister social disciplines—particularly sociology and psychology. Nowhere is this more true than in the study of voting. What I shall argue here is that whatever "indigenous" voting theory traditions we had originally possessed tended to become overshadowed once we had joined the mainstream movement to become more "socially scientific" along with the other social disciplines of sociology, psychology, anthropology, and economics.

Today the three most prominent major varieties of theoretical approaches to voting behavior, which I shall describe in more detail below, all derive from the theoretical efforts of other disciplines. This is true for most of the methodology that we apply in voting research as well. If one were a political science chauvinist, then such a largely derivative status might well occasion some disciplinary alarm, especially considering that it exists in connection with the subfield of the discipline where we have probably made our best scientific effort.

On the other hand, there are several ameliorating features of this "derivative status" that may comfort even the most disciplinarily status-conscious among us. One is that we had, even before the blossoming of the Michigan election studies into a major political science enterprise, an indigenous voting studies tradition that included such influential figures as Gosnell and Key; and their ideas have become incorporated into the mainstream of this research field in important ways. An example would be Key's "critical election" idea (1955). This concept was formatively incorporated into the literature on the nature of realignment of the American electorate.

Second, wherever they may have discovered their theoretical ideas for studying voting, political scientists today are clearly the most numerous and successful group of voting researchers of any discipline; and indeed, they constitute a more active band of psephologists than exists in all the other contributing disciplines combined (political sociologists, political psychologists, political economists, political geographers, political historians, political communication specialists, political anthropologists, and so on).

A third amelioration of the acculturation paradox of voting research is the more fundamental philosophical basis of electoral studies, as, for example, the desirability and workability of democratic institutions. The latter question is still more the province of political theorists than of philosophers, intellectual historians, or other abstract thinkers; and indeed, these political theory questions still provide a major part of the underlying intellectual momentum of even the most arcane, sophisticated, and hyperfactual studies of elections. One of the main questions of this research that has never been successfully answered, for example, is whether the average voter is capable of "rational" voter decision-making. This question is, in a somewhat different form, very like the question that Plato and Aristotle were presenting arguments about in fifth-century B.C. Athens. We have actually made some progress on this question since that time; and I shall try to say more about that later. But the point is that such a basic philosophical issue still plays an important role in driving even the best contemporary research in this field. This part of our effort, at least, comes from earlier political thought and thus is largely an indigenous political science contribution.

AN OVERVIEW OF PROGRESS TO THIS POINT

When we survey the field of voting studies today we are thus looking at the products of investigations that extend over most of the present century. One might try to overview these now overwhelmingly voluminous products of scholarly inquiry in a number of ways. One could usefully focus on the historical landmarks and turning points in the development of this subdiscipline (e.g., Rossi 1959) to give a narrative account of the major steps through which the field evolved as a rigorous, cumulative scientific enterprise. This is what we might term the intellectual history alternative, which has some merit as a description of how the field has advanced. Another possibility would be to select major operative concepts that define the field, regardless of their historical sequence or the electoral context in which they appeared. This is more of an analytic theory alternative. A third possibility would be to produce a propositional inventory that best summarizes the findings or known relationships, both those that serve as axioms for wider postulatory systems and those that are the testable (or tested) derivatives of such postulatory systems. A fourth perspective might be to focus on the operationalizations of the concepts, and thus on how the relationships were tested.

A fifth possibility would be to focus, more abstractly perhaps, upon the paradigmatic frameworks that hold these various elements—historical development, driving concepts, operationalizations, and major tested hypotheses about voting—together. We would ask, for this alternative, what are the chief metaphors or explanatory models, the most essential set of concepts, the operations and relationships that provide the underlying theoretical structure for these studies? Here we would ask what are the essential visions of the nature of humankind, of the political process, and of the situational forces that structure the interpretative application of the concepts, operations, hypotheses, and findings.

I have chosen, in the small space allotted here for comprehending this very large and diverse field, to focus mostly upon the last. While this choice will certainly include some elements of the other four ways of approaching this task, it will try to move beyond these matters to address more directly the underlying structure of ideas that gives this field its special character and how particular systems of ideas or theories of voting, concepts, operations, relationships, and findings thus relate to each other.

What I shall try to do in particular is to encompass the three major systems of ideas that now drive this field of research. This means leaving aside many minor themes. It also means narrowing the focus to mostly American studies and those geared to national elections, despite the fact that both elections in cross-national perspective and subnational elections have revealed many of the limitations of all three of these predominant theoretical approaches. Each of these theoretical systems is important enough to deserve a summary statement about its distinctive perspective. I have thus to reflect upon these dominant theories of voting as they exist in the most voluminous part of the voting literature, which concerns American national elections; and I leave for some later point any attempt to overview the other, equally interesting, aspects of this literature.

THREE THEORETICAL APPROACHES

Julius Caesar once observed, after many campaigns, that all Gaul is divided into just three parts ("Omnia Gallia in tres partibus divisa est"). Similarly, I divide the theory of voting that applies to American national elections into three essential types: those that are derived from the discipline of sociology, those that come more from psychology, and those that issue from economics. There has been a more sporadic, less well-defined indigenous voting study tradition in political science that surfaced in such earlier works as those by Gosnell, Key, Titus, Litchfield, and Ewing. But these "purely political" researches—those that turn upon an analysis of the impact of the state and its political institutions, or of the outcomes of major political events and programs—have gradually become submerged and syncretistically absorbed by the acculturative forces of other disciplines. Oddly, perhaps, as for the Japanese in their remarkable exploitation of Western technology, political scientists, using the disciplinary perspectives of others rather than relying upon their own indigenous culture, have done as much or more to develop this field than have the practitioners from any of the three contributing sister disciplines. The contributions from recent sociologists, psychologists, and economists themselves have actually been quite minor in this area; and they are so mostly because there are few disciplinary incentives to study voting within these other social disciplines as they are presently constituted. Thus, we have immediately the anomaly that political science rules the study of voting but does so, not so much with its own indigenous forms of conceptualization, but through adapting well the contributions of other disciplines to form the theoretical bases for its own studies of voting.

Now what are the three major paradigms of which we speak? The shorthand versions of these well-known paradigmatic systems are: (1) The "Columbia School," "Lazarsfeld et al.," or the sociological/demographic approach; (2) "The Downsian," or economic/"positive theory"/rationalist approach; (3) "The Michigan Model," "Campbell et al.," "SRC/CPS/NES," or "the social-psychological approach." All three of these approaches are reasonably well recognized in this field, given their prominence in the study of voting for more than thirty years. What I shall try to do is say something brief about what each paradigm seems to consist of, what its chief achievements have been, what its chief limitations are thought to be, where each theoretical approach might go next, and, in general, where do we go from here?

The Sociological Approach The scientific study of voting began more as a sociodemographic enterprise. Franklin Giddings and his Columbia University students, such as Stuart A. Rice (1928), put into motion a tradition that has never died in the study of voting despite its having been superseded by other approaches. The methodological tools used and developed by these pioneer, aggregate-data-focused investigators remained dominant until the 1940s, when their natural successors, Lazarsfeld et al., successfully introduced into academic studies of voting the revolutionary methodology of the sample survey, in their much heralded Erie County, Ohio, study of the 1940 presidential election (1944).

What the sociological approach has consisted of is not, however, coterminous with the field of sociology as we know it today. Rather, it had, particularly at the early stages, a mostly descriptive focus upon the geographic and demographic correlates of electoral behavior, together with the seldom well-articulated assumption that people's social, spatial, or group memberships largely determine their political actions.

This basic relationship was conceived as a direct one—that is, as describing an inescapable consequence of being Protestant or Catholic, white-collar or blue-collar, urban or rural, and so on. In a society that has consisted of strong religious, class, regional, and racial, or other ethnic groupings, it seemed natural, at least to sociologists, to assume that such memberships had relatively fixed, direct, strong effects on the vote. The primary electoral reality was thus a group reality, in this view.

Lazarsfeld and company extended what had been mostly descriptive analyses of voting in sociodemographic terms by bringing individual-level survey data to bear, demonstrating that their initial assumption of individual-choice behavior (rather than group-directed behavior) was not supported by their evidence. Indeed, "the psychology of choice" hypothesis of Lazarsfeld, analogized from his earlier studies of consumer, radio program, and occupational choices, did not receive confirmation from the evidence collected in Erie County, given the strong lack of evidence that individual political decision-making had occurred. What these authors concluded, especially after their Elmira Study (Berelson et al. 1954), was that voter decisions are better characterized as group decisions, or indeed, more accurately as cultural tastes than as individual political choice-making behavior. They also surmised that democracy probably would not be workable were it dependent for its existence on there being large numbers of autonomous, well-informed, active individual voters. What keeps democracy going, according to Berelson (1954), is rather the fact that people's voting is grounded in group experience, and thus voters operate successfully without having to make individual information-processing efforts during the campaign.

The essential idea here is that the political awareness of individuals is founded upon social experience and exists very little apart from such experience. Social context thus accounts for the high stability of behavior and intention during and between elections. These authors observed that relatively few people change their minds over the course of the campaign period; and those who do are precisely the ones who are most out of touch with, or marginal to, their own social context. The roles of campaigning and of the media were also thus minimized, given that the relatively few people who changed their votes remained unexposed to most of the campaign stimuli. Furthermore, the campaign stimuli were received only after being filtered through interpersonal communication; and thus such stimuli had mainly reinforcing or implementing effects. Such stimuli, if received, were also highly subject to selective bias on the part of the individual voter, especially selective perception.

What made all of this work in such a stable collective fashion at a political level were strong "brand loyalties" to the political parties. The latter were established through identification with the aspirations of particular sociodemographic groups, especially those which maintained organizations that communicated their political choices to their members.

The Social-Psychological Approach Now both the Michigan group and Anthony Downs learned a good deal from these earlier Columbia researchers, or so they thought. The Campbell, Kahn, Gurin, Converse, Miller, Stokes, et al. team that began their electoral studies in the late 1940s and early 1950s at the University of Michigan were evidently impressed with, and built upon, the finding of relatively little change in voter choices occurring during the course of the election campaign. These scholars also fastened on, and considerably sharpened the concept of "brand loyalties" (to the parties). And indeed, they placed such long-standing feelings of partisanship at the center of the voting-decision universe.

While they agreed to some extent with the sociological approach's conclusion that group forces are important, they distinguished sharply between long-term and short-term (proximate, efficient cause) influences. They then effectively pushed social memberships to the periphery of their explanatory system. They saw mostly these exogenous social variables as having importance only as they contributed to, or detracted from, the longer-term, traitlike attitudinal forces such as partisanship, or to the short-term attitudinal forces that caused deviations or defections from underlying patterns of partisanship, viz., issue positions and candidate images.

Individuals and their personal political psychology were brought back, however, as primary analytical foci. And individuals were brought back in terms of their most potent attitudes toward political objects: orientations to the political parties, to the policy issues debated in the campaign, or to the candidates contesting for office. Thus, the departure was to move voting study analysis away from what appeared to these authors as the less potent, more indirect, relatively static effects of membership in social groupings to the more dynamic, individual, attitudinal determinants of voter intentions and decisions. The triumvirate among the attitudes affecting candidate choices was led by political party identification, which was the core concept and operationalization of the emerging "Michigan Model" (1960), but which was followed in influence by the voters' images of the candidates, and finally by positions on issues.

In addition, the Michigan Model downplayed several other prominent concepts. There was little emphasis upon the impact of the campaign itself. This assumption of sparse campaign effects allowed these investigators to design for each election a static set of two connected surveys, which produced a late preelection, followed by a postelection, cross-section voter study. Nor did the media figure much in their assessment of causal forces. If the campaign was not very relevant to decisions, then neither would be the media inputs. Thus, the Michigan group started where the Lazarsfeld group had left off, with the assumption that the contributions of campaign stimuli were minimal.

Ideology also became a debased concept in this paradigm. Campbell et al.'s attempts to conceptualize and to measure ideological consciousness yielded extremely low incidence, little consistency across issues and issue domains, and weak correlations with the vote (Converse 1964). Thus, while less than 10 percent exhibited the usually assumed left/right consciousness and were thus guided in their decisions by such a political belief and value system, the overwhelming majority lacked such a consistent, comprehensive, principled understanding of politics; thus most voters did not apply ideology to their voting choices.

Political Independents, those heroes of Progressivism, high school civics textbooks, and political science critiques of an earlier era's political party machines, turned out to be a most dismal lot. They were found to be those least likely to live up to the demands of Lockean-style democratic theory, which called for a large and hardy band of rational, principled, active citizens vigilantly monitoring the actions of leaders and the course of public policy. Most Independents—in contrast to partisans—were poorly informed, little interested in the campaign, and therefore barely motivated to take part in elections.

The central emphasis of this theory was upon partisanship—partisan affiliation being seen not as dues-paying or voter-registering behavior but as a psychological, traitlike self-image. Partisan feelings normally originated in childhood, especially in the context of the family, thus reflecting indirectly a sociological basis of such political identification. The power of partisan feelings might thus be traced to some group-process basis; but once taken up as an important aspect of one's self-image, partisan identity became independent of groups, ideology, issues, or the particular candidate choices of the past, even though all of these may have contributed to its power as a central unifying theme in the individual's ongoing electoral experiences.

More transient electoral phenomena, such as the great issues of particular campaigns (including any grand sweeps of ideological currents and shifting value systems), or the contestants themselves, became subject to this underlying partisan reality's theoretical domination. Partisan affiliation became the "unmoved mover" in this explanatory system; and it has, at least for some of its defenders, continued to play this predominant role, even under very different societal and institutional conditions than those existing when this scheme was invented. In the 1980s, for example, when many of the signs of departisanizing influences are rampant across the land, partisanship's paradigmatic defenders have given up little of their theoretical ground (Converse and Markus 1979).

The Economic Approach Now one might have suspected that either a reassertion of the older political institutional tradition, à la Key, might have constituted a challenge, or alternatively, with the new "rediscovery of the state literature," that people would have traced the causal chain back a step to investigate more carefully the political, institutional circumstances surrounding the formation and maintenance of partisan outlooks and commitments, as has been true in the separate subdiscipline of political socialization research. (I shall return to these possibilities later in this essay.) But instead, the main challenge today to the predominant causal paradigm of the Michigan Model comes, surprisingly, from the rationalist voting behavior camp, led by the neo-Downsians. Anthony Downs published his seminal work *An Economic Theory of Democracy* in 1957. This important innovative volume thus predates the all-time greatest landmark piece of voting behavior literature, *The American Voter*. But even with this lead, the rationalists experienced difficulties in attempting to mount their assault, since most of the empirical weapons were already in the hands of the enemy. But under the determined leadership of William Riker and the "positive political theory" school, centered mostly at Rochester, and more lately at such technically oriented universities as Carnegie Mellon, California Institute of Technology, Washington University, and now, perhaps, Harvard University, there has been increasing subdisciplinary pressure from this group. This is especially marked by their recognition from, and modest inclusion in, the Michigan study data collections under the aegis of the National Election Study (NES)—as for example, in the bridging person of Morris Fiorina, who recently served as chair of the Board of Overseers of NES.

   The point of Downsian and post-Downsian rationalist approaches to the study of voting is that we should assume that voters are "rational" people. Indeed, this may be so even in limited-decision contexts such as voting. Downsians thus ask us to suspend disbelief and to regard it as plausible to assume that people have some large capacity for "rational" behavior in the voting context in that they are able to allocate their available means to achieve their own self-interested ends efficiently when voting. Furthermore, Downsians argue that we should regard ordinary voters as prone to weighing costs and benefits when they make their candidate or issue choices in elections, or when they decide about whether to participate at all. Second, their recommendation is that one needs to accept the analogy of the marketplace in some form—that votes are somehow like dollars, which one invests in the anticipation of some definable return. And third, we assume that at the time of the election individual voters are free of undue social pressure to conform to group wants and aspirations, thus, that they are truly individualistic decision-makers (that is, autonomous agents acting on the basis of free will), so that they can adapt their behavior to their own self-interested ends. Downs thus postulates that voters are able and willing to employ a voting calculus by which they weigh each party's promises for future policy initiatives against the record of past performance, relative to their own needs, for maximization of utility.

The common index against which government performance is to be measured is a "fixed conception of the good society," or what we might term ideology, conceived in terms of the degree of proposed intervention by the government in the economy (which is one version of the usual left/right scale). Thus, the question for the voter is essentially how well the party in power has done in achieving one's ideological objectives versus how well the other party would do if it were in power.

The candidates, as arranged across the ideological spectrum as teams of competitors by political parties, will vie with each other in trying to convince the voters that they are the ones most likely to bring greater benefits to each voter—which means moving public policy toward the desired point on the ideological spectrum for the voter. The theory is thus a combined theory of voter and candidate behavior, or how voters and "parties" interact in elections within the context of a common ideological framework for understanding politics, which also provides a common measure of relative performance in providing benefits.

On a variety of grounds, which I shall specify below, most social scientists involved in voting studies have experienced great hesitation (indeed, even violent negative reactions in some cases) about adopting this rationalist perspective. Nonetheless, it has received more attention over the past thirty years; and it has increasingly begun to be taken into the mainstream of voter studies. As a theory, it still does not challenge the preeminence of the Michigan Model; but it appears to be coming up fast on the outside, despite its apparent difficulties as an applicable theory, particularly in the American context. We shall turn to those difficulties presently, as well as to a discussion of the respective advantages of using this and the other types of approaches to studying voting.

Virtues and Vices of the Three Main Explanatory Paradigms Each of these three types of voting theory has certain advantages and disadvantages as the basis for a conceptual and propositional framework for this field of study. I will review what I take to be some of the major virtues and vices of each approach, in an attempt to put into perspective where we are, from a voting theory point of view, as we approach the final decade of twentieth-century voting studies.

Sociological Voting The greatest appeal of the sociological theory lies in the fact that much of what is contested in American politics has been defined in group, ethnic, regional, and social-strata, or socioeconomic terms. Thus, the heavy hand of the wider society and its patterns of stratification and group conflict is always upon politics; and this applies to voting as well. It is, for example, a quite plausible, if simplistic, idea that people's politically formative experiences must occur within various group contexts. Thus, group membership, identification, supportive interaction, and processes of communication about politics, as well as group support for individuals and control of deviance from group values, are likely to be important ingredients in how individuals form their political attitudes, and thus in their political behavior (Dennis 1987). In our collective academic gravitation toward accepting the importance of more proximate influences of political attitudes in determining voter choices, we are indeed apt to neglect the wider social context that shapes and maintains such attitudes and the fact that group distinctions often have great significance among the attitudes of consequence for voting (Brady and Sniderman 1985; Conover and Feldman 1984). To carry this argument a step further, we might also assume that individuals become indelibly stamped with the various social attributes that reflect wider social realities—attributes such as religious or racial membership, values, beliefs, and identifications, level of formal educational attainment, and the like. Some of these social attributes are voluntary and achieved, while others are involuntary and ascribed by others; some are quite central to people's own self-images and sense of place in society, while others are at best peripheral; some are strongly enforced, while others are merely encouraged or tolerated; and some are mostly implicit, while others take on highly elaborate, tangible, organizational forms. And some become the basis for comparing or referencing one's own sense of well-being, while others do not. What we most often have in voter surveys is a shorthand mode for observing these multidimensional complexities of how one is defined in various social contexts—which is to say, simply how to describe who people are in sociodemographic terms.

Third, one can raise these social distinctions to the level of aggregate behavior, to suggest especially that, because of these "naturally occurring" social or group distinctions, people are apt to see the commonality of their interests, wants, relative advantages (or deprivations), values, aspirations, policy concerns, and so on. Such group consciousness sets up the necessary condition for establishing and maintaining political cleavages. The political sociology branch of the sociological approach—which is at least an indirect descendant of the Columbia School, as in the work of such investigators as Lipset (1960), Alford (1963), Hamilton (1972), or Knoke (1976), puts this most pointedly. Political parties are formed in such an analysis in response to underlying social cleavages. Thus, not only is societal location primary for the individual in shaping her or his behavior, but socially based political competition—whether conceived in party, issue, candidate, ideological, or other terms—boils down to an underlying social reality. Social reality rewards some groups and social formations relative to others and thus sets in motion conflict along the lines of predominant social divisions, or cleavages within society. The voter simply mirrors such bases of cleavage in his or her behavior.

All this seems quite plausible on the face of it; yet there are a number of objections one may raise about such analyses of electoral behavior; and such objections have helped to make this the least popular option among political scientists for studying voting of the three major theoretical frameworks.

One major species of objections raised to the sociological approach is that of V. O. Key, Jr., who attacked the tendency of such studies toward social determinism—suggesting, relative to the work of Lazarsfeld et al., that sociologists' conclusion that there are few individual voting decisions but only "group decisions" in elections, or that voter choices are more like cultural tastes than individually deliberated decisions, threatens to take politics out of electoral behavior. Key believed that people do decide as individuals, and that they do so on the basis of weighing successive governments' policy performances. Moreover, the highly stable patterns of collective political behavior found over long periods in particular areas, such as Indiana or Tennessee, more accurately reflect the prior political experiences of the people there than simply the socioeconomic makeup of these electorates. In fact, the latter may have varied considerably over such long periods as from the middle of the nineteenth to the middle of the twentieth century, while voting patterns have stayed roughly the same.

The second most common objection to the sociological approach, which is somewhat the opposite to the objection above, has been to the relatively static nature of social attributes. The characteristics of people defined sociodemographically change relatively little in the short term, whereas voting patterns, and thus election outcomes, vary considerably. One thing that follows from this static state of social attributes is that when one puts these group characteristics of individuals into a multivariate, predictive model of (short-term) candidate choice, they do poorly—especially when unaided by attitudinal data—in accounting for the result. *The People's Choice* furnished us with the first combined instrument thought to be useful for this purpose (using class, urban versus rural residence, and religion)— that is, the well-known Index of Political Predispositions. But this turned out to predict the vote barely better than chance; and it was probably only a weak surrogate for partisan affiliations, insofar as these are to a small extent distinguishable in sociodemographic terms.

The worst failing, however, at least for that aspect of this approach which relies on demographic attributes of individuals for its account of voting (and I include here turnout or other foci of electoral participation, as well as candidate or party choices) is the inherent causal ambiguity of these categories. As I have pointed out earlier (Dennis 1986a), one does not know, for example, without fairly complex auxiliary evidence, what such relatively robust correlations of age or education with turnout actually mean. To ferret out what "age" means causally requires such complex designs as real-time, longitudinal data—i.e., panel studies, or long time-series, cross-sectional cohort analysis—or some other complex form of long-term attitudinal change analysis, such as the study of political socialization. Thus, to give a causal account of what the correlation with age means, it becomes necessary to sort out generational from maturational effects, for example, or to deal with age-related questions such as potential mobilization and/or conversion of voters of different ages—especially when new people are entering the electorate or when the balance of partisan, ideological, value, or group forces are changing in some important way.

Equally, "education," when found to be a correlate of turnout, may mean a great variety of things from a causal point of view. Education may entail simply coming from the kind of family background where politics is salient and thus, for example, going to the right kinds of schools to reinforce that political propensity. It might also mean longer exposure to, and enculturation in, the norms of the civic duty to participate, the learning of cognitive skills and knowledge that give one a better grasp of the complexities and abstractions of politics and government, the grasping of how to deal effectively with bureaucracies such as those that register voters, the habits of efficient collection and processing of political information, the ability to analyze critically the options available in elections, a greater capacity for using efficient means to achieve desired ends, holding ordered preferences, having attained a wider schema of political beliefs and values into which one can fit the particulars of the electoral situation at hand, and so on. Thus, as for most such variables of the sociodemographic variety, one needs a lot more information to make any sense of which ones of a fairly long list of possible causal forces were at work to produce this result. Even the best sociodemographic studies of voting, such as that of Wolfinger and Rosenstone (1980), present this difficulty. At best, these studies are descriptive rather than explanatory, as they stand.

The obvious solution for these difficulties is to design research around hypotheses about the social processes that stand behind such differences. But this would mean bringing this brand of "theorizing" up to present-day sociological standards. One of the difficulties in making group analysis of electoral behavior more popular is that it has been lifted out of a relatively early stage in the development of its parent field. Thus, while the framework contains references to social stratification, social roles, small-group dynamics and reference, or comparison-group phenomena, it developed too early for such newer approaches within sociology as social network or social organization emphases to have become incorporated. To make it more viable, therefore, one would need to incorporate newer concepts and operations.

More important, perhaps, one would need to give this approach greater currency by specifying clearly the conditions under which group membership, identification, communication, standards, wants, dynamics, and so on could be expected to affect electoral behavior, and when these group forces would be less relevant—as Converse did in his discussion of the changing levels of status polarization in American society across elections. Another example might be such conditions for group electoral relevance as the perceived legitimacy of group action, the extent of making group-referenced comparisons of well-being, and the effects of competing value systems to group politics, such as majoritarianism on the one side, or individualism on the other (Dennis 1987b).

Another potential feature of this approach—at least à la Lipset et al. contributions—is the quite old but still valuable focus on political cleavages. Where we have well-defined, enduring patterns of group competition, these are likely to be a more fundamental reality than are the parties, or their ideologies, or current issues and candidates. To some extent, all of the three theoretical approaches discussed here incorporate this idea into what is to be studied. Yet the sociological approach, given its rather loose formulation and only modest incorporation into the mainstream of contemporary voting research, has not fully taken advantage of these possibilities—at least within the American context.

Given the Michigan Model's resistance to the notion of ideology, at least in its formative period, a focus upon political cleavage (and thus upon political coalitions) was not given top billing. Since the period between 1964 and 1972, and the greater admission that issues, and thus ideology, might be looming larger in the electoral area (see Miller, Miller, Raine, and Brown 1976; and Miller and Levitin 1976), this possibility has been given new life, if not yet in the terms of political sociology.

Economic Voting Downsian or other rationalist analysis is the one of the three main approaches that has built this notion of ideology into the fabric of a well-articulated, explicit theory of voting; and indeed, the assumption of socially based political cleavages leading to ideology, or to "a fixed conception of the good society," becomes the common conceptual framework for linking masses and elites in elections. But Downs and post-Downsians merely *assume* this prior state of political cleavage (or of coalitions among groups that have overlapping programmatic preferences). These theorists provide no empirical analysis of this ideological discourse, given the essentially individualistic focus of their analysis. They assume from the outset that electoral politics runs on the engine of self-interested, economically attuned individuals who cast their ballots in favor of the team of promisers whose future performance as officials is most likely to result in their own (the individual voters') gain. The problem with Downsianism on this ground is thus twofold. First, group-related phenomena have no independent existence but are merely the assumed framework for, or outcome of, individual actions. The vote is merely a convenient mechanism for aggregating individual choices. Group processes of communication, interaction, collective effort, defining and enforcing common goals (that may override the individual interests of their members) become difficult problems for such analysis—and indeed often lead to one or another "paradox." Aggregated individual choices thus threaten to keep the outcome from being in some sense a "rational" one. Any analysis of the group is at best heuristic, given that the prime reality is the individual person as decision-maker.

Second, Downsianism runs up against the low incidence and variability of substantial ideological consciousness in the American system, and probably many other places, when we are talking about ordinary people. The Michigan studies revealed that average Americans have relatively infrequent and inconsistent ideological consciousness, even though they seem increasingly to exhibit some liberal versus conservative self-identification. They respond poorly to the content of public policy debates (namely, issues) and exhibit some mixture of ignorance, lack of motivation, and somewhat idiosyncratic interpretations of any larger issues being debated. This is not to say that structured political thinking is entirely absent among American mass publics. Ideology's appearance is rather, by comparison to partisanship, quite variable; and it depends upon the kind of election, and thus the kinds of candidates who come forward to articulate the substance of public debate. The late 1960s and early 1970s were evidently a time of heightened ideological consciousness in Americans; but the 1980s (despite a very ideological president) probably showed a subsidence of this effect in a direction akin to the unideological era of Eisenhower.

Is the bottle half full or half empty? Does Downsian analysis apply to voting phenomena, or does it not? What evidence we have (due mainly to the efforts of the Michigan studies) suggests, for the whole period from 1952 to 1988, that only a relatively small portion of the electorate are in any operative sense stable ideologues—although this effect becomes enhanced under certain electoral circumstances, such as the 1964 and 1972 presidential elections. In other words, people's "conceptions of the good society" are only partially fixed; and they are subject to changing electoral circumstances and to the "educational" efforts of candidates, the mass media, and political groups or other interpersonal attempts at persuasion, socialization, indoctrination, and swaying of opinion. The unanswered question here is how extensively available or well utilized does ideology (i.e., as a broad, consistent political belief and value system) need to be in order for Downsian or rationalist analysis to have real cash value?

We are probably able to show that such a belief system applies better to elites and activists than to the average person. Ideology thus provides at least a necessary common ground for those contesting the election to differentiate themselves from, or coalesce with, each other. In Europe, where it is common to speak of "party ideology," not only is this form of political discourse assumed with some confidence to hold for nearly everyone—candidates, activists, voters, and even bureaucrats (See Aberbach et al. 1981), but it is the main differentiator among the political parties as well. In the more muddied American case, this is simply not so true.

Now the answer to the question of the applicability of the rationalist scheme for studying elections is central also to whether we are willing to be Platonists (à la Converse) or Aristotelians (à la Key or Downs) about the purported wisdom of the masses. Aristotle, of course, did not go so far as to say that the workability of democracy depends upon the capacity of individuals per se to hold well-informed views and ordered preferences with respect to the great issues of public policy. But he did exude considerably more optimism than Plato did about the capacity of common people to show good sense or "wisdom" when it comes to deciding about the matters that affect their own lives, including who should lead them. Aristotle also argued that there is a real danger to the legitimacy, and thus the stability, of a regime if the masses are prevented from participating in their own governance.

What Downsianism comes down to, the factual premise that is fundamental to its normative system, is whether the individual person, in Lockean, or indeed Millian fashion, is capable of acting wisely on his or her own behalf through participatory (i.e., electoral) activity. The central assumption of the rationalist approach is individual "rational" behavior—even though this may lead to some interesting puzzles once individuals make their decisions and these decisions are aggregated (for example, the Condorcet/Arrow problem (1951), or the paradox of not voting, à la Riker and Ordeshook (1973). In order for this theory to work empirically (or worse, even normatively), the voter must consciously survey and compare the available alternatives, develop a set of ordered (especially transitive) preferences or decision rules, and apply this preference ordering or set of rules to the available alternatives in such a way that costs are minimized relative to expected gains.

To make all this happen consistently and smoothly depends at the very least both upon some motivational factors and some cognitive ones for the individual, as well as upon some facilitating environmental circumstances that have to do with the nature of the electoral process. Here we go beyond merely assuming, with Aristotle, that wisdom resides somewhere, collectively, in the great mass of individuals who comprise the potential electorate. And we are probably going well beyond V. O. Key, Jr., or Abraham Lincoln, who assumed that you can't fool all of the people all of the time. Downs is proposing, rather more positively, that voters are motivated enough by the prospects of politics that they will identify what are their own best interests, needs, and concerns relative to what is being debated; and they will have the necessary cognitive capacities to calculate their expected utilities in the light of various available courses of action. Voters will also have, it is assumed, the necessary external resources available, such as accurate knowledge of the options, to make reasoned choices—once they have in place the internal resources of motivation and cognitive capacity to find out what they need to know in order to decide what is best from their own (especially economic) perspective.

A number of possible difficulties with such assumptions have occurred to nonrationalist-minded students of electoral behavior (which I would estimate to be something like 90 percent of all of those who do this kind of work). This approach, in essence—without necessarily intending to—denies both the relevance of group-centered (sociological) analyses and of long-term, relatively fixed attitudinal forces (Michigan Model), except for those that surround the notion of "one's conception of the good society."

The first respect in which the utility of the Downsian and post-Downsian rationalist models (for example, Riker and Ordeshook 1973, or Ferejohn and Fiorina 1975) seems high—for those of us brought up in an individualistic culture—is in bringing back the individual decision-maker to a respected status after his or her eclipse in the wake of *Voting* and *The American Voter*. Neither Berelson or Converse, as spokesmen for their respective camps, has conveyed to us any great faith in the individual voter's capacity to carry the cognitive and motivational burdens assumed in the usual models of democracy, especially in what is assumed about citizens in the Lockean, or rational-active, model of democracy. Downs conclusively puts the individual at the center of the voting universe; and he therefore directly challenges the notion that individual people are not able to be masters of their own political fates.

The second point where Downsianism scores well is in matching up voter and candidate cognitions and motivations, and in linking together into a mutual strategic system both electoral elites and masses. In neither the Lazarsfeld et al. sociological approach nor in the Michigan et al. social-psychological approach is there more than a static, cursory, and mostly separate-track analysis of electoral masses and elites, even though one must applaud such brave efforts as that of Miller and Stokes (1966) to put this all together through their parallel surveys and analysis of representation.

Where such representation studies probably miss the mark, so far as Downs is concerned, is in not focusing sharply enough on the processes of strategic interaction that go on within the campaign—the mass/elite interplay that leads to pressure for ideological convergence by the parties and their candidates over the course of the election campaign. A party's candidates must try to convince each bloc of voters that it is indeed the one that stands closest to them, and thus the group or bloc will be rewarded with greater sought-after benefits once the candidates are put into office.

Despite the increasingly elegant mathematical formulations made by the descendants of Downs (and the positive theory school), and the very serious intellectual efforts on their part to work out the theoretical problems that arise within this framework (and such problems are many, given what seem to be a host of implausible assumptions and inferences), this approach has never had much currency among the great band of economics-doubting voting behavior researchers. Most of the latter are sufficiently mathematically and statistically sophisticated not to be unduly impressed and thus diverted by the technical prowess of these applied mathematicians—especially as the whole enterprise is perceived to run against the grain of the leading paradigm. This impression of irrelevance has been greatly reinforced by the usual lack of impressive empirical efforts on the part of these theorists to test major portions of this theoretical apparatus in the real world of electoral behavior.

Advocates of the leading paradigm suggest that only in very limited respects could such an axiomatic system have much explanatory relevance. The ideological core for common political discourse is not there. People can hardly be imagined to engage in any calculations of the marginal advantages of one set of political options versus another if there is a high level of misinformation or no information about the nature of the alternatives. Too often, these critics argue, real people do not meet the minimal tests for ideological thinking, or even the more partial, restricted requirements for voting on issues. In particular, most people fail to acquire any realistic idea of what government policies have been in effect, even on matters of significant concern to them, or of how well the performance of the party in power has matched its promises made before the last election. Indeed, there is a real question, given the lack of widespread issue voting, and thus a lack of the government in power's having received any mandate for some given set of policy initiatives, whether the whole idea of responsibility for policy performance is an appropriate criterion to apply, at least in what are for the most part highly candidate-centered American elections. Despite the protestations of scholars like Key and Fiorina, backed up by at least weak positive empirical findings in behalf of mandate/performance theories, most students of the process remain unconvinced that policy performance judgment is more than an incidental feature of what is taking place in our elections.

A connected general problem with the rationalist approach is the whole set of ambiguities surrounding the notion of *rationality* itself, especially when applied to the highly circumscribed role of the mass election voter. What one finds over a variety of works by proponents of the rationalist approach—and indeed, this is true even within the confines of *An Economic Theory of Democracy*—is that *rationality*, like *democracy*, to which in this literature it is closely connected, means much more than a single thing.

In Downs's original formulation—which at first glance looks to be a parsimonious rendering of a deductive theory of voting based on a few simple axioms—one finds a variety of meanings (I would estimate around seventeen) for what it means to be rational. At the voter's level of behavior, simply being deliberative—that is, weighing the possible consequences of one's decision prior to making it—may suffice, even though this weighing of consequences may leave out important options or wrongly assign probabilities to various outcomes, or misrepresent the true payoffs associated with alternative courses of action.

In post-Downsian accounts, Downs's quite explicit emphasis upon *efficiency* has largely been replaced by *consistency*, especially ordered or transitive preferences. But what Downs more frequently incorporated into his notion of rationality was conscious goal selection, and thus goal-oriented behavior, or the capacity for making decisions when faced with a range of alternatives. This meaning arises especially in connection with using transitively ordered preferences and doing so consistently over time—namely, when faced again with the same set of alternatives. Downs also refers to "the self-interest axiom," which means "whenever we speak of rational behavior, we always mean rational behavior directed primarily toward selfish ends." He talks a good deal about weighing probable costs against probable benefits, about reducing uncertainty by collecting and processing (relatively efficient) information, and so on.

Where this has all gone is in several directions, definitionally. Later students operating in a Downsian mode have variously emphasized different parts of this definition, such as utility maximization (the cost/benefit ratio-weighing aspects), transitively ordered preferences, self-interest (especially economic self-interest), the idea of informed or uncertainty-reducing decision-making, the idea of being conscious and deliberative about the options before acting, or more simply, decision-making driven more by the head (cognition) than by the heart (emotion). More specific adaptations of various of these ideas within the context of voting have been to self-interested versus sociotropic voting; ideologically driven voting; salient issue, hard issue, position issue, or just plain issue voting; informed voting; retrospective, prospective, or performance-driven decision-making; flexible partisanship; and other rationalist-oriented and motivated voting.

Downsian analysis thus opens up a variety of analytic possibilities by what appears to be an unintentional ambiguity about its most central concept. Indeed, as the neo-Downsian trailing literature demonstrates clearly, there is more than one royal road to the kingdom of rationality, given its diversity of meanings. These possibilities exist quite apart from any meanings or distinctions normally considered outside this theoretical tradition, such as substantive versus procedural rationality, short-term versus longer-term rationality, or collective versus individual rationality. One might simply throw up one's hands at this point and say that we need more stability of meaning here before proceeding with empirical work that would test whether voters are rational and therefore in one sense whether democracy is workable.

What I would suggest is that a more hopeful posture with respect to such conceptual ambiguity is to recognize it for what it is, but then to focus upon its various dimensions for legitimate research purposes. This posture would force us to be clearer about what we are talking about when we refer to someone as rational. Unless we believe that this confusion is endemic and fatal in the rationalist approach (as well as in its parent discipline of microeconomics) because it must necessarily oversimplify and thus distort political reality—particularly in its monomotivational assumption that everyone is unavoidably (and commendably) an egoistic hedonist—then we can proceed. What we must do first is to formulate more clearly the whole set of relevant rational attributes or criteria of judgment. Then we can test which ones apply and which do not in voting. We have a few instances of this type of research already (e.g., Brady and Ansolabehere 1989), where it can be shown, for example, that a substantial number of people have transitively ordered preferences among candidates but may not have done what Downs believed would be axiomatic—viz., attain full knowledge of the range of available candidate alternatives.

Second, when people fail to live up to some presumed criterion of rationality, we need to find out why. Is it some inherent incapacity to act rationally? Is it the result of a failure of prior education or political socialization? Does the general culture fail to support it, given that the culture itself does not value such rational traits, skills, or performance? Or are the circumstances of the election itself inhibiting, due to a lack of clear information or definition of differences among groups, ideologies, parties, issues, or candidates?

The questions we should be asking, therefore, are more fine-grained and would include the following:

1. Which aspects of rational voter behavior are more likely; and which are more unlikely, in general?
2. Who is more likely to act in a rational manner as a voter, and who is not?
3. Under which circumstances will voters become more rational in their approach or capacities (such as when clear, sharp differences on issues are provided by candidates)?
4. What is the life-span developmental sequence like for those who do or do not become more rationally oriented in their voting behavior?
5. Which kinds of cultural, social, historical, institutional, or other forces create a climate conducive to rational voting behavior, and which do not?

To put the matter in this way assumes precisely the reverse to that which is taken as given in this approach. Axioms, such as assumptions about rationality, are simply not questioned and are considered by proponents to be not subject to empirical testing in the same way as are the postulates derived from such axioms. But since the plausibility of this paradigm is at the moment relatively low among students of voting (although not among students of the theory of the business firm), perhaps more forceful steps must be taken to demonstrate its value. One of these persuasive steps could be to test the axioms directly, and to see therefore whether they provide a worthy basis for further reasoning. Here at least, if not in economics, such a task must be faced, given the dominance of a contrary paradigm.

One thing that proponents of this general approach should find comforting, however, is the growing number of instances where there have been empirical tests of limited aspects of rationalism among voters. While the results in each case are far from overwhelming, they are beginning to show that Downsian and other rationalist hypotheses are indeed empirically worthy, both for electoral elites and masses, and both in this country and elsewhere. (See, for example, Fiorina 1981, Brunk 1980, Filer and Kenny, 1980, and Dennis 1986.) What such studies suggest is that, in carefully delimited respects, rational behavior is significantly present, both among those who conduct campaigns and in those who are trying to decide both whether to turn out to vote and, among the available candidates, which to prefer.

As we approach the next decade of research in this area, we may well expect to find increasing numbers of extensions of this form of analysis. Most research in the field of voting research is unlikely to accept fully the analogy of the marketplace, given the great differences in how the situations of buyers and of voters are constrained. There is, especially, the fact that no direct and tangible individual benefits are forthcoming to voters as result of their individual choice behavior, which is, in contrast, true in the marketplace. This greatly limits the applicability of the economist's metaphor. There is, nonetheless, some point in asking in which respects, if any, people do take economically-rational-like actions when they confront electoral choices. These choices will no doubt turn out to be conditionally rational—that is, more rational under some circumstances than under others, more rational for some types of individuals than for others, and more rational in what Almond (1960) referred to as rational-calculating-secular political cultures than in those not so valuatively structured. The rationalist's basic question remains a relevant one so long as we regard it as important to understanding how democracy operates. This is especially true if we accept the premise that individual citizens behave in a positively motivated, informed, and principled manner.

The Michigan Model: Psychological Voting The paradigmatic expression of voter behavior by the Michigan Model is quite different both from the sociological model and the economic model. Relative to the latter, Campbell, Converse, Miller, and Stokes (1960) provide more of a Platonist than an Aristotelian judgment. They do not begin with any special concern for the rational propensities of individual voters. Nor do their findings, at least from the evidence of the 1950s and 1960s, support such a notion. In contrast to Downs, they provide a subtle, diffuse, and rather indirect theoretical approach. It is very much inductive rather than deductive; and it begins not with a grand normative question—such as the desirability or workability of democracy—or with a set of axioms about the nature of human motivation as applied to elections, but rather with the practical aim of giving the best empirical account possible of what causes people to decide as they do in voting. The fundamental causal concept is that of political attitudes, which are individual predispositions to act or to decide in a predictable manner.

The attitudes of relevance to voting are both short-term and long-term in terms of their formation and maintenance; and they constitute the most potent and proximate influences upon how individuals decide at election time. Political knowledge and skill in calculating the probable benefits from one's electoral choices may be of interest, but only as they pertain to the attitudes of greatest consequence for voter decisions, such as long-standing partisan commitments or personal evaluations of the available candidates. At Michigan, affect precedes cognition.

The theoretically central, or "core" political attitude is that of partisanship, which operationally is most directly observed as political party identification. What gives this attitude special potency is that it is a long-term, traitlike self-image that unites whatever other political forces bear upon the electoral outlook of the individual. At the individual level, partisanship also reflects the larger institutional context that is provided by the political parties as they compete over leadership and policy and, more fundamentally, as they define the terms of competition for elections and campaigns. What partisanship does, therefore, is to translate a major part of the wider institutional forces at work in society into individually meaningful electoral terms and to provide, for the observer, a major portion of the causal account of voter decision-making.

The two other most consequential attitudes of the Michigan trilogy are relative positions on issues—which translates the manifest content of debate in the election campaign into personal terms—and candidate images, evaluations, or orientations. The latter refer to the comparative judgments voters make among the contestants—measured as global affect, particular likes and dislikes, or, since 1980, in terms of the emotions generated in response to these candidates, their personal qualities, perceived competence, and leadership experience.

The beauty of the Michigan Model as originally formulated was that it was extremely close to the data, and thus to the empirical operations on which it stands or falls as a theory. This approach is very unlike the Downsian, which seems at first glance to be a single deductive structure, but which in reality is a series of well-connected deductive substructures, with a formidable array not only of postulates but of assumptions necessary for deducing these many postulates.

What perhaps best characterizes the founders of the Michigan School of voting research is their strong propensity for theoretical abstinence. This self-denying propensity, relative to explicit theory, comes clearly, for example, in their removal of the diagram of the "funnel of causality" from the published version of *The American Voter* after it had been circulated in prepublication form with the diagram included. Their style has been one of always staying close to the evidence; and later, younger acolytes of the "Mother Church," especially those with Michigan degrees, even when challenging one or another of the hallowed substantive tenets, have stuck very close to the data (see, for example, Rusk 1982 or Weisberg 1980). And indeed, the great attraction of the Michigan voting study enterprise for the rest of the field has been a keen impulse to collect generally useful, valid, and reliable voter survey evidence—even if the terms of collection, despite their opening this enterprise very widely to other scholars, are still very much within the traditions of the original formulation. What the Michigan researchers have been able to do is to take command of the voting behavior subdiscipline, in part through providing a workable, if not unduly theoretical, approach combined with highly usable data. Indeed, under the organizational leadership of Warren Miller, these efforts have been greatly expanded over the decades; and they are now established as a worldwide research enterprise (some would say "empire") and an apparently permanent, if relatively permeable, research cartel. The Michigan voter studies are undoubtedly the most remarkable and successful collective research effort ever mounted in political science, and are indeed unique among the annals of all social disciplines.

We should be clear that, despite such canonization, the commandments of the Mother Church are not etched forever in stone: the original "divine commandments" on how to conduct voting research were not meant to be permanent once *The American Voter* was published. We find, on the contrary, substantial paradigmatic movement at Michigan, particularly as the more troubled, issue-focused era of the 1960s and 1970s replaced the halcyon days of the Eisenhower electoral era.

Philip Converse, of the originators of the team at Michigan perhaps the most prone to explicate and uphold the theoretical implications of the original vision of the voter, has generally stuck to his guns, both in reaffirming the fundamental causal nature of partisanship, the low salience of ideological thinking among voters, and the generally pessimistic view of the rational propensities of the average citizen. The latter applies particularly to his analysis of the low state of voter information, the lack of strong electoral motivation, and the absence of a consistent wider political belief structure necessary in the Downsian scheme for rational choice behavior. Converse has indeed borne much of the burden of repelling the repeated assaults over the years on the Michigan paradigm, both the attacks of the pro-ideologists and issue-voting proponents and the more recent attempts to undermine the causal primacy of party identification.

Campbell, in his later years, turned away from studies of voting entirely and concerned himself more with racial attitudes, quality of life studies, and other matters. Miller and Stokes, by contrast to Converse, showed a more adaptable research posture—indeed, what developmental psychologists like to refer to as "greater openness to experience." Stokes joined with Butler to produce the justly famous *Political Change in Britain* (1969), which adapted the Michigan model to a foreign, if comparable, setting. But in doing so he incorporated many elements of a more class-based, demographically attuned sociological perspective. Miller has been not only the key organizational force in keeping the NES time series alive, on-track, and expanding, but has even welcomed the idea that partisanship is perhaps not everything—and thus that issues and even ideology may, under appropriate circumstances, count for as much or more in some presidential elections (Miller, Miller, Raine, and Brown 1976; and Miller and Levitan 1976).

Thus, the key Michigan Model players themselves have moved variously as the time series has become extended and as new assaults on *The American Voter* conclusions (and thus upon its theory) have been mounted. These challenges have included questions about the low weight given to ideological consciousness in the Michigan Model (for example, Nie and Andersen 1974; Stimson 1975) and the connected objections to the third-place ranking of issues among the dominant trinity of voter attitudes (see, for example, Key 1966; Pomper 1972; and Nie, Verba, and Petrocik 1979), or toward the retrospectively judged performance of incumbents, and thus the assertion of other major attitudes such as those connected to the economy (Fiorina 1981). There has also been disagreement with the hypothesis of low motivation to participate by the average person (Verba and Nie 1972), and lately, more subtly, the attempted substitution of other psychological, especially cognitive, approaches to the study of voters' attitudes for the reference group/small group dynamics/political socialization approach referred to (albeit rather briefly) in *The American Voter*. Such subtle paradigm substitution assaults from cognitivist psychology include the concepts of cognitive balance (Brody and Page 1972), cognitive schemata (Conover and Feldman 1984), and attributions (Brady and Sniderman 1985).

The most potentially damaging attack mounted thus far on the theoretical structure that underlies this work probably comes from a loose collection of people who for the most part basically believe in the Michigan Model but who nonetheless have uncovered some disturbing problems with the meaning and measurement of partisanship. What the researchers in this disparate band of challengers have revealed is that party identification is not necessarily an unmoved mover through the course of the campaign (Brody 1977; Franklin and Jackson 1981), that partisan identities are weakening as public disapproval of and indifference to partisanship have grown (Dennis 1980, 1986b; Wattenberg 1984; and Burnham 1970), that partisan structuring of the vote has declined substantially (Nie, Verba, and Petrocik 1979), and that partisan affiliations may have become more fleeting and insubstantial. Indeed, party identification may now consist more of a cognitive ledger or balance sheet for recording the bottom line on a person's past experiences with the parties than as an integral part of one's political self-image or identity (Fiorina 1977).

The worst effects on the Michigan Model of this new critique of the core concept probably come from those who find special problems with the traditional measurement index—namely, the well-known seven-point index of political party identification. What the latter studies demonstrate (Petrocik 1974; Keith et al. 1977; Valentine and Van Wingen 1980; Weisberg, 1980; and Dennis, 1989a, 1989b) is that there are clear nonmonotonicities in the scale, relative to a prediction of increasingly consistent partisan behavior as one moves along the scale in either direction from pure Independents to strong party identifiers. Second, this critique suggests that partisanship and independence are not necessarily on the same attitudinal dimension. Third, when one measures partisanship and independence separately, the Michigan account of independence essentially falls apart.

Now, we may ask, with these kinds of demonstrable empirical defects at the core of the theory, and indeed discovered on the approach's own empirical grounds, how does the Michigan paradigm not only still survive today in a robust form and continue to guide research, but even dominate the whole field? To what causes can one attribute this persistence in the face of such adversity? As is probably true for any other world religion, Michiganism in electoral studies has wisely founded its success on a few simple, plausible dicta, the most noteworthy of which is that most people unavoidably incorporate the nature of political competition (in this case, via the two major political parties) into their own thinking and feelings about electoral objects. Second, voters are apt to receive plenty of reinforcement for these baseline orientations through their own subsequent electoral experiences. In addition, such orientation may well be grounded in prior political history and pervasive social pressures. Such a long-term attitudinal structure thus leads one to form new short-term attitudes at each election that are in keeping with the preexisting ones. This portrait of the process of making and keeping the electorate partisan has the corollary observation, as Paul Beck rightly points out, that conventional portraits of elections in America as struggles among alternative ideologies consciously rooted in voter's minds are vastly overdrawn (Beck 1986, 245).

Once one adds these plausible, and evidentially supported, simple dicta to the impressive organizational presence of the Michigan studies via SRC/CPS/NES and a certain degree of monopolization of major national electoral data collection in this country, plus the unmatched efforts in professional socialization and networking via ICPSR and the Michigan Summer Program, then one has a formidable professional, indeed societal, presence. It is one that the voter study profession, for whatever it may think of the theoretical terms of the model or of the extent of applicability of its conclusions, can ill afford to do without. Therefore, even the Michigan Model's worst enemies are likely to feel they have some stake in its research enterprise, and thus to endorse its long-term maintenance as a research cooperative/cartel.

Given the Michigan Model's mostly inexplicit theory (in that its raison d'être has been more factual than theoretical), it might be better characterized not as a "model" at all, but rather as a heretofore partially revealed general analytical framework into which a variety of more specific models of voting can be fitted. Some of these new fittings involve rearrangements of the pecking order across elections of party, issue, and candidate (Shulman and Pomper 1975). Some involve modest adjustments in the direction of admitting more focus on issues, or even more ideological content, to the account of voter decisions. Some may set the stage for admitting other kinds of variables (e.g., rationalist), such as posited voter orderings of preferences across a range of issues, and thus preferences over a range of government performances. Prospective, synchronous, and retrospective judgments not simply about policy performance, but the larger, more symbolic performances of incumbents relative to group aspirations, might in time also become part of this judgmental scheme. The model as it stands contains great adaptiveness; and it is therefore quite capable of model add-ons or model renovation. Even under the pressure of more complex data analysis methods (e.g., nonrecursive simultaneous equation modeling) or more efficient modes of data collection (e.g., computer-assisted telephone interviewing), this framework has shown its capacity to persist and grow.

The Michigan Model continues to beat the opposition; and it does so on a number of grounds. Organizationally it has achieved virtually the status of a world religion, or at least a Japanese-style multinational corporation. Part of the substantive success of this movement is its parsimonious (some would say unnecessarily terse, diffuse, and inexplicit) presentation of its major theoretical terms. It thus has an advantage, paradoxically, over more clearly drawn, internally coherent, deductive-appearing approaches such as that of Downs and the positive theorists. Michiganism has another advantage over rationalist theory as well in that, in keeping with the widely approved, long-standing taste for hyperfactualism among students of voting, it has been unduly vigorous in the production of voting "facts." The rationalist theorists, by contrast, have remained mostly mere theorists (if mathematically elegant ones); and they therefore have not become a significant part of the evidential basis of the subdiscipline. Mathematics, while certainly one of a variety of useful tools available to the election behavior analyst, is an insufficient basis for achieving full legitimacy among most students of voting behavior.

The inheritance from economics of rationalist premises has also

come with a high tax on it—viz., a substantial unrealism and oversim-
plification of the nature of human motivations, particularly in assuming
the voter's motivation to follow electoral proceedings to be high yet
limited in focus to his or her economic self-interest. In the world that we
all think we know about, and which psychology as a discipline tells us
much about systematically, we are usually prepared to believe that voters' motivations are often low, mixed, and highly subject to external,
especially social, pressures. The "economic person" model thus lacks
for most students of voting strong intuitive appeal—except perhaps for
those among us whose thought processes have become more "efficient"
through learning economics, or by pursuing advanced degrees at such
meccas of "economic rationality in politics" as the University of Rochester, Carnegie-Mellon University, Washington University, or California Institute of Technology.

Where the Michigan Model perhaps does not necessarily beat the
rationalist model is in the broader questions of democratic theory that
both raise implicitly. Being generally confused about whether it is a de-
scriptive/causal or a normative/prescriptive discipline, economics has
felt no discomfort about asking whether people as individuals are rational, and within the election context whether such rationality may be
assumed sufficient to make democracy workable. This question probably sounds too value-laden to interest most of the hard-core behavioralists that populate the voting behavior research area. There is a sense in
which the Michigan researchers do give an answer to this broader question—and it is a more elitist, Platonic, and pessimistic one than Downsians would give. While neither formulates these broader questions of
where it all leads as explicitly as one might prefer, the Michigan School,
with its terse theoretical language, leads discussion away from such
questions more rapidly.

Indeed, the Michigan team's best attempts at wider theory explication probably have to do with the macro-level features of partisanship,
as in "the normal vote," or in the analysis of maintaining, deviating,
and realigning elections, or perhaps in the early representation studies.
But these efforts at micro-macro linkage lack the kind of crisp, intuitive
strategic linkage of electoral elites and masses that Downs accomplishes
in his *An Economic Theory of Democracy*. Downs sees that it is an interactive process, like supply and demand in microeconomics, between those
who would seek office and those who have the capacity to keep them
from attaining it. Masses and elites are thus interactively dependent in
the Downsian scheme of things, not simply operating in parallel fashion
or splendid isolation—which is more the view, and thus the analysis, of
the early Michigan studies.

We may suspect, on the other hand, that where the Michigan Model
may have some advantages over Downsian analyses (and post-Downs-

ianism, for that matter) is precisely in its lack of purity, explicitness, and precision about its major theoretical themes. As I have argued earlier (Dennis, 1986a), the theory of turnout, for example in *The American Voter* and afterward, looks to be quite straightforward: it is simply that the more the potential voter is politically involved—i.e., motivated to take part—the more she or he is in fact likely to do so. This is, when one thinks about it, rather flat as a causal interpretation of the phenomenon. It says that the more one is involved psychologically in politics, the more one is likely to become involved behaviorally by turning out to vote. Now, admittedly, there are some nice specifications of which aspects of politico-psychological involvement are of greatest consequence in this connection—viz., political efficacy, citizen duty (to vote), interest in the particular election at hand, concern about which party wins, and intensity of partisan feelings. Yet what one craves causally here is some wider account of how it is that people come to have this sense of political involvement, in these and other senses, in the first place, or what sustains it.

One possible way of extending this analysis backward along the causal chain is to take account of the psychic events leading up to a state of commitment to, or alienation from, the system of electoral politics, and indeed feelings toward the wider institutional context that surrounds elections. What I would argue is that a latent theoretical theme present in these Michigan studies is political alienation or commitment, and this theme of political alienation has gradually become more manifest, especially since the 1970s (as in the *Continuity Guide*, a section of which deals with such variables). This, I would argue, is a strength of the approach, because it intersects with and accommodates the interests of those who want to pursue other kinds of macro-level themes than what was most manifestly part of this effort at the beginning. Another such latent theoretical theme that has gradually emerged in the Michigan studies, after much struggle, is that of the role of political ideologies, coalitions, and cleavages. This theme has been handled more from a social-psychological than an economic point of view, however.

A further main feature of the Michigan studies, however, relative to the sociological approach, has been its exiling of the variables causally central to Lazarsfeld et al. to the periphery of analysis (and thus to the later chapters of *The American Voter*). Campbell et al. make the more static, descriptive, demographic characteristics exogenous to the main explanatory system of proximate political attitudes; and the Michigan approach focuses most data collection and analysis efforts away from such variables. As I observed earlier, the Michigan Model in this way has never threatened to kill off social attributes as being contributors to the account one gives of voting, but only to hold them as permanent hostages. This research strategy essentially undermines any efforts by those dependent upon NES to treat such social attributes in more than a superficial way. Whatever recent interest in group effects on voting has resurfaced in these studies (e.g., Miller, Gurin, Gurin, and Malanchuk 1981; Conover 1989) has done so mostly at the margins, without there being more than modest accommodation of such theoretical interests. The manner in which the Michigan Model has treated the sociological model is by simply absorbing it and attaching it as a set of auxiliary questions to the main force of the analysis.

A Fourth Dimension?

Now whatever happened, we may ask, to the contribution of pre-Michigan, indigenous political science to the development of this field? We know that a variety of scholars with political science department membership have worked in the field of electoral studies without being part of these dominant theoretical approaches. For the most part, these more institutionally and historically oriented scholars, such as Gosnell, Key, or Burnham—who are representative of those prominently outside these three "mainstreams" of voting analysis—have remained isolated theoretically. But, in some part, they have also been absorbed by the larger and more powerful currents of voter studies.

Key, for example, opposed in varying degrees both the sociological school and the Michigan School, believing that the former took the politics out of electoral behavior and that the latter ignored the responsiveness of voters to the two major parties' policy performance. He came closest in spirit to the assumed Downsian emphasis upon the reasonableness of longer-term voter decision-making. But some of his ideas, such as "critical elections," were accepted from the outset by the band of researchers from Ann Arbor; and indeed, Key's concept became the basis for their more elaborate version of the types of elections—especially the general concept of realignment that they elaborated. Unfortunately, this Key-inspired aspect of the dominant theory has fallen upon hard times, given the lack of a clear and general realignment in the post-New Deal period. Key's concept has been weakened by disagreements among realignment scholars about what the concept really means and what brings it into being.

What we find today is a reasonably large body of political scientists who study elections from an institutionalist point of view, but without any overall guiding theory. They focus upon the nature of party organization, competition, and realignment, as well as such topics as registration requirements for eligibility to vote, suffrage restrictions, the form of the ballot, effects of holding various types of primaries, and the like. All of this is done primarily within an atheoretical framework—at least by usual social science theory standards. This lack of a strong theoretical

focus is perhaps not surprising, given that the whole field of voting behavior research developed in part as a revolt against the formalism and
lack of scientific validity of institutional political analysis earlier in this
century. We often see in this more institutionalist literature a variety of
untested guesses being made about the causal processes that stand behind these differences in voting made by institutions. Some of these
hunches often take the form of one of the main three theoretical options. For example, lacking any causal theory of its own, an institutional
analysis of registration effects might speculate—as we find instances in
this literature—that such requirements raise the costs for the potential
voter à la rationalist theory, or that they often interact with preexisting
states of electoral motivation, à la psychological theory, or that they
reduce turnout either because they suggest high social support for im-
posing restrictions, or that they recognize that people with status advantages are less likely to be deterred by such restrictions—both according
to sociological theory.

The question here is whether one might be able to do more to develop a general approach that brings to bear more explicitly the effects
of major political events, processes, institutions, programs, or leadership—in something of the spirit and the terms addressed normally by
less behavioral political scientists working in other subdisciplines. To
argue that electoral behavior and orientations are shaped solely on the
basis of such factors seems doubtful. But we have not thus far, despite
the vigorous exhortations of scholars like V. O. Key, Jr., done a very
good job of exploring the individual- or group-level implications of
such factors. Nor have we incorporated such causal processes into more
behavioral studies very well. We need to take more account of the fact
that, consciously or unconsciously, individuals and groups of individuals are affected by the nature of the choices presented to them and by the
legally and socially defined ease of making those choices, relative to the
economic, psychic, and social resources available for doing so.

We need to look more closely in the electoral context at how organizations, both official and nonofficial, act to shape behavior through
structuring choices, and at how setting the agenda, for example, affects
behavior. What we are mostly missing here is more information about
the larger structures and processes that affect how groups and individuals are able to transform their goals, shared or not, into electoral decisions.

Elections as Legitimation

From the opposite point of view, we probably need to address, in our
research theory and data collection and analysis designs, the extent to
which voting is a learning process and thus more often a mechanism for

legitimating, not only leadership, but the institutions of democracy per se. Although there have been some beginning efforts along this line (for example, Dennis 1970; Ginsberg 1982; and Dennis and Chaffee 1978), there is still more room for exploring the macro-level functions and implications of the electoral process other than that connected only to the electoral balance between the two major parties or to the winning and losing of particular candidates. Elections not only have a series of leadership and policy implications, but also a larger impact of mutual education of masses and elites, with a whole series of interested parties attempting to influence each other (and perhaps to distort the message and the process as well). Elections are an exercise in generating and expressing legitimation, or delegitimation, of a democratic regime and its electoral system. This might not seem so important or be so apparent to those whose sole phenomenological point of interest is the choice of candidates. But we should not leave uninvestigated an important feature of Americans' growing electoral malaise, which represents a loss of the sense of the connectedness of elections to the implementation of policy and to a perception of inadequate leadership. The efficacy of elections has increasingly come to be doubted by the average American, thus suggesting at least a breakdown in the educational side of elections. When this happens, one is eventually led to expect a further decline in electoral system legitimation. When we find, as we do, that voting duty, or the sense of obligation to participate, is typically the strongest motivation to turnout, and that this has remained strong, despite the long-term decline in aggregate turnout of this country, then something not yet well identified has weakened the conversion of the average voter's sense of obligation into behavior. Somehow, despite our very great volume of research in this area, we have failed to find the causes of the breakdown of this conversion and of the lack of implementation of what is apparently a high manifest voter sense of obligation to vote.

CONCLUSION

Where do we go from here? This is a difficult question if one is attempting to anticipate some deflection and redefinition of the great glacial drift of this now well-established "normal science." The easiest and safest answer is simply "ever more of the same." In many respects, this is an exceptionally rich and varied dimension of the study of politics. And it is likely to remain so as we move to the close of the twentieth century. Despite the narrowness of its usual dependent variables—the few kinds of decisions chosen to be in need of explanation—the subdiscipline has attracted some of the best minds and the largest resources of any in political science to conduct its investigations. Compared with other subdisciplines that systematically observe the phenomena of politics, electoral behavior research has been blessed with high achievement. Yet, as for any highly developed scholarly area, we expect a continuing flow of new ideas to reshape the nature of such investigation as an automatic product of past successful development.

At the broadest level, I would think that some of the near-term progress would come from cross-fertilization across paradigmatic boundaries. For example, if we have arrived by intersecting psychological and economic approaches at the hypothesis that voters are often reasonably, if imperfectly, calculating in their choice behavior, we can begin to ask more precisely in which senses each side of this hypothesis applies empirically. I would guess that there are many areas of compromise or combination among the theoretical approaches outlined above (see Simon 1985).

What I would not expect, however, is a grand synthesis of all of these approaches into some Hegelian, or perhaps Parsonian, scheme. Much of the richness of this field has depended upon having available competing sets of guiding concepts to apply to the changing electoral and research environments in which we find ourselves. I would hope, instead of a grand synthesis, and a greater substantive monopoly that might result from such theory merger, that we would spend more of our collective efforts in articulating clearly the major terms and implications of these various theoretical approaches. We therefore need to sharpen and update such models and metaphors more than we need to fold them into any single "gravitation theory" or set of "laws of thermodynamics." In particular, I would hope that the time is ripe for updating existing sociological analysis of voting, for more explicitly developing the implications of the social-psychological theory that grows out of the Michigan tradition, and for making Downsian/rational/economic theory more realistic and empirically based. All of these subdisciplinary actions are feasible with the tools available.

Such updating, sharpening, and making more operationally meaningful these currently available theoretical approaches might have the virtue of allowing much closer analysis of their areas of overlap versus their areas of divergent hypothesization. For example, what does each of them have to offer in interpreting such "new" phenomena as negative-image campaigns of the type increasingly common in American elections of the late 1980s, or increasingly PAC-centered campaign financing? Can electoral behavior theories invented well before the time when these new sources of variation in American elections became recognized adequately incorporate them into their systems of concepts and propositions? I suspect that they can; but we way need to assist such explication and its operationalization through deliberate subdisciplinary action.

What this field perhaps lacks—and this may be in some large part a result of the professional socialization of those who enter it—are those who, while understanding well the operational problems that data collection and analysis pose in this area, can nevertheless rise above them to discover new modes of thinking about the phenomena of elections at a purely theoretical level. Where we come closest to this at the moment is in the deductively oriented rationalist theories. But so far, the perceived unrealism of the factual assumptions of this approach has rendered such theoretical work unpalatable to the vast majority of those who labor in the voting research vineyards.

What we need are more intuitively compelling, parsimonious, coherent, explicit, cumulative, and operationally pragmatic ways of reformulating and extending our present theoretical capital in this field. While this effort might in limited respects involve combining these various paradigmatic approaches, a more productive strategy over the next decade would likely be to enunciate each more clearly as connected series of concepts and propositions. We need to say more sharply what each of these theories tells us, and to extend each in new directions as we encounter heretofore unexperienced, novel electoral phenomena, or even discover some things that we should have known about all along. Once we have such better defined and extended theories, we will be able to confront them more successfully with appropriate evidence, and thus reveal the true structure of knowledge that has emerged across the whole spectrum of electoral behavior inquiry in this century.

REFERENCES

Aberbach, Joel, Robert Putnam, and Bert Rockman. 1981. *Bureaucrats and Politicians in Western Democracies*. Cambridge, Mass.: Harvard University Press.

Alford, Robert. 1963. *Party and Society*. Chicago: Rand McNally.

Almond, Gabriel A. 1960. "A Functional Approach to Comparative Politics." In G. A. Almond and J. S. Coleman, eds., *The Politics of Developing Areas*, 3–66. Princeton, N.J.: Princeton University Press.

Arrow, Kenneth J. 1951. *Social Choice and Individual Values*. New Haven: Yale University Press.

Beck, Paul Allen. 1986. "Choice, Context and Consequence: Beaten and Unbeaten Paths toward a Science of Electoral Behavior." In Herbert F. Weisberg, ed. *Political Science: The Science of Politics*, 241–83. New York: Agathon Press.

Berelson, Bernard R., Paul F. Lazarsfeld, and William N. McPhee. 1954. *Voting*. Chicago: University of Chicago Press.

Brady, Henry E., and Paul M. Sniderman. 1985. "Attribute Attribution: A Group Basis for Political Reasoning." *American Political Science Review* 75: 1061–79.

———, and Stephen Ansolabehere. 1989. "The Nature of Utility Functions in Mass Publics." *American Political Science Review* 83:143–64.

Brody, Richard A. 1977. "Change and Stability in the Components of Party Identification: Presidential to Off-Years." *DEA News* (Spring 1977): 13–18.

———, and Benjamin I. Page. 1972. "Comment: The Assessment of Policy Voting." *American Political Science Review* 66:450–58.

Brunk, Gregory G. 1980. The Impact of Rational Participation Models on Voting Attitudes. *Public Choice* 35:549–64.

Butler, David, and Donald E. Stokes. 1969. *Political Change in Britain*. New York: St. Martin's Press.

Campbell, Angus, Philip E. Converse, Warren E. Miller, and Donald E. Stokes. 1960. *The American Voter*. New York: Wiley.

Conover, Pamela Johnston. 1989. "The Role of Social Groups in Political Thinking." *British Journal of Political Science* 18:51–76.

———, and Stanley Feldman. 1984. "How People Organize the Political World: A Schematic Model." *American Journal of Political Science* 28: 95–126.

Converse, Philip E. 1964. "The Nature of Belief Systems in Mass Publics." In David E. Apter, ed., *Ideology and Discontent*. New York: The Free Press.

———. 1968. "The Concept of a Normal Vote." In Angus Campbell et al., eds., *Elections and the Political Order*. New York: Wiley.

———, and Gregory B. Markus. 1979. " 'Plus ça change . . . ': The New CPS Election Study Panel." *American Political Science Review* 73:32–49.

Dahl, Robert A. 1961. "The Behavioral Approach." *American Political Science Review* 55:763–72.

Dennis, Jack. 1970. "Support for the Institution of Elections by the Mass Public." *American Political Science Review* 64:819–35.

———. 1980. "Changing Public Support for the American Party System." In William J. Crotty, ed., *Paths to Political Reform*, 35–66. Lexington, Mass.: Lexington Books.

———. 1986a. "Theories of Turnout: An Empirical Comparison of Alienationist and Rationalist Perspectives." Paper presented at the annual meeting of the Midwest Political Science Association, Chicago, April 10–12.

———. 1986b. "Public Support for the Party System, 1964–1984." Paper delivered at the annual meeting of the American Political Science Association, Washington, D.C., August 28–31.

———. 1987. "Groups and Political Behavior: Legitimation, Deprivation, and Competing Values." *Political Behavior* 9:323–73.

————. 1989a. "Political Independence in America, Part I: On Being an Independent Partisan Supporter." *British Journal of Political Science* 18:77–109.

————. 1989b. "Political Independence in America, Part II: Towards a Theory." *British Journal of Political Science* 18:197–219.

————, and Steven H. Chaffee. 1978. "Legitimation in the 1976 U.S. Election Campaign." *Communication Research* 5:371–94.

Downs, Anthony. 1957. *An Economic Theory of Democracy*. New York: Harper & Row.

Easton, David. 1953. *The Political System*. New York: Knopf.

————. 1965. *A Framework for Political Analysis*. Englewood Cliffs, N.J.: Prentice-Hall.

Eulau, Heinz. 1963. *The Behavioral Persuasion*. Stanford: Stanford University Press.

Ferejohn, John, and Morris Fiorina. 1975. "The Paradox of Not Voting: A Decision Theoretic Analysis." *American Political Science Review* 69:525–36.

Filer, John E., and Lawrence W. Kenny. 1980. "Voter Turnout and the Benefits of Voting." *Public Choice* 35:575–85.

Fiorina, Morris. 1977. "An Outline for a Model of Party Choice." *American Journal of Political Science* 21:601–26.

————. 1981. *Retrospective Voting in American National Elections*. New Haven: Yale University Press.

Franklin, Charles H., and John E. Jackson. 1981. "The Dynamics of Party Identification." Paper presented at the annual meeting of the American Political Science Association.

Ginsberg, Benjamin. 1982. *The Consequences of Consent*. New York: Random House.

Hamilton, Richard F. 1972. *Class and Politics in the United States*. New York: Wiley.

Keith, Bruce E., et al. 1986. "The Partisan Affinities of Independent 'Leaners.' " *British Journal of Political Science* 16:155–86.

Key, V. O., Jr. 1949. *Southern Politics*. New York: Knopf.

————. 1955. "A Theory of Critical Elections." *Journal of Politics* 17:3–18.

————. 1966. *The Responsible Electorate*. Cambridge, Mass.: Harvard University Press.

Knoke, David. 1976. *Change and Continuity in American Politics: The Social Bases of Political Parties*. Baltimore: The Johns Hopkins University Press.

Lazarsfeld, Paul F., Bernard R. Berelson, and Hazel Gaudet. 1944. *The People's Choice*. New York: Duell, Sloan, and Pearce.

Lipset, Seymour Martin. 1960. *Political Man*. New York: Doubleday.

Miller, Arthur H., Warren E. Miller, Alden Raine, and Thad Brown. 1976. "A Majority Party in Disarray: Policy Polarization in the 1972 Election." *American Political Science Review* 70:753–78.

————, Patricia Gurin, Gerald Gurin, and Oksana Malanchuk. 1981. "Group Consciousness and Political Participation." *American Journal of Political Science* 25:494–511.

Miller, Warren E., and Donald E. Stokes. 1966. "Constituency Influence in Congress." In Angus Campbell et al., eds., *Elections and the Political Order*. New York: Wiley.

————, and Teresa E. Levitin. 1976. *Leadership and Change: Presidential Elections from 1952–1976*. Cambridge, Mass.: Winthrop.

Nie, Norman H., and Kristi Andersen. 1974. "Mass Belief Systems Revisited: Political Change and Attitude Structure." *Journal of Politics* 36:540–91.

————, Sidney Verba, and John R. Petrocik. 1979. *The Changing American Voter*. Cambridge, Mass.: Harvard University Press.

Petrocik, John R. 1974. "An Analysis of Intransitivities in the Index of Party Identification." *Political Methodology* 1:31–47.

Pomper, Gerald M. 1972. "From Confusion to Clarity: Issues and American Voters, 1956–1968." *American Political Science Review* 62:415–28.

Rice, Stuart A. 1928. *Quantitative Methods in Politics*. New York: Knopf.

Riker, William H., and Peter C. Ordeshook. 1973. *An Introduction to Positive Political Theory*. Englewood Cliffs, N.J.: Prentice-Hall.

Rossi, Peter H. 1959. "Four Landmarks in Voting Research." In Eugene Burdick and Arthur J. Brodbeck, eds., *American Voting Behavior*, 5–54. Glencoe, Ill.: The Free Press.

Rusk, Jerrold G. 1982. "The Michigan Election Studies: A Critical Evaluation." *Micropolitics* 2:82–109.

Shulman, Mark A., and Gerald M. Pomper. 1975. "Variability in Electoral Behavior: Longitudinal Perspectives from Causal Modeling." *American Journal of Political Science* 19:1–18.

Simon, Herbert A. 1985. "Human Nature in Politics: The Dialogue of Psychology with Political Science." *American Political Science Review* 79:293–304.

Stimson, James A. 1975. "Belief Systems: Constraint, Complexity, and the 1972 Election." *American Journal of Political Science* 19:393–417.

Valentine, David C., and John R. Van Wingen. 1980. "Partisanship, Independence and the Partisan Identification Question." *American Politics Quarterly* 8:165–86.

Verba, Sidney, and Norman H. Nie. 1972. *Participation in America*. New York: Harper & Row.

Wattenberg, Martin P. 1984. *The Decline of American Political Parties, 1952–1980*. Cambridge, Mass.: Harvard University Press.

Weisberg, Herbert. 1980. "Party Identification: A Multidimensional Conceptualization." *Political Behavior* 2:33–60.

Wolfinger, Raymond E., and Steven J. Rosenstone. 1980. *Who Votes?* New Haven: Yale University Press.

4

Media and Politics

Doris A. Graber

INTRODUCTION

Political science research on the media and politics has accomplished much in a brief time, considering social and institutional impediments to innovations. Yet much more remains undone. Where are we now, and where is new growth most needed? I shall begin on a sour note by identifying four major shortcomings of media and politics as a subfield of political science study and then follow with more specific discussions of the status and needs of this new area of specialization. Throughout, the focus will be on contributions made by our profession. The important work done by social scientists from other disciplines will be excluded.

My first complaint is that political scientists have made many small inroads into virgin territory in the media and politics area but have pursued few of these promising leads extensively. Typical research strategy patterns in the social sciences may provide an explanation. Political science research tends to be unplanned, piecemeal, often opportunistic. Researchers succumb to the lure of following well-trodden easy paths and bow to the conservatism of funding agencies.

Second, and partly because of hesitancy to pursue novel research leads, one branch of media and politics study—media impact on elections—has received an unduly large share of research resources compared to the study of the media's role in other areas of political life.

Christopher Arterton, Kathleen Kendall, Jarol Manheim, and Paul Quirk provided valuable critiques of earlier drafts. I want to acknowledge their contributions and thank them for making this a better chapter.

Election studies have become a bandwagon on which most media and politics scholars choose to ride most of the time. It is a relatively safe perch, close to the political science mainstream.

Third, growth of media and politics studies remains hobbled because the field is still deemed to be on the fringes of political science. Undergraduate and graduate education in political communication remains limited. The major reasons are a continuing debate about whether mass media really play an important role in politics, and a feeling on the part of many academicians that this turf belongs by right to other disciplines, such as sociology.

Fourth, media studies are a truly interdisciplinary field. The political science research discussed in this essay has been impoverished because it rarely draws on work done in sister disciplines such as sociology, communications, and journalism. Many political scientists who dabble in this field rest their case on the small nucleus of political science studies, ignoring the rest of the burgeoning literature. Our parochialism borders on chauvinism, and the boundaries set for this essay perpetuate current trends. Unfortunately, other disciplines are similarly afflicted. Building on the work of all disciplines and undertaking more interdisciplinary collaborations would benefit the field immensely.

Keeping in mind these general deficiencies, what, then, are the major research questions that political scientists have tackled and what contributions have they made to the answers? Political scientists have focused on four major questions: (1) What *shapes* media content? (2) What *is* media content? (3) How do mass media *audiences process* media content? Most importantly, (4) What *effects* does media content produce? Examination of their findings raises two additional questions. One relates to tools of the trade, asking (5) what research designs and methodologies have proved most useful. The other one (6) seeks to discern where the subfield is heading. Analysis of past efforts and achievements provides clues to future directions and goals.

WHAT SHAPES MASS MEDIA CONTENT?

In probing what shapes media content, political scientists have been primarily concerned with exploring ideological influences. Like their colleagues in other disciplines, political scientists disagree about whether media content is shaped primarily by proponents on the right or the left of the ideological spectrum. Scholars like Robert and Linda Lichter and Stanley Rothman (1986) have argued that media elites who work for the leading news media lean to the left and report accordingly. When they tell their stories through interviews, they select respondents who agree with their viewpoints.

Scholars like Lance Bennett (1988), Michael Parenti (1986), Murray Edelman (1964), David Paletz and Robert Entman (1981), and Benjamin Ginsberg (1986), to name but a few, consider the media to be the minions of Big Business and the right wing. These social critics have faulted the media for using news selection power to strengthen white-middle-class values and suppress socialist viewpoints. Some claim that these choices are made deliberately to perpetuate capitalist exploitation of the masses in line with the ideological preferences of media owners. They also claim that the media have intentionally suppressed the facts about dangerous products and technologies to protect the profits of large corporations.

Still others see media as apostles of the status quo. The work of Leon Sigal (1973) is often quoted to demonstrate that media content reflects the views of the political establishment, because government people are the predominant sources interviewed by newspeople. Underlying the debate about the ideological thrust of the media is the assumption that it colors the ideological thrust of political life (Bennett 1988; Entman 1989; Edelman 1988). This is an interesting and important assumption, but little has been done to put scholarly flesh on the bare theoretical bones. The time is ripe to do so.

Other areas largely ignored by political scientists, but covered by scholars in other disciplines, concern the constraints on news choices and presentations imposed by the organizational structure and functioning of the media industry. While organizational structure and functioning may rightfully be deemed the turf of sociologists, questions about the effects of governmental policies on the shaping of the news certainly fall within the purview of political science. Nonetheless, they have been little explored. The American myth that democratic governments should not and do not affect mass media output may explain the reluctance to cover this area. A small number of studies dealing with media policy-making, such as the work of Krasnow, Longley, and Terry (1982) on the politics of broadcast regulation, are exceptions. We need many more, covering a broad spectrum of laws that directly or indirectly affect the interrelationships of media with other political and economic institutions. The research produced thus far by lawyers and economists is not adequate.

Besides probing the influence of legislation on media performance, the influence of the political climate in general on media choice and presentation of news needs to be explored. All too often researchers treat media as an independent variable that only affects other institutions but is not affected by them. That flies in the face of reality. It is essential, therefore, to gauge the impact that politicians have on media coverage in their carefully orchestrated efforts to gain or divert attention regarding issues that concern them. Examples of the kinds of studies that are needed are Martin Linsky's (1986a, b) investigations of the efforts of federal officials to manipulate press coverage to support their political goals and Marjorie Hershey's study (1984) of the ways in which campaigners learn to use the media effectively. Success rates in gaining media support and cooperation vary widely. It would therefore be interesting to investigate the essence of successful media relations and the factors that generate failures, including various contextual factors and interpersonal communications of political figures.

The protection under the First Amendment of press freedom and society's right to know and other constitutional issues have also been important factors in shaping media content. Most studies have been done by historians, communications scholars, and lawyers, but a handful of political scientists have been involved as well (Pool 1983, Berns 1976). A few political scientists have examined control of media content by totalitarian societies. Ellen Mickiewicz's study of Soviet media (1988) is an excellent recent effort. Earlier studies by Richard Fagen (1969), Alan Liu (1971), and others also cover this topic. The landmark work on government-sponsored propaganda in totalitarian societies, which includes media-disseminated propaganda, is a three-volume collection edited by Harold Lasswell, Daniel Lerner, and Hans Speier (1980), which gives a historical account of worldwide propaganda activities. Alexander George's wartime analysis (1959) of the content of German radio news is also important. It was commissioned by the United States government to garner clues to German propaganda goals from German radio broadcasts. The effort met with substantial success.

The role played by media in governmental public relations has also received a modicum of attention in work by Manheim and Albritton (1984), who investigated changes in media coverage after foreign governments have hired public relations firms, and a study by Stephen Hess (1984), who describes how public relations personnel within the United States national government operate. Martin Linsky (1986b) provides case studies of the media's role in government public relations efforts. While these all are laudable efforts, much more needs to be done to construct an information base for assessing how governments use media to foster governmental purposes.

WHAT IS MEDIA CONTENT?
General Studies

This question has been of interest to practicing politicians since the days of the Founding Fathers because mass media are the primary source of current political information. How rich or poor or slanted or negative mass media images of the world are depends on the story choices made by media staffs, whose freedom of choice is limited only by technical constraints and by the media policies and cultural dikes in their societies. For many images of reality presented by the mass media, audiences lack the capacity to verify the situation for themselves or to examine alternative versions of reality. They must therefore rely on those images.

Since political scientists want to understand how citizens perceive their political world and how these perceptions influence political decisions, one might expect extensive investigations of political images. This has been true to a limited extent only. In the 1950s and 1960s, a group of prominent social scientists collaborated in what came to be known as the Hoover Institution's RADIR (Revolution and Development of International Relations) studies. The idea behind these studies was that the values and consequent political developments in various nations could be inferred from the images disseminated through their mass media (Lasswell et al. 1952; Pool et al. 1952, 1959). Presumably, although there are many cautions, "the sequence of movements in history can be conveniently read by scanning the dominant symbols of successive periods" (Lasswell 1952, 505). The RADIR scholars argued that media images reveal what kinds of things are likely to be widely known within a society and what sort of information has remained shrouded. Media images indicate what sorts of things are labeled as important in particular societies and become priorities, as well as what that society officially deems right or wrong. Media images also show relationships made in a given society among concepts—whether poverty, for example, is linked to sloth or to social injustice, and whether it is classified as a private or public problem.

Scholars involved in the RADIR studies examined mass media output from five countries over a sixty-year period. They checked 25,000 editorials in prestigious newspapers in France, Germany, England, Russia, and the U.S.A. between 1890 and 1950, tracing 416 distinct verbal symbols. They found considerable differences in the nature and frequency of use of symbols. For example, totalitarian societies, compared to democracies, appeared to concentrate on relatively few symbols.

Karl Deutsch, who analyzed mass media reporting about international events, even suggested the possibility of establishing media monitoring and early warning systems to detect mounting tensions and take preventive steps. "It should be possible to say whether the amount of attention given to a specific conflict area or to the image of a particular 'enemy' country is reaching the danger point, in the sense that continuing hostile attention in the mass media may tend to harden public opinion to such a degree as eventually to destroy the freedom of choice of the national government concerned" (1957, 201–2).

Deutsch was also the leading exponent of attempts to trace cohesiveness and value-sharing among nations through an analysis of communication flows and mass media and elite images (Deutsch et al. 1957, 1967). He and Richard Merritt analyzed the impact of unfavorable publicity on national images (Deutsch and Merritt 1965). Follow-up on this type of work has been meager. A recent effort, which focuses more on the nature of images and less on their impact than the RADIR studies consists of two books by William Adams (1981, 1982), one on media images of Middle Eastern conflicts and the other, more generally, on images of other international situations. However, in both books fewer than half the selections are by political scientists.

While sociologists, psychologists, and communications scholars have probed media offerings for the extent and nature of news about social deviance to assess it relative to asocial public behaviors, political scientists have sat on the sidelines. Similarly, American political scientists have made little effort to analyze news as a clue to the reality images dispensed by public officials. Historians, rhetoricians, and communications scholars have done most of this work, with a little peripheral help from political scientists like Murray Edelman (1964), David Paletz and Robert Dunn (1969), and Lance Bennett (1988). In sociology, ethnomethodologists like Gay Tuchman (1978) and Mark Fishman (1980) have studied news as a mode of reality construction and have examined the ideological slants of that reality. But political scientists have not followed in their footsteps, aside from overall statements about political orientations and an occasional study of the slant of coverage of a particular event (Lang and Lang 1983). Political scientists have almost totally ignored movies and television entertainment shows as important sources of political images.

Election Research

The bulk of mass media content research in political science has dealt with political images in elections. The crop has been comparatively ample (Arterton 1978; Robinson 1981, 1987; Robinson and Sheehan 1983a, 1983b; Patterson 1980; Nie et al. 1976; Nimmo and Combs 1983; Nimmo and Savage 1976; A. H. Miller et al. 1985a, 1985b; Ranney 1983; Nimmo 1981; Adams 1983; Graber 1986). Political scientists have been especially interested in the frequency and quality of candidate coverage, because it can be crucial to a candidate's success or failure. The candidacy of Jimmy Carter, for instance, would have been well-nigh impossible if he had not been able to secure extensive media coverage (Arterton 1978; Robinson 1978). However, the precise role played by media images seems to vary, and the magic formulae that accurately predict it remain to be discovered (Orren and Polsby 1987).

Researchers agree that winner and loser images are very important because the American public seems to love winners. Catering to public tastes, a large portion of election news dwells on the horse-race aspects of political competition, projecting winners and losers throughout the preprimary, primary, and final contests. The outcomes are presented against the backdrop of expectations created by earlier news stories (Patterson 1980; Nie et al. 1976; Nimmo and Combs 1983; Broh 1980). Speculations about the impact of media-circulated popularity polls have been plentiful. Nonetheless, few scholars have assessed how such polls actually affect public attitudes and voting decisions (Bartels 1985, 1987). The fact that major media organizations now have their own polling departments has vastly increased the emphasis put on winner and loser images. While the public loves winners, research indicates that news stories often treat frontrunners unkindly, be they candidates or incumbents (Robinson 1983a).

Studies of television, newspaper, and news-magazine coverage of recent presidential elections reveal many trends likely to affect voter choices. For example, news stories depict only a limited number of the personal and professional attributes of candidates. Personal qualities, such as trustworthiness, strength of character, leadership abilities, and compassion are stressed most (Patterson 1980; Weaver et al. 1981; Graber 1986; Robinson 1983a). On an average, three out of every four attributes mentioned in news stories refer to such personal qualities. The remainder refer to professional competence, such as the ability to handle foreign affairs well or to rally public opinion support.

Even though the types of qualities by which candidates are judged are quite similar, comparisons among candidates are often difficult because emphasis on individual traits and competencies differs sharply. This lack of comparability makes the voters' choices very difficult. Moreover, news stories report the views of a multitude of news sources and usually provide contradictory images of the same candidates. Adherence to journalistic canons of objectivity prevents newspeople from making explicit value judgments in ordinary news stories to give audiences guidance about the merits of these contradictory images.

On the whole, research indicates that television and newspaper images are quite similar. However, the brevity of television stories necessitates drawing images in bolder, simpler strokes and using pictures to reinforce and supplement brief verbal messages. To conserve time, television newscasters often create stereotypical images of candidates during the early stages of campaigns and then shape stories to fit into these images (Robinson 1981). This technique creates serious political problems when the stereotype misrepresents reality or when candidates have changed their policy stands (Arterton 1978).

Whereas pictures often convey positive images, verbal commentary about candidates tends to be negative whenever judgments are made

(Robinson 1981, 1987; Graber 1986). Political scientists have speculated that such negative coverage causes or contributes to the rising political cynicism of the American public. The negative portrayals of political candidates have been blamed for making it increasingly difficult for public officials to govern with public support after election and to win a second term in office (Ranney 1983). However, not all scholars agree that coverage of candidates is predominantly negative. For example, Nimmo (1981, 252) claims that "The bulk of research pertaining to United States presidential elections since the 1950's indicates that the images of candidates remain fairly positive and stable throughout the course of most campaigns." Nimmo concedes that negative coverage is substantial. As negative images are generally more potent than positive ones, they are likely to dominate perceptions even when the images are less frequently presented. Hence the concerns about the impact of negative coverage remain even if the balance slants in favor of positive images.

Political scientists also disagree about the degree of stability of media images. A number of investigators claim that images remain fairly stable throughout campaigns, and even from campaign to campaign for candidates who run repeatedly (see Nimmo 1981; Patterson 1980; Weaver et al. 1981). Others (e.g., Robinson 1983a) point to ups and downs, linked to particular events in the campaign. As usual, a search for reasons for the disparity points to differences in judgmental criteria. Some investigators measure stability by the consistency in criteria used by newspeople to evaluate candidates throughout an election and from election to election. Others judge consistency in terms of fluctuating appraisals of the ratings earned by candidates when judged by these criteria. While criteria tend to remain stable, ratings tend to fluctuate. Moreover, the picture is usually mixed; some ratings change, others remain stable. It then becomes a matter of choice whether one declares the cup to be half full or half empty.

Rather than looking at media images as a series of characterizations of individual candidates, one can examine them as parts of a single dramatic presentation. Nimmo and Combs (1983) use such a dramatist perspective when they describe elections as melodramatic rituals in which the protagonists in the drama are locked in a heroic struggle. The final election becomes the climax in which the victor triumphs while the loser goes down in defeat. To increase the dramatic qualities of the contest, the images are drawn in bold, oversimplified strokes, at the expense of realism with its more modulated images. Nimmo and Combs believe that the public can be fooled by these rhetorical visions, mistaking the drama for reality and gearing its expectations of candidate performance in office accordingly. Disillusionment with presidential performance ensues.

Images stressing the candidates' stands on issues and their conducting of the campaign are less prevalent in news stories than images involving their personal qualities and qualifications. In presidential elections, the balance has hovered around two to one. Although only limited evidence has been collected thus far, this distribution seems to hold true in other types of elections and for print as well as electronic media (Patterson 1980; Graber 1983; but see Kessel 1988). In presidential campaigns, when the country is not involved in war, selected issues of domestic policy are emphasized. Generally, stories are superficial, focusing on current problems and avoiding discussion of complex issues. Newspeople try to present issues as conflicts among candidates. For television, they prefer issues that lend themselves to interesting pictorial coverage (Patterson 1980). Their goal, of course, is to generate simple, clear-cut, exciting, colorful stories. Consequently, trivial issues frequently receive the media limelight while serious ones are neglected (Arterton 1984). A few political scientists have investigated coverage of specific issues during campaigns, such as U.S. dealings with Iran or the formulation of energy policy. Their analyses routinely point to major deficiencies that impair public understanding of the issue in question (e.g., Sahr 1983).

In part, the complaints that issue coverage during campaigns is scarce may arise from measurement problems. Current content analyses are relatively crude and generally fail to analyze the full content of stories; information about content distribution is therefore suspect. Many content analyses are limited to headlines or to front pages, or to coding an entire story as a single topic. Such approaches serve to depress issue counts. Content analyses that code all the topics covered in a story and that pay heed to issue information conveyed by pictures are almost nonexistent. The perceived deemphasis of issues and the shallowness of analyses has given rise to frequent charges of press irresponsibility (Pomper and Lederman 1980).

Are the images presented in campaign news biased? A few scholars have tried to identify what constitutes bias in election news—which is a tricky enterprise—and to explain the reasons for it (Hofstetter 1976, 1978, 1979; Kressel 1987; Sorauf 1987). Bias appears to be predominantly structural rather than political. Imbalances in space and time or critical comment allotted to various candidates are best explained by the need to produce interesting stories rather than by political preconceptions. However, the effects of imbalances are no less real, regardless of the motivations that prompted them. If lack of coverage constitutes bias, there is extreme bias against most trailing candidates during primaries, against vice-presidential candidates during the general election, and against minor party candidates in most national, state, and local elections. Since biases of various types can have a profound impact on electoral fortunes, more bias research seems desirable. The development of reliable measures to identify biases and test for their presence seems particularly urgent.

Gaps in Content Research

Many major gaps remain in the study of media coverage of politics. Relatively few studies of media impact on elections have analyzed media content systematically (Hofstetter 1976; Graber 1989; Patterson 1980; Adams 1983; Robinson and Sheehan 1983a). Instead, the impact of media content has been gauged by asking audiences about their attitudes and opinions and attributing their views to their alleged reading, viewing, and listening habits. In most studies, audiences are not even asked about exposure to the specific stories whose impact is under investigation. There has been practically no attention directed to the meanings conveyed by visual messages on television. The few visual image studies that have been reported have concentrated largely on the impact of facial displays (Lanzetta et al. 1985; Rosenberg and McCafferty 1987; Rosenberg et al. 1986; Graber 1986). Only a few studies have matched content data with survey data from respondents whose exposure to the analyzed media has been ascertained (e.g., Weaver et al. 1981; Patterson 1980; Miller et al. 1979; Graber 1988).

The technical and financial problems involved in content analysis and in executing linked research designs have been the chief obstacles. Most studies have therefore judged media content impressionistically and have used weak indirect measures of media exposure. Exposure has usually been appraised by self-assessments couched in vague terms about the frequency of media use, or about the most important information source. To draw conclusions about media exposure from such data requires dangerously large inferential leaps. The general news context in which election stories are embedded has largely escaped scrutiny, despite experimental evidence indicating that contextual news strongly affects political evaluations (Iyengar et al. 1982; Iyengar and Kinder 1987; Graber 1987b).

Instead of scrutinizing how the media present election-related stories, political scientists have speculated about the kinds of information used by voters to make voting decisions. For example, numerous studies have focused on the likely impact of information about major economic issues, such as inflation and unemployment, on voting decisions. In constructing and testing theories about economic criteria for voting, researchers have largely ignored practical issues, such as the ready availability of relevant information and the appropriateness of its format for the media audience (Kinder 1981a, 1981b; Peffley et al. 1987; Niemi and Bartels 1983).

There has also been a lag in studying images created by newspaper and television advertisements, press releases, and other media beyond the major news sources. Judging from research in other disciplines, these media are also leaving their mark on the minds of average Americans. The few political science studies of campaign advertising support this finding (Patterson and McClure 1976; Vermeer 1982, 1988; Joslyn 1984; Nesbit 1988; Kern 1989).

HOW DO MASS MEDIA AUDIENCES PROCESS MEDIA CONTENT?

One of the fastest growing areas of media research is the study of how human beings process information. It is a natural outgrowth of findings which established that media stimuli are not absorbed unchanged by audiences. Instead, the relationship is transactional. The media stimuli are transformed by audiences who bring their own cognitions and feelings to bear in the process of extracting meanings from them. Several parts of the process have been studied by political scientists, mostly as they relate to election information. They include how people of varying political orientations and sophistication decide to pay attention or to ignore certain media stimuli, how they pare down information that is of interest to them so that it can be managed more readily, and how they incorporate it into their thought processes. The inferences they draw from this information have also been examined.

The research has been grounded in a variety of information-processing theories. Among them, schema theories are currently enjoying the broadest support. Simply put, such theories postulate that people develop mental models about various aspects of their world on the basis of direct experiences and information transmitted by mass media and other sources. The models contain conceptions of general patterns along with examples that illustrate these patterns and indicate relationships among the component parts of the schema. Schemata guide information selection, provide the framework for assimilating new information, and furnish the basis for developing repertoires of inferences. For example, when a news story reports a strike by schoolteachers, ideas about the consequences of such a strike can be readily drawn from schemata in the audience's memory. The precise impact of the story may thus depend on the presence or absence of relevant schemata and on the nature of the fit between media images and the schemata held by audience members (Graber 1988; Miller et al. 1985a; Lau and Sears 1986; Axelrod 1976; Putnam 1973; Fiske and Kinder 1981; Sears and Citrin 1982; Conover and Feldman 1980, 1984, 1986; Lodge and Wahlke 1982; Lau and Sears 1986; Hamill and Lodge 1986; Lodge and Hamill 1986).

If initial media-based schemata indeed become the molds into which later information is fitted, then media images disseminated early in life and early in the development of particular events such as election campaigns may be far more important than later ones. It is therefore fortunate that, at least in election research, numerous political science studies now focus on the early stages of campaigns, when new candidates are first introduced, rather than only on the final weeks, as has been past practice (Patterson 1980; Weaver et al. 1981; Robinson and Sheehan 1983a; Keeter and Zukin 1983). Aside from tracing the inception of election images, political scientists have not as yet attempted to measure the impact of childhood and adolescent media exposure on political image formation in later life. This could be a fertile new field for political socialization research.

By and large, how varying contexts may affect what audiences actually learn from media content has received only slight attention from political scientists. For example, little effort has been made to discover whether learning of campaign images varies depending on whether voting choices are made early or late during the campaign (Cundy 1986). We do not know nearly enough about whether first exposure to information leaves a lasting legacy or whether and to what extent it is superseded by information offered at a later date. Only sparse attention has been devoted to mapping how learning processes and outcomes differ depending on whether information is conveyed through the printed word, other visual and aural symbols, or picture images (Adams 1982; Patterson 1980; Weaver et al. 1981; Lau and Erber 1985). We do not even know how long information is retained. Overall, the long-standing debate among political scientists about the nature of belief systems could benefit immensely from further work on the cognitive and emotional outcomes of political information processing.

WHAT EFFECTS DOES MEDIA CONTENT PRODUCE?

The study of mass media is based on the premise that they have some kinds of significant effects, though it remains arguable what precisely these effects are under a variety of circumstances. As Bernard Berelson (1948, 172) once said facetiously: "Some kinds of communication on some kinds of issues, brought to the attention of some kinds of people under some kinds of conditions, have some kinds of effects." Researchers have found it fairly difficult to disentangle media effects from other influences with which they are intertwined.

It has been particularly troublesome to distinguish the impact of media stories about events from the impact of those events themselves. Newspeople often create idiosyncratic images of reality through the unique ways in which they present and frame particular stories. The media-created *Zwischenwelt* may then produce effects directly traceable to stories about the event rather than the event as such, which may produce its own consequences as well. Panic stories about the severity of radiation fallout from the Chernobyl nuclear plant accident, for example, caused a massive exodus of foreigners from the Soviet Union. More factual accounts, describing the extent of damage and placing the accident into an appropriate scientific context, would have elicited a far more moderate response.

Sometimes, the media's main contribution may lie in bringing events to the attention of important audiences who might otherwise remain unaware. Under other circumstances, media simply serve as transmission channels for information prepared and framed by public and private authorities who may have nearly automatic access to media. In that case, the independent impact of the news media is minimal, except for the fact that they are able to give much wider exposure to these messages than would be possible through other means.

The start of political science research on media effects is usually placed in the mid-1940s when students of elections realized that they could not fully tell their story without considering media impact. The "voting studies" therefore tested media impact as a possible major factor in voting decisions and found it wanting (Lazarsfeld et al. 1944; Berelson et al. 1954; Campbell et al. 1954, 1960, 1966). In the wake of findings of minimal impact, all types of political science research on media effects withered.

As indicated earlier, the RADIR scholars, Karl Deutsch and many others, had also investigated the interface of media and politics during this period. Harold Lasswell, a sociologist–political scientist hybrid, had been a key figure in outlining the importance of mass media effects in his essay on "The Structure and Function of Communication in Society" (Lasswell 1969). He pointed out that media perform three functions that produce important effects. They acquaint people with ongoing events, which is part of their agenda-setting role. They interpret the meanings of those events, shaping the perspectives from which the world will be viewed. And, in the process, media socialize individuals into their cultural settings. Lasswell's classification suggested three major areas of media effects research: examination of the political impact of the images selected by the media for wide dissemination; examination of the effects of various types of interpretations given to these images; and assessment of media impact on political socialization. It should be clear by now that political scientists did comparatively little to follow up on these suggestions despite the fact that other disciplines had laid the groundwork.

The study of media influence on elections resumed in the late 1960s and 1970s, since the notion of nearly total media impotence to affect elections clashed with apparent reality and with political folklore (Nie et al. 1976; Miller and Levitin 1976; Patterson and McClure 1976). These renewed investigations, which focused almost exclusively on election contexts, were undertaken in the wake of major social and political changes relevant to media and politics interactions. Examples are the rise of television as a popular communication source and the steady decline of party influence on candidate selection, which left a void that media could fill. Parties now have tried to recapture influence by guiding candidates in their interactions with media in the hope that the candidates and their party mentors, rather than newspeople, will dominate the process.

Among the many media-related research questions beckoning for answers, political scientists have continued to be most interested in the effects of mass media information on voting and election outcomes. They have wanted to know how mass media information shapes voters' views and opinions about candidates and issues and how this, in turn, affects their vote. Studies have either concentrated on media impact alone, or have tried to assess its relative influence among a variety of factors such as voters' party allegiance, psychological characteristics, or past and current experiences and information.

The new studies have overturned many earlier findings that attributed minimal influence to mass media. Most importantly, they have created a large and strong base of research findings which establish that the mass media can, indeed, be important election influences. Nonetheless, many political scientists continue to slight media impact. The research horse does not shed its blinders readily, especially since the design of many political science studies serves to minimize media impact. Media influence is acknowledged only when messages presented by news stories reach audiences directly. When media messages are transmitted in multiple-step processes, as often happens when they are diffused through interpersonal contacts, researchers routinely fail to credit the media as the original source of the information. Similarly, media influence has been slighted when it involves a chain of attitude changes. For example, media emphasis on a candidate's political party affiliation may make partisan concerns salient to audiences. In turn, attention to partisan concerns may change votes. Media-generated cynicism about politics may contribute to low voter turnouts at election time. Although turnout may decide the outcome of the election, it is not usually recorded as media influence on elections.

Most scholars would agree with Dan Nimmo's conclusion (1981, 257): "In sum, then, the verdict concerning the part played by the mass media in relation to individuals' voting behavior is that of influential informers and impotent persuaders. Just what aspects of mass communication inform and/or persuade, however, is not clear." Many factors have been shown to be important. These include the voter's receptivity to the message, the potency of the message, the appropriateness of its form, and the setting in which it occurs. Nimmo's conclusion runs counter to the claims made by public relations professionals that voters are highly susceptible to media persuasion. Such claims receive only mixed support even with respect to election commercials. Joslyn (1984) reports that data gathered in 1970, 1972, and 1974 show that exposure to political commercials can actually bring about voting defection. On the other hand, an experimental study by Meadow and Sigelman (1982) points toward minimal effects.

The disagreement about the significance of media effects may spring from the fact that scholars have been concerned with persuasion of large, statistically significant numbers of people, while the public relations professionals are primarily concerned with election outcomes. A close election may well be decided by persuasive appeals when a switch in even a small, statistically insignificant number of votes may determine the election outcome. A further problem springs from the fact that the size of media audiences is grossly exaggerated and media impact grossly understated when the size of the target audience is equated with the actual audience. Normally, only a small fraction of the target audience is reached by each message. The rate of persuasion should be computed on the basis of people actually reached rather than those physically reachable but practically beyond bounds.

Gaps in Media Effects Research

Aside from testing how media stories influence potential voters' thinking and feelings about candidates and issues, other media effects on the electoral process have been neglected. A few studies have examined how voter turnout is changed when election outcomes or outcome projections or exit poll results are publicized before the voting booths have closed throughout the country (e.g., Epstein and Strom 1984). Scant attention has been given to the impact the media have on nominations through bestowing name recognition and through fostering or discouraging contributors of campaign resources, publishing popularity polls, and designating likely winners and losers (Patterson 1980; Nie et al. 1976; Nimmo and Combs 1983; Broh 1980). Media impact on such matters is undoubtedly significant (Arterton 1978; Robinson 1978).

Serious political science research has also ignored the impact of many effects of media-oriented campaigns on major political processes. For instance, how has the high cost of televised campaigns affected candidate recruitment and altered the role played by interest groups and PACs? Assertions are legion but not well-grounded in research. Candidates now gear their campaign locations, the subjects they discuss, and the manner of presenting themselves largely to media needs. How have media-oriented strategies affected political outcomes? What difference does it make that New Hampshire and Iowa have become political hot spots, thanks to the disproportionate amounts of media coverage bestowed on them (Orren and Polsby 1987)?

The waning influence of political parties on nominations, campaigns, and elections apparently is closely tied to the rising influence of the mass media. Capturing this trend in a rhetorical question, one commentator recently asked, "Would you ever vote for a man you had never seen on television?" Understanding the role that mass media images play in elections and other political processes is also hampered by imbalances in the levels of research. Most political science studies, as well as most studies in sister disciplines, have focused on the presidency. We know relatively little about the role of media images at the congressional, state, and local levels. Only a few scattered articles and a very small number of books focus explicitly on media images in these neglected areas (e.g., Goldenberg and Traugott 1983, 1987; Vermeer 1982, 1987; Dunn 1969; Graber 1983). Aside from congressional elections, studies are so few that one dare not draw general conclusions from them.

Turning to more broadly gauged research, political scientists by and large have been less concerned than communications scholars with the role played by frequently or prominently featured stories in setting the public's agenda of concerns. The credit for starting agenda-setting research accrues chiefly to communications scholars Donald Shaw and Maxwell McCombs (1977), even though there are important political science godfathers. These include Bernard Cohen (1963), who pointed out that the mass media are powerful in telling us what to think *about* even though they may not tell us what to think, and Norton Long (1958, 256), who ascribed to the newspaper "a great part in determining what most people will be talking about, what most people will think the facts are, and what most people will regard as the way problems are dealt with . . . to a large extent, it sets the civic agenda." Again, political scientists lit the fires but did not tend them, while other disciplines jumped into the breach.

Political scientists have devoted sparse attention to the impact of media images on general political socialization and resocialization of citizens, on various forms of political participation, and on many other phases of the political process. In fact, media influence has rated only a few lines in most political socialization texts until very recently (Greenstein 1965; Easton and Dennis 1969). As late as 1989, a major collection of readings on adult socialization contained not even an index entry to the issue (Sigel 1989). As regards the political process in general, we do not know to what extent media stories about environmental pollution, homeless people, life in Japan, or the travels of Mikhail Gorbachev have affected public policies. The influence of major national crises on learning from media images has been investigated all too rarely (Lang and Lang 1983). Political folklore about such matters abounds, but it remains to be substantiated.

There have been relatively few studies of the contributions of media to major changes in the political system. The reason, at least in part, has been the difficulty of specifying the extent of media influence in situations that entail complex interactions among many different political forces. For example, how much have media contributed to the decline of political parties? What role did they play in the Civil Rights movement and the integration of minorities into political life? Has the rise of truly national media altered national politics? When a story about unsafe financial institutions is broadcast nationwide, how great a danger does it pose for the country's economic soundness?

Only a handful of political scientists have studied the media in relation to specific governmental institutions and policies. Examples are studies focusing on the president's relations with the news media (Grossman and Kumar 1981; Rubin 1981), several studies dealing with Washington reporters' treatment of government and public officials (Nimmo 1964; Hess 1981, 1986), and studies of the role played by government public relations personnel (Hess 1984; Linsky 1986b). The president's use of news media to support his foreign policies has been examined by Montague Kern and Patricia and Ralph Levering. They investigated the uses that President John Kennedy made of the press in conducting foreign policy (Kern et al. 1983). Susan Welch's study of newspaper coverage of the Vietnam War is an example of studying media coverage of one particular policy and its impact on public perceptions of the conflict. Such studies illustrate the extent to which the media can shape and dominate public views of issues, particularly when the events occur in remote geographical locations (Welch 1972). They highlight the need for much additional work.

Political scientists have rarely looked at the impact of coverage of the Supreme Court on public knowledge and attitudes toward it. A study of reportage problems affecting landmark cases, like *Baker v. Carr* and *Engel v. Vitale* (reapportionment and school prayer), is a rarity (Newland 1964). A number of studies of governmental institutions have, however, discussed media impact as a subordinate focus. Presidency studies like those by Kernell (1986) and Kessel (1988) are examples. Bernard Cohen's 1963 study of foreign policy amounted to a backdoor entry into agenda-setting research. Media impact on community cohesiveness and as a factor in community conflict has been assessed as a byproduct in studies focused primarily on other concerns (Janowitz 1980; Wolfsfeld 1984).

In the wake of the breakup of colonial empires, several political scientists did explore the impact of news media on political development. The hope was that the governments of new nations would foster

media presentation of modernizing ideas that would then stimulate
people to emulate these ideas. The unparalleled ability of the mass media to reach people and expose them to new ideas opened vistas of rapid
worldwide technological and political advancement. Some early research showed substantial correlations between mass media growth and
economic growth in developing societies (Pye 1963; Pool 1963). But,
as with other effects, it soon became clear that presence or absence of
effects hinged on numerous intervening conditions. Political scientists
lost interest, even though public optimism persists about the power of
mass media to provide the knowledge base on which modernization
must rest.

Even scarcer are studies that raise broad public policy questions related to media coverage and its effects on American democratic institutions. Thomas Jefferson believed that the media were essential to
maintaining democracy. Little has been done to put his theories to the
test. In fact, a few studies have produced contrary evidence, indicating
that media may be bad for a healthy democracy. Michael Robinson's
research (1976) shows that the negativism that is so apparent in television news can produce cynicism about government in the audience.
Jarol Manheim (1976), Lance Bennett (1988), and Robert Entman
(1989) have argued that the media trivialize and slant politics. As a result, people lose interest in politics and lack understanding of political
phenomena. This makes it easier for elites to control them. Jeffrey Tulis
(1987) documents that presidential rhetoric loses substance when presidents strive to produce catchy sound bites. Others contend that the
need to gain media attention has brought candidates to the fore who are
able to win elections but who lack the skills to govern afterward. Consequently, the quality of political life has been steadily deteriorating.

While media coverage may be deleterious to the nation's political
health, lack of coverage can also be harmful. The Kerner Commission
report (1968), for example, condemned the media for lack of attention
to the problems of black citizens. It blamed the riots of the 1960s on
media neglect. Similarly, a presidential commission that investigated
the nuclear mishap at Three Mile Island charged that inadequate media
coverage worsened the impact of the problem (1979). Political scientists have been only peripherally involved in such studies.

RESEARCH METHODOLOGIES AND DESIGNS
Content Analysis

Since most American media research deals with assessing media impact
on audiences, the most widely used research techniques are content
analysis and survey research questionnaires. Content analysis can be ei-

ther quantitative or qualitative, or a mixture of these methods. It may be done by trained human coders, which remains the preferred method, or by computers, or by a combination of the two. When voluminous news media data need to be analyzed, this is a time-consuming, costly, and often tedious technique. Therefore, only a handful of political scientists have used it, mostly in its most primitive forms.

The kinds of features that political scientists have examined in media stories vary widely, ranging from simple frequency counts of stories, to analyses of rhetorical features of messages about particular topics, to more complex analyses of the nature and treatment of specific topics (Adams 1983; Rothman and Lichter 1987; Paletz and Guthrie 1987). Scholars have scrutinized the completeness and accuracy of stories, often looking for particular biases and omissions in coverage (Nimmo and Combs 1985). Content analyses may examine a certain genre of communication, such as presidential debates, or may use case-study techniques, concentrating on analyzing coverage of a single event (Adams et al. 1986; Feldman and Sigelman 1985).

As is true of many other research methods, content analysis is plagued by several serious deficiencies that impair the validity of the results. For example, investigators do not use uniform coding categories. Most scholars create their own, tailored to suit the purposes of their particular investigation. Unfortunately, the choice of individualized categories affects study results, wreaking havoc with any attempts to compare findings. Another problem is the significance assigned to high and low frequencies of mention of coded items. In general, frequent mention is equated with high significance, while rare mention indicates lack of significance. Yet a single story pointing to a major policy blunder, for example, may be far more significant than hundreds of stories indicating satisfactory performance. Few reports based on quantitative analyses heed such significant qualitative considerations (Robinson 1981a; Graber 1983). Their validity suffers accordingly. What is sorely needed, therefore, are formulae for the successful blending of quantitative and qualitative approaches.

The validity of content analysis is also frequently impaired because of failure to analyze the full array of major facts and meanings conveyed by stories. Many content analyses have been limited to headlines or to front pages, assuming, without testing, that back pages lack impact. An entire story is often coded as a single topic, even though most stories contain multiple topics. Such restricted approaches to content analysis severely distort actual story content. Content analyses that code stories fully and pay heed to nonverbal information are almost nonexistent.

As mentioned, coding of audiovisual information has presented major problems in the past because of the richness of pictorial detail offered by television. These problems can be overcome by focusing coding on the meanings conveyed by audiovisuals rather than on isolated pictorial elements. One approach, called "gestalt" coding, mimics the coding decisions made by people when they extract meanings from the pictures appearing on their television sets (Graber 1987a). Gestalt coding starts by identifying the kinds of information that people normally seek as cues in interpreting the news under consideration. During a presidential election, this might be the traits of the candidate (Lau and Sears 1986). The content analyst would then examine the audiovisuals, looking for configurations of cues about presidential traits. The decisions required for audiovisual gestalt coding are neither unduly complex nor unduly idiosyncratic, because the audiovisual language used in television news broadcasts is designed to be easily understood so that it can convey common meanings to a vast, diverse audience unlikely to grasp delicate shadings of information. As television news items rarely exceed two minutes in length, the language must be and is highly stereotypical.

To make accurate, realistic coding decisions, the context of each story within the total newscast, the manner of introducing and sequencing stories, and the meanings conveyed by aural components other than words must also be considered. The anchor's opening statements must be weighed especially heavily, as they often set the frame and tone for the entire story. The general political context at the time of the news broadcast and major contemporaneous news trends must also be incorporated into the analysis. For instance, the fact that Reagan's age had become an important issue in 1984, after the first presidential debate, was likely to enhance people's attention to close-up pictures that might reveal signs of age-related disabilities.

Surveys and Interviews

Studies of the effects of media images are generally executed through surveys and polls of media audiences. Cross-sectional designs and panel designs both have been popular in election-related studies, with panel designs gaining in favor because they are better suited for tracking attitudinal changes over time (e.g., Patterson and McClure 1976; Patterson 1980; Miller and Levitin 1976; Nie et al. 1976). Samples have ranged from several thousand respondents interviewed in a single wave or multiple waves to intensive work done with tiny panels or even single individuals (Weaver et al. 1981; Brown 1980). Few campaign studies have focused on elite audiences like convention delegates or party officials, whose influence on political decisions and on the flow of political information is substantial (Rapoport et al. 1986). However, a number of studies, which have explored attitude and behavior differences linked to education level, prior knowledge, and interest in the election, have shed some light on mass/elite issues (Weaver et al. 1981; Lau and Erber 1985; Hamill and Lodge 1986).

In election studies, research designs normally entail formulating hypotheses about likely media impact a priori and testing them through examination of survey responses. Respondents who are interviewed are usually asked about their media use habits, either in general at a specific time or in reference to a specific broadcast or story. Their knowledge of certain information contained in media messages, or their mental states and feelings about candidates and issues, are then taken as evidence of the extent of media impact. Researchers rarely ask open-ended questions, allowing respondents to report what they believe that they have learned from media stories and how they link their mental states and feelings to these stories. In fact, the range of media-related questions asked in surveys and polls has generally been quite narrow, because other questions have enjoyed a preferred status. When major surveys like the National Election Studies are in preparation, the voices of media scholars have been too few to prevail when it comes to allocation of sizable chunks of research time.

Survey research designs employed in media impact studies have a number of serious weaknesses. In the first place, investigators usually are not able to confirm that respondents have actually been exposed to the information stimuli for which effects are being tested. In fact, in the majority of instances, investigators have not even examined these stimuli in detail. Second, survey researchers generally know little about the information already held by respondents prior to their exposure to specific media stimuli. This deprives them of a baseline for measuring media-induced changes in perception and behavior.

While survey research remains the dominant mode of investigation of media impact, several other approaches have made inroads based on the assumption that media impact cannot be understood unless one looks more closely at the way in which individuals process media information. Such thinking has lead to intensive analyses of small numbers of individuals. Several scholars have undertaken in-depth interviews of small groups of people, using various psychological testing devices (Graber 1988; Iyengar and Kinder 1987; Neuman et al. 1988). Among intensive analysis techniques, Q-methodology appears to be particularly well suited for communication research. It is designed to measure clusters of subjective reactions to information stimuli, based on individual scores, rather than a mean drawn from a large population. The technique enables researchers to detect the kinds of people most likely to exhibit particular patterns of reactions (Brown 1980; Nimmo and Savage 1976). Once types of people exhibiting similar reaction patterns have been identified, survey research can establish the distribution of these reaction patterns in larger populations.

Although interesting results have been obtained through ethnographic studies in which researchers use natural settings to observe how people communicate about political matters, political scientists have shunned this approach. Judging from conversations with colleagues, many potential users of this method fear that it would be automatically condemned as too impressionistic, too anthropological, or too journalistic. However, purely experimental studies to probe media impact have come into vogue, despite the fact that the methodology is not characteristic of political science research. Mostly, they have involved exposing small groups of people to carefully selected segments of typical media information and then measuring their retention of the information or the attitudes deriving from the information (Meadow and Sigelman 1982; Iyengar et al. 1982; Iyengar and Kinder 1987; Rosenberg 1988). The principal advantage of experimental studies is the researcher's ability to control the stimuli to which research subjects are exposed. Such control avoids the kind of stimulus adulteration encountered in natural settings where many stimuli are present and interact. The chief problem posed by experimental research is the artificiality of the context. Media impact may be quite different in controlled laboratory settings than in natural situations.

Studies designed to examine media impact through intensive interviews of small panels of people or through various laboratory procedures run the risk of being unrepresentative, so that the findings cannot be attributed to larger populations without further testing. Nonetheless, they are an attractive alternative to large-scale surveys. Their comparatively low budgets make them affordable for scholars unable to obtain support from major research-funding agencies. Replication by other small or large samples can increase confidence in their representativeness. Mixed research designs that combine experimental and survey research procedures are another alternative to overcoming the problems posed by small samples. In such a design, large sample populations are divided into experimental and control groups. Various treatments, such as exposure to specific broadcasts, are then provided only for selected groups of respondents (Bishop et al. 1984). Thus far, such mixed designs have been used only very rarely.

Other Design Problems

Current research has produced many contradictory findings. They are hard to reconcile because research designs have varied greatly and major concepts have been defined in different ways. What, for instance, is encompassed in candidate personality? Is "personality" a matter of white teeth, or of sizing up a candidate's background and character? What constitutes "momentum" for a candidate or a policy? When setbacks occur, has momentum ceased or merely slowed? Similarly, there is little agreement about what constitutes "learning" from a mass media story. Have respondents "learned" the content of a story if they recognize it as familiar after it is retold? Or does "learning" entail the ability to recount the story without prompting? If facts are told incorrectly, is this evidence that learning has failed to occur? How many facts and what kinds of facts must be recalled from a story in order to say that it has been "learned?" Different studies provide different answers (Weaver et al. 1981; Bartels 1987; Jacoby et al. 1986). Future studies should try to resolve such uncertainties by defining their terms more precisely.

Problems arise also because time lags between a media event and impact measurement have varied widely. They need to be carefully considered and more accurately specified. Some measurements have taken place within minutes, others have been delayed for weeks and months. Obviously, facts and impressions reported immediately after exposure may not match those obtainable after a much greater lapse of time. Research on the length of retention of information has provided few guidelines for judging the degree of change that ought to be expected over time. The political news context in which respondents are interviewed also changes, often during the course of a single survey, especially if it extends over a period of days or weeks. A major political incident unfolding while the survey is in progress may create a rapidly fluctuating political climate.

There are many unresolved problems. Much political science election research rests on shaky, unexpressed and unexamined, often patently unrealistic, assumptions. For example, in political science utopia land, most voters are fully informed about real-world political and social conditions and make fully rational, well-calculated choices. They are amateur statisticians. Emotions, snap judgments, or capricious decisions come into play only rarely. At the start of each election, or even at each new phase in the process, voters' minds are clean slates, so that all their knowledge and opinions about the election can be attributed to currently available information. Long-term memory hardly exists. Voters' judgments are usually original and rarely reflect the judgments made by commentators and quoted in the media. Television pictures count for little or nothing.

Since researchers know what kinds of information are learned, it is not necessary to ask voters to describe what information they deemed important and how they extracted it from the available news supply and used it. Anyway, respondents' descriptions of information use and processing are suspect and deserve less credence than the researchers' hypotheses. Such questionable assumptions can and must be tested empirically to determine to what extent and under what circumstances they are wholly or partially false, and researchers must take full account of actual human information-processing behaviors.

Some uncertainties about the validity of research findings could be resolved through replications of past research. Replications are also needed to judge how universally applicable current findings are and to assess the variations in findings produced by changing political and technological contexts. Many of the studies done at the national level need to be replicated at state and local levels to develop better insights into the idiosyncrasies of politics at those levels in various parts of the country. To compare media performance in various political systems and various types of media ownership and control patterns would also be instructive. Similarly, more attention needs to be paid in all phases of media research to cultural differences among population groups based on demographic factors such as age, race, religion, national origin, place of residence, and economic and occupational characteristics. Media influence on mass publics needs to be distinguished from the often far more politically crucial media impact on political elites.

BUILDING ON THE FOUNDATIONS LAID IN THE PAST

Many possibilities for striking out in new directions have already been noted. They will benefit from a new spirit of daring that should lead to untried research ventures, particularly in the large realm of politics that does not focus on elections. The study of information processing, including processing visual information, appears to be a particularly promising area for significant new findings about mass media impact on thinking and behavior. Computer simulations and research into the physiology of brain functions may open up a number of the black boxes that have hitherto blocked understanding. More experimental research will further deepen our understanding of how the human mind assimilates and uses media information. Memory processes also warrant a great deal more research. We need to know what audiences remember from the past and how long the attitudes and feelings that spring from media information last. These insights should produce new knowledge about socialization and the structure of belief systems.

Much more research also needs to be done on details of the process through which contextual news and the framing of messages prime the audience's attention. For example, we need to know how public-opinion poll results are affected by stories featured at the time the poll was taken. Successes and failures of purposive indoctrination delivered in political advertising messages can illuminate the limitations faced by newspeople in transmitting information accurately through less purposively controlled messages (Joslyn 1984; Meadow and Sigelman 1982). These successes and failures can also shed light on the problems that audiences currently face because news formats are inadequately synchronized with human news-processing skills (Lanzetta et al. 1985; Rosenberg et al. 1986; Graber 1988b; Granberg and Holmberg 1986).

Besides pursuing new paths of inquiry that have not been explored in the past, political scientists need to retest old findings to ascertain their validity under changing technological and political conditions and in new contexts (Abramson et al. 1988). The opportunities for narrowcasting created through cable television and satellite technology may herald the fracturing of mass consensus for many political issues. Assessing the nature and significance of technological changes will require renewed research efforts, including complex new designs. These must encompass a better melding of qualitative and quantitative methods and more attention to both micro-level and macro-level effects. Most of these ventures will benefit from increased interdisciplinary cooperation, as well as replication of inquiries by scholars whose work represents diverse disciplinary perspectives, designs, and methodologies. Reliance on past work from all disciplines may also forestall unnecessary duplication of research.

Most importantly, although major changes in the American political system have been attributed in whole or in part to the nature of media coverage in the television age, few scholars have taken the trouble to investigate the accuracy of these perceptions. We need to know how the media cover public problems and public policies, and how this coverage affects the public dialogue and decision-making. Barbara Nelson's 1984 inquiry into the contributions of publicity to child abuse legislation is an example. If we want to understand how politics really works, we need many more such studies. The time has come to investigate the precise role that media play in propelling political figures into office and in setting and guiding the agenda for political action. We need to fathom media impact on the climate of opinion in which democracy thrives or languishes. Concentrating research efforts largely at the micro-level of media effects on individuals will not give us the answers. Rather, the research focus must now shift massively to long-neglected macro-level systems effects.

REFERENCES

This bibliography is restricted to political science sources.

Abramson, Jeffrey B., F. Christopher Arterton, and Gary R. Orren. 1988. *The Electronic Commonwealth*. New York: Basic Books.

Adams, William C., ed. 1981. *Television Coverage of the Middle East*. Norwood, N.J.: Ablex.

————, ed. 1982. *Television Coverage of International Affairs*. Norwood, N.J.: Ablex.

————, ed. 1983. *Television Coverage of the 1980 Presidential Campaign*. Norwood, N.J.: Ablex.

———— et al. 1986. "Before and After *The Day After*: The Unexpected Results of a Televised Drama." *Political Communication and Persuasion* 3:191–213.

Arterton, F. Christopher. 1978. "Campaign Organizations Confront the Media-Political Environment." In *Race for the Presidency: The Media and the Nominating Process*, ed. James D. Barber. Englewood Cliffs, N.J.: Prentice-Hall.

————. 1984. *Media Politics: The News Strategies of Presidential Campaigns*. Lexington, Mass.: D. C. Heath.

————. 1987. *Teledemocracy: Can Technology Protect Democracy?* Beverly Hills, Calif.: Sage Publications.

Axelrod, Robert. 1976. *Structure of Decision: The Cognitive Maps of Political Elites*. Princeton, N.J.: Princeton University Press.

Bartels, Larry M. 1985. "Expectations and Preferences in Presidential Nominating Campaigns." *American Political Science Review* 79:804–15.

————. 1987. "Candidate Choice and the Dynamics of the Presidential Nominating Process." *American Journal of Political Science* 31:1–30.

Behr, Roy, and Shanto Iyengar. 1985. "Television News, Real-World Cues, and Changes in the Public Agenda." *Public Opinion Quarterly* 49:38–57.

Bennett, W. Lance. 1988. *News: The Politics of Illusion*. 2d ed. New York: Longman.

Berelson, Bernard. 1948. "Communication and Public Opinion." In *Communications in Modern Society*, ed. Wilbur Schramm. Urbana: University of Illinois Press.

————, Paul Lazarsfeld, and William McPhee. 1954. *Voting: A Study of Opinion Formation in a Presidential Campaign*. Chicago: University of Chicago Press.

Bishop, George F., Robert W. Oldendick, and Alfred J. Tuchfarber. 1984. "Interest in Political Campaigns: The Influence of Question Order and Electoral Context." *Political Behavior* 6:159–69.

Broh, C. Anthony. 1980. "Horse-race Journalism: Reporting the Polls in the 1976 Presidential Election." *Public Opinion Quarterly* 44:514–29.

Brown, Steven R. 1980. *Political Subjectivity: Applications of Q Methodology in Political Science*. New Haven: Yale University Press.

Campbell, Angus, Gerald Gurin, and Warren Miller. 1954. *The Voter Decides*. Evanston, Ill.: Row, Peterson.

————, Philip E. Converse, Warren E. Miller, and Donald E. Stokes. 1960. *The American Voter*. New York: Wiley.

————. 1966. *Elections and the Political Order*. New York: Wiley, 1966.

Cohen, Bernard C. 1963. *The Press and Foreign Policy*. Princeton, N.J: Princeton University Press.

Conover, Pamela J., and Stanley Feldman. 1980. "Belief System Organization in the American Electorate: An Alternate Approach." In *The Electorate Reconsidered*, ed. John C. Pierce and John A. Sullivan. Beverly Hills, Calif.: Sage Publications.

———. 1984. "How People Organize the Political World: A Schematic Model." *American Journal of Political Science* 28:95–126.

———. 1986. "The Role of Inference in the Perception of Political Candidates." In *Political Cognition*, ed. Richard R. Lau and David O. Sears. Hillsdale, N.J.: Erlbaum.

Cundy, Donald T. 1986. "Political Commercials and Candidate Image: The Effect Can Be Substantial." In *New Perspectives on Political Advertising*, ed. Lynda Lee Kaid, Dan Nimmo, and Keith R. Sanders. Beverly Hills, Calif.: Sage Publications.

Deutsch, Karl W. 1957. "Mass Communication and the Loss of Freedom in National Decision-Making." *Journal of Conflict Resolution* 1:200–11.

——— et al. 1957. *Political Community and the North Atlantic Area*. Princeton, N.J.: Princeton University Press.

———, and Richard L. Merritt. 1965. "Effects of Events on National and International Images." In *International Behavior*, ed. Herbert Kelman. New York: Holt, Rinehart and Winston.

———, Lewis J. Edinger, Roy C. Macridis, and Richard L. Merritt. 1967. *France, Germany, and the Western Alliance: A Study of Elite Attitudes on European Integration and World Politics*. New York: Scribner's.

Dunn, Delmer D. 1969. *Public Officials and the Press*. Reading, Mass.: Addison-Wesley.

Easton, David, and Jack Dennis. 1969. *Children in the Political System: Origins of Political Legitimacy*. New York: McGraw-Hill.

Edelman, Murray. 1964. *The Symbolic Uses of Politics*. Urbana: University of Illinois Press.

———. 1988. *Constructing the Political Spectacle*. Chicago: University of Chicago Press.

Entman, Robert M. 1989. *Democracy Without Citizens: Media and the Decay of American Politics*. New York: Oxford University Press.

Epstein, Laurily, and Gerald Strom. 1984. "Survey Research and Election Night Projections." *Public Opinion* 7:48–50.

Erbring, Lutz, Edie N. Goldenberg, and Arthur H. Miller. 1980. "Front-Page News and Real-World Cues: A New Look at Agenda-Setting by the Media." *American Journal of Political Science* 24:16–49.

Fagen, Richard R. 1969. *The Transformation of Political Culture in Cuba*. Stanford, Calif.: Stanford University Press.

Feldman, Stanley, and Lee Sigelman. 1985. "The Political Impact of Prime-Time Television: 'The Day After.'" *Journal of Politics* 47:556–78.

Fishman, Mark. 1980. *Manufacturing the News*. Austin: University of Texas Press.

Fiske, Susan, and Donald Kinder. 1981. "Involvement, Expertise and Schema Use: Evidence from Political Cognition." In *Personality, Cognition, and Social Interaction*, ed. Nancy Cantor and John F. Kihlstrom. Hillsdale, N.J.: Erlbaum.

George, Alexander L. 1959. *Propaganda Analysis*. Evanston, Ill.: Row, Peterson.

Ginsberg, Benjamin. 1986. *The Captive Public: How Mass Opinion Promotes State Power*. New York: Basic Books.

Goldenberg, Edie, and Michael W. Traugott. 1984. *Campaigning for Congress*. Washington, D.C.: Congressional Quarterly Press.

————, eds. 1987. "Mass Media in Legislative Campaigns." *Legislative Studies Quarterly* 12, no. 3.

Graber, Doris A. 1978. "Problems in Measuring Audience Effects of the 1976 Debates." In *The Presidential Debates: Media, Electoral, and Policy Perspectives*, ed. George R. Bishop, Robert G. Meadow, and Marylin Jackson-Beeck. New York: Praeger.

————. 1983. "Hoopla and Horse-Race in 1980 Campaign Coverage: A Closer Look." In *Mass Media and Elections: International Research Perspectives*, ed. Winfred Schulz and Klaus Schoenbach. Munich: Oelschlaeger.

————. 1986. "Mass Media and Political Images in Elections." *Research in Micropolitics*, vol. 1, ed. Samuel L. Long. New York: JAI Press.

————. 1987a. "Kind Pictures and Harsh Words: How Television Presents the Candidates." In *Elections in America*, ed. Kay Lehman Schlozman. Boston: Allen & Unwin.

————. 1987b. "Framing Election News Broadcasts: News Context and its Impact on the 1984 Presidential Election." *Social Science Quarterly* 68: 552–68.

————. 1988. *Processing the News: How People Tame the Information Tide*. New York: Longman.

————. 1989. *Mass Media and American Politics*. Washington, D.C.: Congressional Quarterly Press.

Granberg, Donald, and Sven Holmberg. 1986. "Political Perception among Voters in Sweden and the U.S.: Analysis of Issues with Explicit Alternatives." *Western Political Quarterly* 39:7–28.

Greenstein, Fred I. 1965. *Children and Politics*. New Haven: Yale University Press.

Grossman, Michael B., and Martha J. Kumar. 1981. *Portraying the President: The White House and the News Media*. Baltimore: The Johns Hopkins University Press.

Hamill, Ruth, and Milton Lodge. 1986. "Cognitive Consequences of Political Sophistication." In *Political Cognition*, ed. Richard R. Lau and David O. Sears. Hillsdale, N.J.: Erlbaum.

Hershey, Marjorie Randon. 1984. *Running for Office: The Political Education of Campaigners*. Chatham, N.J.: Chatham House Publishers.

Hess, Stephen. 1981. *The Washington Reporters*. Washington, D.C.: Brookings Institution.

———. 1984. *The Government/Press Connection*. Washington, D.C.: Brookings Institution.

———. 1986. *The Ultimate Insiders: U.S. Senators in the National Media*. Washington, D.C.: Brookings Institution.

Hofstetter, C. Richard. 1976. *Bias in the News*. Columbus: Ohio State University Press.

———. 1978. "News Bias in the 1972 Campaign: A Cross-Media Analysis." *Journalism Monographs* 58.

———. 1979. "Perception of News Bias in the 1972 Presidential Campaign." *Journalism Quarterly* 56:370–74.

Iyengar, Shanto, Mark D. Peters, and Donald R. Kinder. 1982. "Experimental Demonstrations of the 'Not-So-Minimal' Consequences of Television News Programs." *American Political Science Review* 76:848–58.

———, and Donald R. Kinder. 1987. *News That Matters: Television and American Opinion*. Chicago: University of Chicago Press.

Janowitz, Morris. 1980. *The Community Press in an Urban Setting: The Social Elements of Urbanism*. 3d ed. Chicago: University of Chicago Press.

Joslyn, Richard A. 1984. *Mass Media and Elections*. Reading, Mass.: Addison-Wesley.

Keeter, Scott, and Cliff Zukin. 1983. *Uninformed Choice: The Failure of the New Presidential Nominating System*. New York: Praeger.

Kern, Montague, Patricia W. Levering, and Ralph B. Levering. 1983. *The Kennedy Crises: The Press, the Presidency, and Foreign Policy*. Chapel Hill: University of North Carolina Press.

Kern, Montague. 1989. *30-Second Politics: Political Advertising in the Eighties*. New York: Praeger.

Kernell, Samuel. 1986. *Going Public: New Strategies of Presidential Leadership*. Washington, D.C.: Congressional Quarterly Press.

Kessel, John. 1988. *Presidential Campaign Politics: Coalition Strategies and Citizen Response*. 3d ed. Homewood, Ill.: Dorsey Press.

Kinder, Donald R. 1981a. "Presidents, Prosperity and Public Opinion." *Public Opinion Quarterly* 45:1–21.

———. 1981b. "Sociotropic Politics: The American Case." *British Journal of Political Science* 11:129–62.

Krasnow, Erwin G., Lawrence D. Longley, and Herbert A. Terry. 1982. *The Politics of Broadcast Regulation*. 3d ed. New York: St. Martin's Press.

Kressel, Neil J. 1987. "Biased Judgments of Media Bias: A Case Study of the Arab-Israel Dispute." *Political Psychology* 8:211–26.

Lang, Gladys Engel, and Kurt Lang. 1983. *The Battle for Public Opinion: The President, the Press, and the Polls during Watergate*. New York: Columbia University Press.

Lanzetta, John T., Denis G. Sullivan, Roger D. Masters, and Gregory J. McHugo. 1985. "Emotional and Cognitive Responses to Televised Images of Political Leaders. In *Mass Media and Political Thought*, ed. Sidney Kraus and Richard M. Perloff. Beverly Hills, Calif.: Sage Publications.

Lasswell, Harold D. 1969. "The Structure and Function of Communication in Society." In *Mass Communications*, ed. Wilbur Schramm. Urbana: University of Illinois Press.

———, Daniel Lerner, and Ithiel de Sola Pool. 1952. *The Comparative Study of Symbols*. Stanford: Stanford University Press.

———, Daniel Lerner, and Hans Speier. 1980. *Propaganda and Communication in World History*. 3 vols. Hawaii: University of Hawaii Press.

Lau, Richard R., and Ralph Erber. 1985. "Political Sophistication: An Information-Processing Perspective." In *Mass Media and Political Thought*, ed. Sidney Kraus and Richard M. Perloff. Beverly Hills, Calif.: Sage Publications.

———, and David Sears, eds. 1986. *Political Cognition: The 19th Annual Symposium on Cognition*. Hillsdale, N.J.: Erlbaum.

Lazarsfeld, Paul, Bernard Berelson, and Hazel Gaudet. 1944. *The People's Choice*. New York: Columbia University Press, 1944.

Levitin, Teresa E., and Warren E. Miller. 1979. "Ideological Interpretations of Presidential Elections." *American Political Science Review* 73:751–71.

Lichter, S. Robert, Stanley Rothman, and Linda S. Lichter. 1986. *The Media Elite*. New York: Adler and Adler.

Linsky, Martin. 1986a. *Impact: How the Press Affects Federal Policymaking*. New York: Norton.

———. 1986b. *Impact: How the Press Affects Federal Policymaking: Six Case Studies*. New York: Norton.

Liu, Alan P. L. 1971. *Communications and National Integration in Communist China*. Berkeley: University of California Press.

Lodge, Milton, and John C. Wahlke. 1982. "Politicos, Apoliticals, and the Processing of Political Information." *International Political Science Review* 3: 131–50.

———, and Ruth Hamill. 1986. "A Partisan Schema for Political Information Processing." *American Political Science Review* 80:505–19.

Long, Norton. 1958. "The Local Community as an Ecology of Games." *American Journal of Sociology* 64:246–58.

MacKuen, Michael B., and Steven Lane Coombs. 1981. *More Than News: Media Power in Public Affairs*. Beverly Hills, Calif.: Sage Publications.

Manheim, Jarol B. 1976. "Can Democracy Survive Television?" *Journal of Communication* 26:84–90.

———, and Robert B. Albritton. 1984. "Changing National Images: International Public Relations and Media Agenda-Setting." *American Political Science Review* 78:641–57.

Meadow, Robert G., and Lee Sigelman. 1982. "Some Effects and Noneffects of Campaign Commercials: An Experimental Study." *Political Behavior* 4: 163–75.

Mickiewicz, Ellen. 1988. *Split Signals: Television and Politics in the Soviet Union*. New York: Oxford University Press.

Miller, Arthur H., Edie N. Goldenberg, and Lutz Erbring. 1979. "Type-set Politics: Impact of Newspapers on Public Confidence." *American Political Science Review* 73:67–84.

———, Martin P. Wattenberg, and Oksana Malanchuk. 1985a. "Cognitive Representations of Candidate Assessments." In *Political Communication Yearbook, 1984*, ed. Keith R. Sanders, Lynda Lee Kaid, and Dan Nimmo. Carbondale: Southern Illinois University Press.

———, and Martin P. Wattenberg. 1985b. "Throwing the Rascals Out: Policy and Performance Evaluations of Presidential Candidates, 1952–1980." *American Political Science Review* 79:359–72.

———, Martin P. Wattenberg, and Oksana Malanchuk. 1986. "Schematic Assessments of Presidential Candidates." *American Political Science Review* 80:521–40.

Miller, Warren E., and Teresa E. Levitin. 1976. *Leadership and Change*. Cambridge, Mass.: Winthrop.

———, Arthur H. Miller, and Edward J. Schneider. 1980. *American National Election Studies Data Sourcebook, 1952–1978*. Cambridge, Mass.: Harvard University Press.

Nelson, Barbara. 1984. *Making an Issue of Child Abuse: Political Agenda Setting for Social Problems*. Chicago: University of Chicago Press.

Nesbit, Dorothy Davidson. 1988. *Videostyle in U.S. Senate Campaigns*. Knoxville: University of Tennessee Press.

Neuman, W. Russell, Marion Just, and Ann Crigler. 1988. "Knowledge, Opinion and the News." American Political Science Association paper.

Newland, Chester A. 1964. "Press Coverage of the United States Supreme Court." *Western Political Quarterly* 17:15–36.

Nie, Norman H., Sidney Verba, and John R. Petrocik. 1976. *The Changing American Voter*. Cambridge, Mass.: Harvard University Press.

Niemi, Richard J., and Larry M. Bartels. 1983. "New Measures of Issue Salience: An Evaluation." *Journal of Politics* 47:1212–20.

Nimmo, Dan P. 1964. *Newsgathering in Washington: A Study in Political Communication*. New York: Atherton Press.

————. 1981. "Mass Communication and Politics." *Handbook of Political Behavior*, vol. 4, Samuel L. Long. New York: Plenum Press.

————, and Robert Savage. 1976. *Candidates and Their Images*. Pacific Palisades, Calif.: Goodyear.

————, and James E. Combs. 1983. *Mediated Political Realities*. New York: Longman.

————. 1985. *Nightly Horrors: Crisis Coverage in Television Network News*. Knoxville: University of Tennessee Press.

Orren, Gary R., and Nathan W. Polsby, eds. 1987. *Media and Momentum: The New Hampshire Primary and Nomination Politics*. Chatham, N.J.: Chatham House.

Page, Benjamin I., Robert Y. Shapiro, and Glenn R. Dempsey. 1987. "What Moves Public Opinion?" *American Political Science Review* 81:23–43.

Paletz, David, and Robert Dunn. 1969. "Press Coverage of Civil Disorder: A Case Study of Winston-Salem, 1967." *Public Opinion Quarterly* 33: 329–45.

————, and Robert Entman. 1981. *Media Power Politics*. New York: The Free Press.

————, and K. Kendall Guthrie. 1987. "The Three Faces of Ronald Reagan." *Journal of Communication* 37:7–23.

Parenti, Michael. 1986. *Inventing Reality: The Politics of the Mass Media*. New York: St. Martin's Press.

Patterson, Thomas E. 1980. *The Mass Media Election: How Americans Choose Their President*. New York: Praeger.

————, and Robert D. McClure. 1976. *The Unseeing Eye: The Myth of Television Power in National Elections*. New York: Putnam.

Peffley, Mark, Stanley Feldman, and Lee Sigelman. 1987. "Economic Conditions and Party Competence: Processes of Belief Revision." *Journal of Politics* 49:100–121.

Pomper, Gerald M., with Susan Lederman. 1980. *Elections in America*. 2d ed. New York: Longman.

Pool, Ithiel de Sola. 1952. *The Prestige Papers: A Survey of Their Editorials*. Stanford: Stanford University Press.

————. 1959. *Symbols of Internationalism*. Stanford, Calif.: Stanford University Press.

————. 1963. "The Mass Media and Politics in the Modernization Process." In *Communication and Political Development*, ed. Lucian W. Pye. Princeton, N.J.: Princeton University Press.

————. 1983. *Technologies of Freedom*. Cambridge, Mass.: Harvard University Press.

President's Commission on the Accident at Three Mile Island. 1979. *Report of the Public's Right to Information Task Force*. Washington, D.C.: Government Printing Office.

Protess, David L., Donna R. Leff, Stephen C. Brooks, and Margaret Gordon. 1985. "Uncovering Rape: The Watchdog Press and the Limits of Agenda Setting." *Public Opinion Quarterly* 49:19–37.

Putnam, Robert D. 1973. *The Beliefs of Politicians: Ideology, Conflict, and Democracy in Britain and Italy*. New Haven: Yale University Press.

Pye, Lucian W., ed. 1963. *Communications and Political Development*. Princeton, N.J.: Princeton University Press.

Ranney, Austin. 1983. *Channels of Power: The Impact of Television on American Politics*. Washington, D.C.: American Enterprise Institute for Public Policy Research.

Rapoport, Ronald B., Allan I. Abramowitz, and John J. McGlennon. 1986. *The Life of the Parties: Activists in Presidential Politics*. Lexington: University Press of Kentucky.

Robinson, Michael J. 1976. "Public Affairs Television and the Growth of Political Malaise." *American Political Science Review* 70:409–42.

———. 1978. "TV's Newest Program: The Presidential Nominations Game." *Public Opinion* 1:41–46.

———. 1981a. "The Media in 1980: Was the Message the Message?" In *The American Elections of 1980*, ed. Austin Ranney. Washington, D.C.: American Enterprise Institute for Public Policy Research.

———. 1981b. "A Statesman Is a Dead Politician: Candidate Images on Network News." In *What's News: The Media in American Society*, ed. Elie Abel. San Francisco: Institute for Contemporary Studies.

———. 1987. "News Media Myths and Realities: What the Network News Did and Didn't Do in the 1984 General Campaign." *Elections in America*, ed. Kay Lehman Schlozman, pp. 143–70. Boston: Allen & Unwin.

———, and Margaret Sheehan. 1983a. *Over the Wire and on TV: CBS and UPI in Campaign '80*. New York: Basic Books.

———. 1983b. "Traditional Ink vs. Modern Video Versions of Campaign '80." In *Television Coverage of the 1980 Presidential Campaign*. Norwood, N.J.: Ablex.

Rosenberg, Shawn W. 1988. *Reason, Ideology and Politics*. Princeton, N.J.: Princeton University Press.

———, Lisa Bohan, Patrick McCafferty, and Kevin Harris. 1986. "The Image and the Vote: The Effect of Candidate Presentation on Voter Preference." *American Journal of Political Science* 30:108–27.

———, with Patrick McCafferty. 1987. "The Image and the Vote: Manipulating Voters' Preferences." *Public Opinion Quarterly* 51:31–47.

Rothman, Stanley, and S. Robert Lichter. 1987. "Elite Ideology and Risk Perception in Nuclear Energy Policy." *American Political Science Review* 81: 383–404.

Rubin, Richard L. 1981. *Press, Party, and Presidency*. New York: Norton.

Sahr, Robert C. 1983. "Energy as a Non-Issue in 1980 Coverage." In *Television Coverage of the 1980 Presidential Campaign*, ed. William C. Adams. Norwood, N.J.: Ablex.

Sears, David O., and Jack Citrin. 1982. *Tax Revolt: Something for Nothing in California*. Cambridge, Mass.: Harvard University Press.

Shaw, Donald L., and Maxwell E. McCombs. 1977. *The Emergence of American Political Issues: The Agenda-Setting Function of the Press*. St. Paul, Minn.: West.

Sigal, Leon. 1973. *Reporters and Officials: The Organization and Politics of Newsmaking*. Lexington, Mass.: D. C. Heath.

Sigel, Roberta S., ed. 1989. *Political Learning in Adulthood: A Sourcebook of Theory and Research*. Chicago: University of Chicago Press, 1989.

Sorauf, Frank J. 1987. "Campaign Money and the Press: Three Soundings." *Political Science Quarterly* 102:25–42.

Tuchman, Gaye. 1978. *Making News: A Study in the Construction of Reality*. New York: The Free Press.

Tulis, Jeffrey. 1987. *The Rhetorical Presidency*. Princeton, N.J.: Princeton University Press.

United States Government. 1968. *Report of the National Advisory Commission on Civil Disorders*. New York: Bantam Books.

Vermeer, Jan Pons. 1982. *For Immediate Release: Candidate Press Releases in American Political Campaigns*. Westport, Conn.: Greenwood Press.

———, ed. 1987. *Campaigns in the News: Mass Media and Congressional Elections*. Westport, Conn.: Greenwood Press.

Weaver, David H., Doris A. Graber, Maxwell E. McCombs, and Chaim H. Eyal. 1981. *Media Agenda-Setting in a Presidential Election: Issues, Images, and Interest*. New York: Praeger, 1981.

Welch, Susan. 1972. "The American Press and Indochina, 1950–1956." In *Communication in International Politics*, ed. Richard L. Merritt. Urbana: University of Illinois Press.

Wolfsfeld, Gadi. 1984. "Collective Political Action and Media Strategy: The Case of Yamit." *Journal of Conflict Resolution* 28:363–81.

5

Political Socialization: Where's the Politics?

Pamela Johnston Conover

The subfield of political socialization is in trouble, deep trouble. How do we know this? Because there has been a veritable explosion in the number of commentaries telling us that it is so (for example, Connell 1987; Conover and Searing 1987; Cook 1985; Niemi and Sobieszek 1977; Rosenberg 1985). Because the number of journal articles dealing with political socialization has plummeted in the last decade (see Cook 1985). Because panels devoted to the demise of the field abound at professional meetings while panels dealing with empirical research dwindle. Indeed, it has reached the point where the critics of the field may well outnumber the actual practitioners.

How did this happen? Can anything be done about it? Should anything be done about it? These are the questions that I shall take up in this paper. I shall begin by briefly reviewing the high points in the development of the subfield, as well as the problems that eventually undermined this research. Then, I shall turn to my own prescriptions for reviving and reshaping the study of socialization.

I gratefully acknowledge the support of the Spencer Foundation in the preparation of this paper. I also appreciate the assistance of Matthew Burbank and Jenifer MacGillvary, and the very helpful comments of Donald Searing.

THE STUDY OF POLITICAL SOCIALIZATION
The Past

Two broadly defined research traditions gave shape and impetus to the emergence of the subfield of political socialization in the 1960s (see Kinder and Sears 1985). One tradition was initiated by Herbert Hyman (1959), with the publication of *Political Socialization*. This influential book summarized socialization findings from other disciplines, gave the subfield its name, and suggested a rationale for studying socialization. Hyman (1959) drew our attention to the fact that political behavior is learned behavior and that, to understand this, learning is important. In particular, he focused his attention on the citizen as a voter, and consequently on the learning of partisanship and other attitudes directly relevant to participation in the electoral arena.

The other tradition is best defined by the work of David Easton and his colleagues (Easton and Hess 1962; Easton and Dennis 1969; Hess and Torney 1967), who placed Charles Merriam's (1931) questions about how nations and governments mold children into good citizens in the context of system's theory. The argument was simple and powerful: political socialization is important to study because it provides the basis for political stability.

In the long run, it was the Hyman tradition, with its focus on the electoral arena and the sources of political participation, that had the most staying power. But, at the time, it was the Easton tradition that captured the discipline's imagination, at least for a brief period. The rise and fall of Easton's approach has been chronicled and analyzed repeatedly (Cook 1985; Connell 1987; Kinder and Sears 1985; Merelman 1972; Niemi 1973; Niemi and Sobieszek 1977; Sears 1975). I have little new to add to these accounts of the story. Nonetheless, it is a story that bears repeating, however briefly, because it is a story that provides important lessons for our subfield.

System Stability and Children's Views of Authorities Enthusiasm for the study of political socialization burst forth in the 1960s in reaction to an intriguing set of findings dealing with children's images of political authorities. In 1960, two articles, one by Robert Hess and David Easton and the other by Fred Greenstein, captured our attention with their discovery of the extremely positive attitudes that young children hold toward political authorities. These findings were quickly placed in the theoretical context of systems theory (see Easton and Hess 1962; Easton 1965). And this new theoretical approach was rapidly put to the test in several key empirical studies. Greenstein's book appeared in 1965, with more interesting data. And two years later, the first major national study by Hess and Torney (1967) provided seemingly solid evidence on the importance of early learning. Finally, in 1969, Easton and Dennis's *Children in the Political System* was published. This was the last of the early studies, and perhaps the best. But it never received the full appreciation and follow-up it deserved—in part, because by the time it was published the field's theoretical foundations were already under attack.

Nevertheless, taken all together, the decade's landmark studies had fixed in the mind of the profession two dramatic findings and one important assumption. The findings were that children "personalized" government to a remarkable degree and, to an even more remarkable degree, they "idealized" what they saw, particularly the president, whom Greenstein (1960) characterized as "The Benevolent Leader." Such feelings, moreover, appeared to be firm bonds rooted in deep-seated needs and anxieties about authority figures. And they appeared to be politically significant as a basis for diffuse system support, presumably a critical source of political stability. The important assumption was "persistence": socialization was likely completed by the end of elementary school; or, if not completed, at least later learning would be modest for most people and not of great significance for their basic orientations.

But, by the 1970s, this research tradition in socialization was under fire, as dramatic events and new data began to shatter the profession's confidence in the whole endeavor. As Fred Greenstein noted (1975, 1973), the events of the late sixties and early seventies involving the now college-age children of the early socialization studies seemed perversely designed to discredit the idealization thesis: Vietnam protests, insurrections in the ghettos, protests during President Johnson's last years, and then the rejection of President Nixon after Watergate. Earlier idealization of authorities seemed to have evaporated.

Or perhaps it had never existed in the first place—at least for some children. That is to say, just as unsettling as the above events were the numerous survey studies that demonstrated that children's idealization of political authorities was not a universal phenomenon: Appalachian children (Jaros, Hirsch and Fleron 1968), black children (Greenberg 1970; Sears and McConahay 1973; Abramson 1977), Mexican-American children (García 1973), and British children, too (Stradling and Zurick 1971; Greenstein et al. 1974) all demonstrated less than idealistic views of the political authorities. Some fifteen years later, calmer voices (Kinder and Sears 1985) would suggest that it was difficult to assess the implications of these protests, which were perhaps unusual, and of the data, which were highly correlated with partisanship. In retrospect, the idealization thesis simply may have been weakened without invalidating its principal claim (i.e., that early idealization will affect later supportive feelings when children become adults). But, at the time, the prevailing effect of these events and findings was to create disillusionment with the study of childhood socialization (see Niemi and Sobieszek 1977).

This disillusionment deepened as the theoretical rationale for studying childhood socialization—the persistence assumption—became more and more problematic. As Donald Kinder and David Sears (1985, 719–20) succinctly noted: "The importance of preadult political socialization lies primarily in the impact its residues have on adult attitudes and behavior. To have such an impact they must of course persist into and through adulthood in some form or another. But do they in fact persist?" Although there was some evidence suggesting the stability of certain kinds of political orientations, such as partisanship and racial attitudes (see Kinder and Rhodebeck 1982; Miller and Sears 1986; Sears 1975), by and large most of the evidence undermined confidence in the persistence assumption (Jennings and Niemi 1981; Marsh 1971; Searing et al. 1973, 1976). The most persuasive evidence came from longitudinal studies that demonstrated considerable change in political attitudes (including partisanship) after childhood (e.g., Jennings and Niemi 1981).

As if the collapse of the childhood idealization and persistence hypotheses were not enough, there were also methodological critiques that threatened to shut down the study of childhood socialization. The use of survey research among young children came under heavy fire as evidence mounted that children's survey responses were very unstable (Connell and Goot, 1972/1973; Vaillancourt 1973) and especially prone to response-set bias (Kolson and Green 1970). To be sure, by the 1970s some innovative researchers had abandoned survey research in favor of methods more appropriate to studying children, such as semi-structured interviews and projective tests (e.g., Connell 1971; Greenstein, 1975), and hypothetical dilemmas (e.g., Adelson 1971; Adelson and O'Neil 1966; and Merelman, 1971). But the innovations came too late and were introduced by too few researchers to make much difference. By 1980, the study of childhood socialization had come to a standstill.[1] And most of the discipline was wondering, as were Richard Niemi and Barbara Sobieszek (1977, 216–17), "other than studying it for its own sake, is there any justification for studying the political views of pre-adults and especially pre-teenagers?"

Later, I shall argue that there is indeed a very important justification; but that is getting ahead of the story. Before turning to the future, it is important to complete our understanding of the past. It is important to see how the Hyman tradition fared.

Political Development and Lifelong Socialization Although the spotlight may have been briefly captured by those who studied children's attitudes toward political authorities, the subfield had another more enduring focus, the one suggested by Hyman. Hyman (1959, 9–10) recognized that the process of becoming a member of a collectivity is central to the concept of political socialization. Yet he approached the study of political socialization more narrowly, directing his attention to the citizen as a voter, and thus to the role of socialization in the development of partisanship. His approach was attractive. It was compatible with the liberal theory of democracy that interprets voting as the citizen's primary function. And the citizen as a voter was already being studied empirically by the Michigan school of electoral studies. By adopting concepts and measures already prominent in these national election studies—concepts such as party identification, political interest, and political efficacy—Hyman's approach to the study of socialization was immediately connected to adult political behavior, and thus its political importance was immediately established.

The consequences of this focus were difficult to foresee in the 1960s. But with hindsight it seems clear that, once the goal became to explain political participation, it perhaps became inevitable that the focus of socialization research would move away from early childhood toward adolescence and adulthood. After all, with the possible exception of party identification, many of the factors that are critical to adult political participation are *not* especially critical to the everyday lives of citizens. It strains credibility, therefore, to argue that such attitudes would be sufficiently central to have been formed early in childhood and to persist into adulthood. Instead, it seems more plausible that such explanatory variables would be formed after childhood, closer to the time when they would actually have some effect. In retrospect, it should come as no surprise that so many researchers became disenchanted with the study of early childhood socialization, disillusioned by the apparent theoretical collapse of the Easton tradition and by the apparent failure of the Hyman tradition to make persistence convincing.

The evolution of the Hyman tradition is best exemplified in the work of M. Kent Jennings and Richard Niemi (1974, 1981) and a host of their students and colleagues. Several characteristics of this research deserve note. For one thing, in this research enterprise the concept of political socialization underwent a gradual transformation. Jennings and Niemi, and others as well, gradually directed our attention away from socialization as the "making of citizens" and toward the more general conceptualization of socialization as a process of learning. It was a definitional shift that caught on quickly. By 1973, Dean Jaros, for example, was already proclaiming that "political socialization is the study of political learning" (Jaros 1973, 23). Moreover, it was a definitional shift that moved our attention away from the importance of socialization for political stability and toward the importance of socialization for individual political development.

With their longitudinal study, Jennings and Niemi (1981) demonstrated that political learning extends well beyond childhood; although young adults change more rapidly than their parents, the parents change too. Such findings helped to push socialization research away from its focus on childhood toward a new focus on lifelong political learning. In the 1980s, a number of researchers began to explore political development through the life cycle (e.g., Franklin 1984; Delli Carpini 1986; Jennings 1979; Jennings and Markus 1984, 1988; Klein 1983; Sapiro 1983, 1988). These studies demonstrated that people change in political orientations throughout life; that generations respond differently to the same events; and that political development varies according to one's social roles and gender. Taken together, such studies effectively bury the belief that, in the future, political learning can be studied adequately simply by focusing on young children.

Another important legacy of the Hyman tradition was to direct our attention away from psychological models of learning and toward sociological frameworks of explanation. In particular, Hyman's 1959 analysis emphasized the importance of the family in the socialization process and, more generally, focused on the "agents" of socialization as the key independent variables for explaining the learning of political beliefs and attitudes. In the years to follow, numerous studies were devoted to establishing the relative effects upon political learning of the family, the school, peer groups, the media, and political events (for a review, see Niemi and Sobieszek 1977). As we shall see later, this exercise has been both beneficial and detrimental to the field.

In summary, the landmark studies of the 1960s established the basic framework that defined the field of political socialization. They also produced startling new data, which began by commanding the profession's attention and ended in disillusionment. The 1970s saw a second generation of studies that responded to some parts of the early work and developed other parts of it, particularly the theories relating to the Hyman tradition and electoral focus. What is needed now? Where should we take our future studies of socialization? To these questions I now turn.

Defining Political Socialization

One of the most unsettling factors in the study of political socialization is the continuing disagreement over the nature of political socialization itself. As Kinder and Sears (1985, 714) note, the most common definition, the definition most in keeping with the concept's intellectual tradition, is the one that focuses on "society's molding of the child to some a priori model, usually one perpetuating the status quo." Yet, research in the dominant Hyman tradition often adopts an alternative definition, one that emphasizes "the child's idiosyncratic personal growth" and the attainment of attitudes that do not necessarily contribute to the maintenance of the political system (Kinder and Sears 1985, 714).

Obviously, both definitions suggest important topics for study, neither of which should be abandoned. But equally obvious is the fact that these topics are quite distinct, albeit related to one another. They cannot both claim to define "political socialization" without continuing to perpetuate unnecessary conceptual confusion. One of them needs a new label. Certainly, the intellectual history of the concept suggests that the first meaning, society's molding of individuals into citizens, has the strongest claim to the label "political socialization" (see Jaros 1973; Gutmann 1987). And socialization researchers themselves have already suggested an alternative label for the second meaning: political learning (e.g., Jennings and Niemi 1974).

However, better definitions are not enough to untangle the conceptual confusion. It is essential to explore theoretically and practically how these two concepts—political socialization and political learning—relate to one another, and how they both relate to education. These relationships hinge on two questions: (1) is the learning relevant to support for the current regime?; and (2) is the transmission of information deliberate?

With these questions in mind, *political learning* may be defined as the broader, more inclusive term. It refers to the learning of any politically relevant material regardless of whether or not this learning promotes support for the existing political regime, and likewise regardless of whether or not the learning is deliberate. Such a treatment of "political learning" is consistent with a focus on how individuals gradually develop their political beliefs and attitudes, some of which may actually be subversive to the current political regime. Moreover, so defined, political learning is a global concept that encompasses political socialization, but much more besides.

Political Socialization's distinctive concern is bound up with the process of becoming a member of a group, organization, or society. The original meaning of the verb *to socialize*, and also the core of its meaning today, is "to render social, to make fit for living in society" (*Oxford English Dictionary*). Thus, political socialization refers to the learning of those values, attitudes, and modes of behavior that help people "fit in" to their political systems, that make them "good" citizens (see Gutmann 1987, 15). Like political learning, then, political socialization includes processes that are unintentional as well as processes that are deliberate; but political socialization is narrower than political learning because it only includes learning that generally promotes support for the existing regime.

Though we often assimilate *education* into our understanding of both socialization and learning, it is important to distinguish among the terms. As Amy Gutmann (1987, 15) notes, without such distinctions "it is easy to lose sight of the distinctive virtue of a democratic society, that it authorizes citizens to influence how their society reproduces itself." Compared to the other two concepts, education is consistently deliberate: "the deliberate, systematic, and sustained effort to transmit, evoke or acquire knowledge, attitudes, values, skills, or sensibilities . . . " (Cremin 1977, 134).[2] In this vein, *political education* would then be the deliberate effort to transmit political information or to create affective political orientations. Whether or not such learning supports the political regime is, in this context, irrelevant (cf. Torney, Oppenheim, and Farnen 1975). As represented diagrammatically in figure 1, political education overlaps political socialization. But not all political education is political socialization, nor is all political socialization political education.

Finally, there is one other concept that needs to be fit into the picture: *civic education*. This refers to both education and socialization, to the deliberate teaching of attitudes and values that are compatible with support for the existing political regime. In a democracy, civic education trains democratic citizens; and, so described, it constitutes the area of overlap in figure 1 between political socialization and political education. Although it refers to deliberate teaching, civic education is not, it should be stressed, restricted to formal schooling. Many other organizations, such as scouts and churches, are actively engaged in this process.

For many researchers, these definitions will do more to clarify the conceptual confusion than to ameliorate the skepticism about the value of political socialization research. In particular, critics are likely to be disturbed by the fact that these definitions seem far from value-neutral; instead, they may seem to reflect the model of liberal democratic society that dominates American political science rather than alternative political theories (Lindblom 1982). Such potential criticisms are not fatal; but they require that the definitions be refined if misconceptions are to be avoided.

Let us begin with the concept of political learning. As defined, it is neutral with respect to the impact of the learning on the individual. But, in practice, we have assumed this learning to be analogous with individual development. As Charles Lindblom (1982, 17) explains, learning is frequently taken to mean a process of development in which people "improve their grasp of reality, improve the accuracy of their perceptions, and develop skills in perception, analysis, and evaluation." What must be emphasized is that political learning, as defined above, can either contribute to individual development or hinder it. The same may be said for political socialization.

Figure 1.
Political Learning: Relationships among Political Socialization,
Civic Education, and Political Education

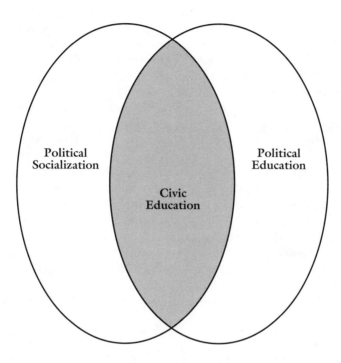

Political Learning

There are still other potential misconceptions about the term "political socialization." As just suggested, political socialization does not always contribute to the political *development* of an individual; but too often the hypothesized alternative is that the effects of socialization are *benign*. Clearly this is not always the case. Women and minorities, for example, may be successfully socialized to accept a political system that perpetuates patriarchy and racism, a system that is detrimental to their personal interests (see Sapiro 1987). As political socialization is defined above, no assumption is made about the nature of its effects on the individual; learning to "fit in" to the dominant society may be either a positive experience or a negative experience. Nonetheless, those who study political socialization must keep in mind that it can have negative consequences for some citizens; it can obstruct the social capacities of individuals rather than "bringing them into society"; it can be little more than indoctrination that allows the advantaged to continue to control and manipulate the disadvantaged (Lindblom 1982, 18).

Finally, political and civic education can also be viewed from two sides. We usually assume that education will have positive benefits for the child. But of course this is not always the case. Education, too, can be a tool of state indoctrination rather than a means to individual development. As defined, political education allows for both kinds of effects. And as researchers we must do the same.

Having sorted out some of the conceptual confusion, where do we go next? The concepts of political socialization and political learning direct us toward very different, albeit related, paths of research (Jennings and Niemi 1974, 13; Sapiro 1987, 154). Political learning focuses our attention on the individual and the *psychology* of learning. Its study centers on the question: what is important and necessary to the political development of the individual? In contrast, political socialization focuses our attention on the political system and the *politics* of learning. Its study centers on the question: what is important and necessary to the viability of the political system? These are both important roads to follow. However, since this essay was commissioned as an overview of the study of political socialization, I shall quite deliberately focus my attention on political socialization as it has been defined herein.

STUDYING POLITICAL SOCIALIZATION
The Macro-Level Rationale

Traditionally, the primary rationale for studying political socialization has concentrated on macro-level consequences: we study the political socialization of citizens because those citizens act and think in ways that influence the political system; we study the political socialization of children—future citizens—because when they grow up they, too, will act and think in ways that influence the political system. Certainly, this was the guiding rationale that originally led researchers to the study of political socialization. But by the 1980s this rationale had lost its credibility. One of the reasons for this discouragement was outlined earlier: disturbing findings and events discredited the Eastonian theoretical framework. But, there was another, perhaps equally important reason: deep dissatisfaction, even hostility, toward the general systems theories in which the Eastonian framework was embedded. If ever again we wish to provide political socialization with a macro-level rationale, we must avoid the pitfalls associated with systems theory, particularly those pitfalls concerning the goals, content, and control of political socialization.

The Goal of Political Socialization: System Maintenance? Central to the early socialization studies was the assumption that *the* major function of political socialization was to ensure political stability and system maintenance (Easton 1965; Easton and Dennis 1969). This assumption has been questioned on several counts.

For some, systems theory carries a disturbing "conservative bias." "Bias," in this regard, may be taken in two ways. First, socialization research was criticized because its emphasis on system stability necessitated a substantive focus on conservative processes (Sears 1975; also see Dawson, Prewitt, and Dawson 1977, 24–26). The "rap" was that socialization was the process through which the dominant classes perpetuated their rule by teaching dominated classes to accept their rule, and even to like it. Therefore, by studying this process researchers were said to be helping "to perpetuate power and economic inequalities and/or a 'false consciousness' " (Kinder and Sears 1985, 714). Who would want to help do that? Cast in such a conspiratorial light, political scientists increasingly grew uncomfortable with the idea of studying the status quo and restive with the study of political socialization. The charge of a conservative bias also had a second, more serious, point: namely, that the definitions of the topics and concepts involved in socialization research were so "tainted" by systems theory and its emphasis on system maintenance that they would distort the vision of researchers and lead them empirically to underestimate heterogeneity, dissensus, and change (Kavanagh 1983, 35; Sapiro 1987; Lindblom 1982).

Looking to the future, how might we best address such charges? By recognizing, first, that they have some validity. To be properly understood, socialization must be recognized as a conservative force that normally promotes continuity in political and social relationships. That is simply what it is. By using conformity to help buttress consensus, socialization processes tend to protect this continuity and, thereby, usually help to perpetuate the status quo. Moreover, socialization is, indeed, a process used by those who rule to reinforce their rule. But it would be a mistake to assume that socialization *invariably* promotes the status quo.[3] Of course it does not. Socialization can also be a mechanism through which cultural and political change is effected (Eckstein 1988).[4] As researchers, then, we must be sensitive to the extent to which socialization can promote both continuity and change. Moreover, we *ought* to be able to recognize that doing research on socialization that promotes the status quo does not ipso facto constitute an endorsement of those effects. Marxist scholars in Western societies, for example, have studied socialization to understand better what they are up against. At the same time, we *must* be sensitive to the very real possibility that the unusual theoretical perspectives involved sometimes hinder our awareness that socialization is indeed promoting the status quo, perpetuating inequities, and disadvantaging some.

Beyond the question of bias, there are still other problems with the assumption that the primary goal of socialization is to ensure system maintenance. Some scholars have argued that the assumption is too broad: a focus on system maintenance mixes together many different kinds of political phenomena (Merelman 1972). Others have argued that this assumption is too narrow: a focus on system maintenance constitutes "a very limited view of the importance of politics and political socialization" (Sapiro 1987, 153). Both charges are probably true, which more than anything else demonstrates that the term "system maintenance" is too ambiguous and too abstract. If we broaden the definition of system maintenance to encompass everything from obeying the law to engaging in interest-group politics, we shall render the concept so general as to be useless. In the most general sense, political protest could be described as an act of system maintenance. The alternative—one that I favor—is to adopt an understanding of system maintenance which recognizes that not all political behavior contributes *directly* to system maintenance, and that in fact some behavior makes no contribution whatsoever to it.

To elaborate, the problems of system maintenance, narrowly defined, are the problems of rule and control. But politics also involves problems of the allocation of resources. The two are obviously related. If the problems associated with the allocation of resources cannot be solved, this will exacerbate the problems of rule and control.[5] Consequently, citizens must learn to behave in those ways that directly contribute to the rule of the existing regime (e.g., system maintenance) *and* they must learn to engage in allocative politics in a manner that *indirectly* reinforces the rule of the existing regime. By definition, political socialization embraces both kinds of learning. It involves learning those values, attitudes, skills, and virtues that contribute to the persistence of the regime regardless of whether the contribution is a direct or an indirect one. Specifically, it includes learning both to support the authorities and to support the political culture that is embodied in the regime. Recognizing this, we must ask: what behaviors and attitudes contribute directly to system maintenance; what behaviors and attitudes contribute indirectly to system maintenance; and to what extent does socialization engender those attitudes and behaviors? These questions are best answered in the context of a more specific understanding of the content of socialization. I turn to that topic now.

The Content of Political Socialization: Diffuse System Support?
What is the content of political socialization? Easton (1965) offered
one of the early and most influential responses to this question when he
argued that socialization concerns the political community, the regime
or the authorities. However, he narrowed our empirical approach to
these objects of socialization by his assumption that socialization's
most important contribution to system maintenance is through the development of diffuse system support, "a generalized belief in the legitimacy of the regime and its authorities" (Kinder and Sears 1985, 715).
Given this assumption, it is not particularly surprising that the bulk of
the early research focused on attachment to regime norms and symbols—the flag, political slogans, national heroes, majority rule, minority rights, obeying the law, generalized trust, and so on.[6]
    But there is a serious problem here. As a general theory must do,
general systems theory specifies the content of socialization without reference to any particular political system, without reference to the concrete and particular goals of particular authorities and institutions that
control particular socialization processes. In so doing, this approach
restricts our attention to the content of political socialization that presumably characterizes *any* political system—diffuse support or loyalty,
law abidingness, and, some would add, the willingness to defend one's
country (see Galston 1988). No doubt this is the core of political socialization. But it is only the core. All political systems supplement this
core with very important learning that is essential to preserving, either
directly or indirectly, their particular political system. Unfortunately,
because our vision has been focused on diffuse system support, we have
neglected these more distinctive and no less important elements of socialization: the central values that define a particular political culture
and the crucial skills that citizens must have to preserve that culture and
system. It is time that we expanded our vision of political socialization
to incorporate these other elements.
    To specify the content of socialization more fully and meaningfully,
we must take seriously the fact that socialization is a political process.
We must take seriously the question of who controls—and who benefits
from—the socialization process. For only if we know who controls the
socialization process will we be in a position to understand the particular content of the process. In the American context, this question has
been evaded by claiming that it does not matter who controls the system
since there is an overwhelming consensus on the principles of government, and thus presumably on the content of socialization. But, as
Lindblom (1982) points out, this begs the question, for it leaves unanswered the obvious further question of where the consensus came from
in the first place. We simply cannot understand political socialization in

a cultural and historical vacuum. To understand contemporary political socialization we must use our history; we must understand how competing cultures gained control of ideas and of the institutions that allow them to perpetuate those ideas (Wildavsky 1987). In effect, political socialization usually perpetuates a particular political culture; consequently, its content cannot be fully specified, nor properly understood, without reference to this particular political culture, its historical origins, and its embodiment in political institutions.[7]

Therefore, to study political socialization in the United States, we must begin by asking what are the particular values and skills that citizens must possess if the American political culture and the American form of government are to persist. In this regard, Herbert McClosky and John Zaller (1984) have chronicled how the values of individualism and egalitarianism have evolved historically to become the central values defining the American ethos. And Amy Gutmann (1987) has explained why the abilities to deliberate and think critically are central to the formation of the American democratic character (also see Barber 1984).

Most recently, William Galston (1988) has outlined the "liberal virtues," traits of character that liberal societies like the United States must engender in their citizens if these societies are to be viable. Specifically, Galston (1988) argues that liberal *societies* depend upon the virtues of independence and tolerance, and that liberal *market economies* rely on specific virtues associated with the roles of entrepreneur (e.g., imagination, drive) and the organizational employee (e.g., punctuality, reliability), as well as more general virtues such as the work ethic, a capacity for moderate delay of gratification, and adaptability. But most relevant is Galston's identification of the virtues upon which liberal *politics* depend. Liberal citizens must have the "capacity to discern, and the restraint to respect, the rights of others"; the "capacity to discern the talent and character of candidates"; the willingness "to demand no more public services than their country can afford and to pay for all the benefits they demand"; a disposition "to engage in public discourse"; and a disposition to reduce the gap between "principles and practices in liberal society" (Galston 1988, 1283, 1285).

Of course, all of this presumes that there is a unified American political culture—a liberal culture—when, instead, there may be competing cultures (see Wildavsky 1987). No doubt, different strains of political culture would instill different values and skills through socialization. As Galston (1988) notes, for example, the virtues of the liberal citizen are *not* the same as those of the civic-republican citizen: "In a liberal polity there is no duty to participate actively in politics, no requirement to place the public above the private and to subordinate personal interest to the common good systematically, no commitment to accept collective determination of personal choices" (Galston 1988, 1284). To the extent that there are such challenges to the dominant political culture, conflict may emerge between elites as well as within institutions. What, then, becomes important is to examine carefully the dynamics of this conflict so as to sort out which particular strains of political culture characterize the dominant political elites and institutions that most control political socialization.

Let us assume for the moment that the dominant political culture of the United States is, indeed, a liberal one. And, if we assume that these are the values, the abilities, and the virtues that are essential to preserving such a liberal political system, then we have studied relatively little of the content of political socialization. The learning of core values like individualism has received scant attention (an exception is McClosky and Zaller 1984). And even less attention has been paid to the learning of the virtues that Galston argues are central to the preservation of liberal society. To be sure, considerable research has been devoted to explaining the development of tolerance (see McClosky and Brill 1983; Sullivan, Piereson, and Marcus 1981), and certain partisan predispositions (see Jennings and Niemi 1974, 1981). But, for the most part, we have ignored empirically the question of how citizens develop the sort of "deliberative character" that Gutmann, Galston, and others (e.g., Barber 1984) judge to be so central to a liberal democractic society. Instead, we have restricted our focus to the common core of socialization, diffuse system support and law abidingness, and the learning of dispositions (e.g., partisanship, political efficacy) that may explain electoral participation but are not, if we accept these arguments, central to the preservation of a liberal society, economy, or politics.

Thus, if we take seriously the task of studying political socialization as opposed to political learning, we must redirect our focus to take in the values, abilities, and virtues that, theoretically at least, are central to the preservation of the particular political culture and institutions of the country under study. Moreover, in doing so, it is likely that we will be drawn back into childhood. It is, after all, in childhood where character begins to form. And it is, after all, in childhood where political institutions have the most opportunity, through the educational system, to shape the developing character of future citizens.[8]

The Control of Political Socialization: Agents and the Political System? Who controls the socialization process? It is an ambiguous question. Nonetheless, in the past Plato and Rousseau and a host of others have directed our attention to the rulers and their involvement in the politics of socialization. Perhaps the most obvious way to get at who controls political socialization is simply to focus directly on the state. But until recently the state has been largely ignored in the discipline, and particularly in our efforts to understand who controls socialization (see Krasner 1984).[9] In retrospect, this claim may at first seem odd, given that some elements of the state—the regime and the authorities—have long been the major focus for specifying the content of socialization. Yet it is the state as a controller of socialization that has been neglected. And this neglect is understandable when one considers the intellectual history of the concept of the state. By the time that socialization research had begun to take off in the 1960s, the concept of the state had fallen out of favor and had been replaced by concepts such as the political system (Almond 1988; Krasner 1984).

Unfortunately, the concept of the political system may have done more to obscure than to clarify our understanding of who shapes the process of political socialization. Typically, the political system has been conceptualized in a vague and abstract fashion, a "little black box" into which go system inputs and from which emerge, almost magically, system outputs. This level of abstraction is especially jarring when juxtaposed with the concreteness of the individual level attitudes and behaviors that were presumably being influenced by the system (Lowi 1988).

To some extent, the problem was ameliorated by breaking down the political system into its principal components: (*a*) the "legally empowered and legitimately coercive institutions" of the state; (*b*) "extralegal and paralegal institutions like political parties, interest groups, and the mass media"; and (*c*) "social institutions such as family, school, church, and the like" (Almond 1988, 855). Yet, once having decomposed the political system, our natural inclination—an inclination reinforced by the field's ties to sociology—was to concentrate on those aspects of it that most directly influence the development of future citizens. Hence, we concentrated the great bulk of our attention on the role of social institutions as *agents* of socialization. Numerous studies probed the relative effects of the family and schools on children. And later, peer groups and the media joined the list of prime agents (for a review of this literature see Niemi and Sobieszek 1977).

But, by focusing so intensely on these social institutions, we lost sight of something important: the politics of socialization. In decomposing the concept of the political system, we lost sight both of the state as a *controller* of socialization and of social institutions as *agents* of socialization (Connell 1987). We lost sight of the fact that the political system's components are related, that there is a connection between the state and those social institutions that most directly shape the character of future citizens. In this way, we also lost sight of socialization as a *political* process through which rulers seek to ensure their rule.

How, then, can we best study the politics of socialization? There are two alternatives. The first is to focus on the state as a controller of socialization. This would lead the field away from the individual, and away from its roots in behavioralism. The second is to focus on the politics that characterize the agents of socialization. This would reinforce the field's existing focus on the individual while simultaneously expanding our definition of what constitutes the political. Let me briefly consider each alternative.

It is not necessary to jump onto the "return of the state" bandwagon in order to benefit from some of the insights produced by the movement (for a review, see Krasner 1984). In particular, statist orientations draw us away from an atomistic view of politics in which political leaders are simply a collection of individuals constrained more by societal forces than by political institutions, a view in which institutions are merely instrumental devices for the aggregation of preferences. Instead, we are directed toward a view in which institutions, formal rules, and enduring ideologies restrict the behavior of political leaders and structure governmental activities, a view in which institutions themselves are intrinsically significant (Elkins 1987; Krasner 1984). With respect to socialization, a statist orientation reminds us of "the formative bearing" of political institutions: the manner in which political institutions help constitute the political way of life of a citizenry (Elkins 1987). Moreover, as we are drawn away from an atomistic conception of the rulers we are also lured away from a purely individualistic conception of the ruled. Rather than consider the socializing impact of institutions on isolated individuals, we are led to focus on their effects on the collectivity (Connell 1987).

Two recent studies provide concrete examples of the direction such research might take. In *City and Regime in the American Republic*, Stephen Elkins (1987) explores the way in which a city's political institutions shape the nature of its citizenry. In particular, he seeks to determine which city institutional arrangements (e.g., neighborhood assemblies, citywide referenda, city legislatures) are most likely to promote the development of a commercial public interest which he deems central to the success and prosperity of a commercial republic.[10] Thus, we have in Elkin's work an examination of the way in which political institutions socialize—or fail to socialize—the citizenry as a whole to a way of political life that is judged central to the preservation and success of the regime.

In "Politics, Markets, and the Organization of Schools," John Chubb and Terry Moe (1988) examine how public and private schools differ in terms of institutional control and the implications of this for understanding the effectiveness of schools and the content of education. Critically, Chubb and Moe recognize that public schools, unlike private schools, are subject to the authority and democratic control of the state precisely so that important social goals—such as the transmission of democratic values—can be imposed upon them. That the institutional settings of school do, in fact, matter is forcefully demonstrated by their findings concerning the respective goals of private and public schools. Public schools place considerably greater emphasis on basic literacy, citizenship, good work habits, and occupational skills. They are, in effect, working to engender the virtues essential to being a liberal citizen and an organizational employee in a liberal economy. On the other hand, not surprisingly, given that they are under the control of the market rather than the state, private schools are less concerned with socializing students to be good citizens. Instead, they best prepare their students to become entrepreneurs in a liberal market economy by encouraging academic excellence and personal growth, and thus presumably the entrepreneurial virtues—imagination, initiative, drive, and determination (Galston 1988). Thus, as in the case of Elkin's 1987 study, Chubb and Moe (1988) draw our attention to the manner in which political institutions shape the development of a citizenry so as to instill those values, abilities, and virtues essential to the preservation of the regime.

Studying the formative bearing of political institutions is one way to bring politics back into the study of political socialization. The second way is to focus on the politics within the social institutions commonly studied as agents of socialization, such as the family, the schools, and the media (Connell 1987; Sapiro 1987). As Virginia Sapiro (1987) points out, this may require us to expand our definition of the political to encompass the ostensibly "private" social interactions that occur within the confines of these social institutions. Nonetheless, this expansion becomes essential when we recognize that the state does, indeed, influence social institutions; that social institutions such as the family do, in fact, contain a politics; and that, critically, the politics embodied within social institutions often reflect the politics of the state. As R. W. Connell (1987, 221) notes, "the state is actively connected with the structure of power, and hence with the patterning of politics, within non-state institutions." Moreover, recognizing that social institutions embody a form of politics creates a further justification for studying children. Whereas in the past we deemed their participation in social institutions as mere preparation for politics later in life, now it becomes apparent that through their social relations children are already participating in a kind of politics (Connell 1987).

Feminist scholars provide the leading example of this sort of research in their work on the politics of the family. In particular, they have noted that families constituted within what might generously be termed a democratic patriarchal state such as the United States are, themselves, democratic patriarchies (Elshtain 1981; Sapiro 1987). This is no coincidence. The development of future citizens who will support an existing patriarchal state is best accomplished within families that are structured in the same fashion. Similarly, the internal structure of schools can shape the development of students. Schools that embody democratic practices are better able to instill democratic character than those in which the authority patterns are perceived to be autocratic and unfair (see Gutmann 1987, chap. 2). And again, this is no coincidence. Such studies suggest the importance of both the politics that goes on within the agents of socialization, and the link between such politics and the politics of the state.

STUDYING POLITICAL SOCIALIZATION
The Micro-Level Rationale

Studying political socialization in order to understand how rulers ensure the perpetuation of their rule is important, but it is not the only rationale. Political socialization has implications not just for the maintenance of the political system but also for the personal development of individual citizens. In the past, many researchers have argued that we should study the consequences of political socialization for the individual (see Cook 1985; Lindblom 1982; Merelman 1972; Sears 1975). But, to do so, we must focus on a particular set of questions.

When we study political socialization we necessarily focus on the learning of those values, abilities, and virtues that are essential to the preservation of the political system: they define the content of political socialization. Consequently, when we study the impact of socialization on the individual we must focus our attention on precisely the same content. In the past, it has been assumed that political socialization contributes positively to the development of the individual, or at its worst that it has a benign effect (Lindblom 1982). Clearly such an assumption is inappropriate. Instead, the central research question must be: in what sense, *if any*, does the learning of this particular content contribute to the political development of the individual? Or, to put it differently, we must consider to what extent the needs of the system match—or fail to match—the needs of the individual.

In general, in liberal polities we might anticipate some inconsistency between those qualities that make someone a "good person" and those that make someone a "good citizen." They are not one and the same. For example, to obey an immoral law fulfills one's duty as a citizen but likely violates one's personal morality and thereby diminishes one's self-respect and dignity (Galston 1988). Therefore, socializing citizens to be indiscriminately law-abiding may prove eventually to be detrimental to their personal well-being. Similarly, socializing citizens to be courageous and loyal—to be willing to sacrifice their lives for the state if necessary—may obviously clash with the sense of self-direction and individual choice that some deem essential to self-development (Galston 1988). To some extent, then, successful political socialization may unavoidably diminish a citizen's capacity for self-development. Thus, the first task for those who study the impact of political socialization on the individual is to identify those ways in which the socialization needs of a particular system may inherently conflict with, as well as contribute to, the individual development of *all* its citizens.

It must be recognized, however, that the impact of socialization on individual development will vary across citizens. Socialization is, after all, a political process. Those individuals who are most disadvantaged by the current system will be precisely the same ones whose personal development is most at risk from the socialization process. Inequities associated with gender, race, and class are perpetuated, in part, by socializing women, minorities, and poor people to accept their disadvantaged positions in society. This is not to suggest that socialization has invariably negative effects on the disadvantaged. It most definitely does not. But, it does force us to recognize that the politics of the disadvantaged may often involve a rejection of, and rebellion against, a portion of the socialization being attempted by the dominant political culture. Thus, a second task for those who study the impact of political socialization on the individual is to focus on the "dark side" of socialization: the extent to which socialization limits the choices and hinders the personal development of the disadvantaged.

THE STUDY OF POLITICAL LEARNING: A FOOTNOTE

I have deliberately concentrated my attention on the study of political socialization rather than political learning. Nonetheless, a few comments about the future study of political learning are appropriate because, though distinct, the two topics are obviously related. However, the study of political learning demands a different and, in some ways, far broader focus than the study of political socialization.

Specifically, the study of political learning necessarily encompasses the full range of political attitudes and behaviors that define how a person relates to the political world. These may range from partisan orientations to information on specific public policies, and from voting to political protest. In comparison, the content of political socialization constitutes a considerably smaller portion of the political attitudes and behaviors that people learn during the course of their lives. Nevertheless, in many ways researchers have done a better job in exploring the range of content that characterizes political learning than they have done in identifying and studying the content of political socialization. The work of Jennings and Niemi (1974, 1981) stands out in this regard and provides an excellent basis for the next generation of work.

Similarly, though the psychology of learning is important to understanding the micro-level dynamics of the socialization process, it cannot constitute the core of socialization theory. Politics, not psychology, occupies that central position. In contrast, given its focus on the individual, the psychology of learning necessarily lies at the heart of the study of political learning. In this regard, some scholars (e.g., Rosenberg 1985) have criticized previous studies for their lack of grounding in psychological theories. But the complaint is overstated. The work done in the 1970s—again, most notably that of Jennings and Niemi (1974, 1981)—drew on social learning theory with good results. And in the 1980s, there have been conscious efforts to induce a more sophisticated understanding of the psychology of political learning. Timothy Cook's 1985 urging that students of political learning make greater use of cognitive developmental models such as Vygotsky's fits comfortably with others' (Sapiro 1987; Torney-Purta 1989) recommendation that schema theory be applied more deliberately to the study of political learning.

Both Vygotsky's (1978) model and the more amorphous schema theory share the assumption that an individual develops cognitively through interactions with the environment. This is critical. Such a perspective requires that political learning necessarily be embedded in and constrained by the social structure and the immediate context. Thus it draws attention to the importance of gender, race, and class in structuring the learning experience; and it suggests the ways through which political culture and the state shape political learning. Furthermore, this theoretical approach forces the recognition that individuals are not simply passive recipients of learning. Rather, they play an active role in shaping the course of their political learning, sometimes to the point of rejecting what is being taught.

But, while embracing cognitive theories of development, we would do well to keep in mind the limitations of those theories. Schema theories and cognitive developmental theories focus on cognition. But there are other aspects to individual political development. Emotions also play an important, though all too often neglected, role in politics.[11] Thinking about the contribution of emotions to political development naturally leads us to a more complete and integrated view of the evolution of the political self than does the narrower focus on cognitive development. Moreover, it also draws our attention to the neglected topic of political identity. Rather than study the learning of distinct attitudes and beliefs, we might profit more from examining how political identities evolve over the course of a life.

Two strains of research supply a foundation for the construction of such a research agenda. Research on the emergence of group identities and group consciousness provides a basis for developing a more coherent view of the political self, particularly in the case of the disadvantaged (see Gurin 1985; Klein 1985). Similarly, work on the patterning of life-cycle events suggests a way of analyzing the path of lifelong political development (see Sapiro 1987, 1988). Both bodies of research suggest a substantially more holistic view of political development than had previous approaches.

CONCLUSIONS

In summary, thirty years ago the field of political socialization exploded upon the discipline. It generated enthusiasm and high expectations. Those expectations have not been met. Nonetheless, political socialization is not—nor should it be—a dead field. Its revival depends upon the recognition that the term "political socialization" has in the past encompassed two different research agendas: political socialization and political learning. Over the last fifteen years, most research has concentrated on political learning, with the goal of understanding individual political development over the life cycle. This research program has steadily progressed and gradually developed a more sophisticated theoretical foundation. Despite rumors to the contrary, it is doing just fine. In contrast, the study of political socialization, as originally conceived, has sputtered to a stop.

Renewing the study of political socialization requires a rationale. In that regard, the study of political socialization has long been justified on the basis of a macro-level argument: that socialization is important to understanding the persistence of the state. Yet, if that rationale is to justify future studies of socialization, we must take it seriously. We must accept that the study of political socialization is, indeed, often the study of how the status quo perpetuates itself, and that, consequently, in some cases, socialization is manipulative. We must recognize that the study of political socialization cannot be conducted in a cultural and historical vacuum; it is impossible to specify fully the content of socialization without reference to who rules, to the institutions, the enduring ideologies, and the political elites that constitute the state. Finally, we must take seriously the fact that socialization is a political process, that it is controlled by those who rule and is affected by conflicts with those who do not rule. And thus, above all, we must work to restore politics to the study of political socialization.

NOTES

1. There are exceptions to this. One of the more notable was a longitudinal study of elementary schoolchildren conducted by Stanley Moore, James Lare, and Kenneth Wagner (1985).

2. Some define education so broadly that it includes unconscious factors. But, as Gutmann (1987, 15) has pointed out, when broadly defined, "it is much easier to extol the significance of education than it is to say anything systematic about it."

3. From a theoretical perspective, Easton and Dennis (1969) certainly recognized that socialization could be an agent for change. Nonetheless, their empirical work focused on the contributions of socialization to the maintenance of the status quo.

4. Similarly, at the individual level, a lack of persistence from childhood to adulthood does not necessarily mean that socialization has failed (see Cook 1985). Resocialization during periods of change may produce shifts from earlier socialization.

5. This is, of course, the rationale that underlies a broad, all-encompassing definition of system maintenance.

6. There were some studies that focused on the community level, but they were not nearly so numerous or prominent as those concerning the regime level (see, for example, Adelson 1971; Adelson and O'Neil 1966; Lare, Wagner, and Moore 1985). And, at the same time, research in keeping with the Hyman tradition tended to focus on those characteristics most relevant to system maintenance through participation in the electoral process: partisanship, political interest, political efficacy, political knowledge (e.g., Jennings and Niemi 1974, 1981; Sigel and Hoskin, 1981).

7. Cultural theory is undergoing a minirevival at this time (e.g., Eckstein 1988; Inglehart 1988; Wildavsky 1987). Socialization researchers would do well to take note of this literature.

8. This would revive the persistence question. But, by focusing on the formation of democratic character, we would be concentrating on variables that intuitively should be more likely to develop in childhood and to persist into adulthood.

9. No doubt, my use of the term "the state" is in and of itself provocative and alien to the systems theory approach (see Easton 1981). One might substitute the term "government" or "regime" where I have used "the state" without doing fatal damage to the thrust of my argument. Nonetheless, I will use the state, because recent efforts at "bringing back the state" suggest ideas that may benefit socialization research.

10. Elkins (1987, 120) describes the commercial public interest as a willingness "to judge economic policies by their contributions toward solving the central problems of a republican government."

11. For example, how do people develop enduring affective orientations

toward politics? Over time, how do emotions help to define one's political consciousness?

REFERENCES

Abramson, Paul R. 1977. *The Political Socialization of Black Americans: A Critical Evaluation of Research on Efficacy and Trust*. New York: The Free Press.

Adelson, Joseph. 1971. "The Political Imagination of the Young Adolescent." *Daedalus* 100:1013–50.

————, and Robert P. O'Neil. 1966. "Growth of Political Ideas in Adolescence: The Sense of Community." *Journal of Personality and Social Psychology* 4: 295–306.

Almond, Gabriel A. 1988. "The Return to the State." *American Political Science Review* 82:853–74.

Barber, Benjamin. 1984. *Strong Democracy: Participatory Politics for a New Age*. Berkeley: University of California Press.

Chubb, John E., and Terry M. Moe. 1988. "Politics, Markets, and the Organization of Schools." *American Political Science Review* 82:1065–88.

Connell, R. W. 1971. *The Child's Construction of Politics*. Carlton, Victoria, Australia: Melbourne University Press.

————. 1987. "Why the 'Political Socialization' Paradigm Failed and What Should Replace It." *International Political Science Review* 8:215–23.

————, and M. Goot. 1972/73. "Science and Ideology in American 'Political Socialization' Research." *Berkeley Journal of Sociology* 17:167–93.

Conover, Pamela J., and Donald D. Searing. 1987. "Citizenship Regained: A New Framework for the Study of Political Socialization." Revision of a paper presented at the annual meeting of the American Political Science Association, Chicago.

Cook, Timothy E. 1985. "The Bear Market in Political Socialization and the Costs of Misunderstood Psychological Theories." *American Political Science Review* 79:1079–93.

Cremin, Lawrence A. 1977. *Traditions of American Education*. New York: Basic Books.

Dawson, Richard E., Kenneth Prewitt, and Karen S. Dawson. 1977. *Political Socialization*. 2d ed. Boston: Little, Brown.

Delli Carpini, Michael X. 1986. *Stability and Change in American Politics: The Coming Age of the Generation of the 1960's*. New York: New York University Press.

Easton, David. 1965. *A Systems Analysis of Political Life*. New York: Wiley.

————. 1981. "The Political System Besieged by the State." *Political Theory* 9: 303–25.

————, and Robert D. Hess. 1962. "The Child's Political World." *Midwest Journal of Political Science* 6:229–46.

————, and Jack Dennis. 1969. *Children in the Political System.* New York: Mc-Graw-Hill.

Eckstein, Harry. 1988. "A Culturalist Theory of Political Change." *American Political Science Review* 82:789–804.

Elkins, Stephen L. 1987. *City and Regime in the American Republic.* Chicago: University of Chicago Press.

Elshtain, Jean B. 1981. *Public Man, Private Woman: Women in Social and Political Thought.* Princeton, N.J.: Princeton University Press.

Franklin, Charles H. 1984. "Issue Preferences, Socialization, and the Evolution of Party Identification." *American Journal of Political Science* 28:459–78.

Galston, William A. 1988. "Liberal Virtues." *American Political Science Review* 82:1277–92.

García, F. Chris. 1973. *Political Socialization of Chicano Children: A Comparative Study with Anglos in California Schools.* New York: Praeger.

Greenberg, Edward S. 1970. "Orientations of Black and White Children to Political Authority Figures." *Social Science Quarterly* 51:561–71.

Greenstein, Fred I. 1960. "The Benevolent Leader: Children's Images of Political Authority." *American Political Science Review* 54:934–43.

————. 1965. *Children and Politics.* New Haven: Yale University Press.

————. 1975. "The Benevolent Leader Revisited: Children's Images of Political Leaders in Three Democracies." *American Political Science Review* 64:1371–98.

————, V. Herman, R. N. Stradling, and E. Zureik. 1974. "The Child's Conception of the Queen and the Prime Minister." *British Journal of Political Science* 4:257–87.

Gurin, Patricia. 1985. "Women's Gender Consciousness." *Public Opinion Quarterly* 49:43–63.

Gutmann, Amy. 1987. *Democratic Education.* Princeton, N.J.: Princeton University Press.

Hess, Robert D., and David Easton. 1960. "The Child's Image of the President." *Public Opinion Quarterly* 24:632–44.

————, and Judith V. Torney. 1967. *The Development of Political Attitudes in Children.* Chicago: Aldine.

Hyman, Herbert H. 1959. *Political Socialization: A Study in the Psychology of Political Behavior.* New York: The Free Press.

Inglehart, Ronald. 1988. "The Renaissance of Political Culture." *American Political Science Review* 82:1203–30.

Jaros, Dean. 1973. *Socialization to Politics.* New York: Praeger.

————, H. Hirsch, and F. J. Fleron, Jr. 1968. "The Malevolent Leader: Political

Socialization in an American Subculture." *American Political Science Review* 62:564–75.

Jennings, M. Kent. 1979. "Another Look at the Life Cycle and Political Participation." *American Journal of Political Science* 23:755–71.

————, and Richard G. Niemi. 1974. *The Political Character of Adolescence: The Influence of Families and Schools*. Princeton, N.J.: Princeton University Press.

————. 1981. *Generations and Politics: A Panel Study of Young Adults and Their Parents*. Princeton, N.J.: Princeton University Press.

————, and Gregory B. Markus. 1984. "Partisan Orientations over the Long Haul: Results from the Three-wave Political Socialization Panel Study." *American Political Science Review* 78:1000–1018.

————. 1988. "Political Involvement in the Later Years: A Longitudinal Survey." *American Journal of Political Science* 32:302–16.

Kavanagh, Dennis. 1983. *Political Science and Political Behavior*. London: Allen and Unwin.

Kinder, Donald R., and Laurie A. Rhodebeck. 1982. "Continuities in Support for Racial Equality, 1972–1976." *Public Opinion Quarterly* 46:195–215.

————, and David O. Sears. 1985. "Public Opinion and Political Action." In *Handbook of Social Psychology*, vol. 2, ed. Gardner Lindzey and Elliot Aronson. 3d ed. New York: Random House.

Klein, Ethel. 1984. *Gender Politics*. Cambridge, Mass.: Harvard University Press.

Kolson, K. L., and J. J. Green. 1970. "Response Set Bias and Political Socialization Research." *Social Science Quarterly* 51:527–38.

Krasner, Stephen D. 1984. "Approaches to the State: Alternative Conceptions and Historical Dynamics." *Comparative Politics* 16:223–46.

Lindblom, Charles E. 1982. "Another State of Mind." *American Political Science Review* 76:9–21.

Lowi, Theodore J. 1988. "The Return to the State: Critiques." *American Political Science Review* 82:885–91.

Marsh, David. 1971. "Political Socialization: The Implicit Assumptions Questioned." *British Journal of Political Science* 1:453–65.

McClosky, Herbert, and Alida Brill. 1983. *Dimensions of Tolerance: What Americans Believe about Civil Liberties*. New York: Russell Sage Foundation.

————, and John Zaller. 1984. *The American Ethos: Public Attitudes toward Capitalism and Democracy*. Cambridge, Mass.: Harvard University Press.

Merelman, Richard M. 1971. "The Development of Policy-Thinking in Adolescence." *American Political Science Review* 67:161–66.

————. 1972. "The Adolescence of Political Socialization." *Sociology of Education* 45:134–66.

Merriam, Charles E. 1966. *The Making of Citizens*. New York: Teachers College Press, Columbia University.

Miller, Steven D., and David O. Sears. 1986. "Stability and Change in Social Tolerance." *American Journal of Political Science* 30:214–36.

Moore, Stanley W., James Lare, and Kenneth A. Wagner. 1985. *The Child's Political World: A Longitudinal Perspective*. New York: Praeger.

Niemi, Richard G. 1973. "Political Socialization." In *Handbook of Political Psychology*, ed. Jeanne N. Knutson, 117–38. San Francisco: Jossey-Bass.

———, and Barbara I. Sobieszek. 1977. "Political Socialization." *Annual Review of Sociology* 3:209–33.

Rosenberg, Shawn W. 1985. "Sociology, Psychology and the Study of Political Behavior: The Case of the Research on Political Socialization." *Journal of Politics* 47:715–31.

Sapiro, Virginia. 1983. *The Political Integration of Women*. Urbana: University of Illinois Press.

———. 1987. "What Research on the Political Socialization of Women Can Tell Us about the Political Socialization of People." In *The Impact of Feminist Research in the Academy*, ed. Christie Farnham, 148–73. Bloomington: Indiana University Press.

———. 1988. "Life Course, Gender, and Individual Political Development." Paper presented at the annual meeting of the International Political Science Association, Washington, D.C.

Searing, Donald D., Joel J. Schwartz, and Alden E. Lind. 1973. "The Structuring Principle: Political Socialization and Belief Systems." *American Political Science Review* 67:415–32.

———, Gerald Wright, and George Rabinowitz. 1976. "The Primacy Principle: Attitude Change and Political Socialization." *British Journal of Political Science* 6:83–113.

Sears, David O. 1975. "Political Socialization." In *The Handbook of Political Science*, vol. 2, ed. Fred I. Greenstein and Nelson Polsby, 93–154. Reading, Mass.: Addison-Wesley.

———, and John S. McConahay. 1973. *The Politics of Violence: The New Urban Blacks and the Watts Riot*. Boston: Houghton Mifflin.

Sigel, Roberta S., and Marilyn B. Hoskin. 1981. *The Political Involvement of Adolescents*. New Brunswick, N.J.: Rutgers University Press.

Stradling, Robert, and Elia Zurick. 1971. "Political and Non-political Ideals of English Primary and Secondary School Children." *The Sociological Review* 19:203–28.

Sullivan, John L., James Piereson, and George E. Marcus. 1982. *Political Tolerance and American Democracy*. Chicago: University of Chicago Press.

Torney, Judith V., A. N. Oppenheim, and Russell F. Farnen. 1975. *Civic Education in Ten Countries: An Empirical Study*. New York: Wiley.

Torney-Purta, Judith V. 1989. "From Attitudes and Knowledge to Schemata:

Expanding the Outcomes of Political Socialization Research." In *Political Socialization and Citizenship Education*, ed. Orit Ichilov. Forthcoming.

Vaillancourt, P. M. 1973. "Stability of Children's Survey Responses." *Public Opinion Quarterly* 37:373–87.

Vygotsky, L. S. 1978. *Mind in Society: The Development of Higher Psychological Processes*. Cambridge, Mass.: Harvard University Press.

Wildavsky, Aaron. 1987. "Choosing Preferences by Constructing Institutions: A Cultural Theory of Preference Formation." *American Political Science Review* 81:3–22.

6

Political Psychology: Where Have We Been? Where Are We Going?

Betty Glad

INTRODUCTION

Political psychology* since the end of World War II has had an uneven history. A short creative burst in the field was followed by a subsequent period of relative neglect, followed again in recent years by a new creative outpouring. The reasons for the earlier neglect and its costs are explored in this article. Suggestions are made for the best ways to sustain the present revival of interest and to clear away the conceptual roadblocks that have impeded the development of political psychology as a scientific effort. Methodological critiques based on the assumption

As panelists at the Midwest Political Science Association meetings at which this essay was first presented, Kathleen Knight, Kathleen McGraw, and Paul Sniderman called to my attention some important works in the areas of attitudes and voting behavior that I might have otherwise overlooked. Harvey Starr, a colleague at the University of South Carolina, also made some helpful suggestions in terms of the relevant literature. Due to space limitations, I could not incorporate all their recommendations into this work, but I am grateful to all of them for their suggestions and am sure the following essay is more balanced as a result.
*"Political psychology" for the purposes of this article is broadly defined as that subdiscipline which explores the impact of the cognitive processes, the emotions (that is, affect), and the defense mechanisms of human beings, both individually and collectively, on their political behavior. As I argue in this essay, a full psychological explanation of political behavior would have to cover all the above phenomena. But because some psychologists have stressed cognition as the funnel through which emotions and defenses become manifest, the term "political psychology" may sometimes be used in that narrower sense. The sense in which the term is used should be evident from the context.

153

that one must choose between structural and psychological analyses are rejected, as well as the opposition of reason to passion. To understand political behavior fully, it is argued, one needs to look more closely at the emotions and unconscious defenses that motivate human beings. This attention to affect, however, need not issue in a new "dismal science." Emotions such as empathy and realistic fear, it is argued, may have a positive impact on political behavior. Moreover, affect may anchor behavior in ways that make it relatively predictable and therefore subject to scientific analysis.

CREATIVE BEGINNINGS

Political psychology for a short time after World War II tackled some major problems about how people relate to political authority. The liberal faith in the virtue of the common man and the ultimate triumph of democracy in the world had been undermined by the rise of fascism in Germany and Italy, by the development of totalitarian communism in the USSR, and the barbarisms of the war. Several researchers explored the nature of these apparently atavistic forces, focusing first on the psychological underpinnings of fascism, and later on the specter of what appeared to be the most critical threat to the postwar world—an expanding world communism.

Among the first puzzles investigated was the maintenance of the morale of the Wehrmacht during the latter phases of the war. According to Shils and Janowitz (1948, 553), loyalty to Hitler, as well as the psychological ties of the soldiers to their comrades, were the sources of this morale. Others looked into the factors that made individuals susceptible to propaganda. Several psychoanalysts meeting at the Washington School of Psychiatry in 1950 concluded that crises and other factors which weaken the ego of the individual can lead to widespread regression in a mass public (Stanton and Perry 1951). Ironically, as Lasswell noted, governmental lies and other acts undermine the individual's ability to assess reality, thereby creating a public that clings to the threatening but all-powerful authority. Proof that these kinds of factors worked upon the German public in the early days of the Nazi regime was provided by Charlotte Beradt's *The Third Reich of Dreams*, published in 1968. Through analyses of the manifest content of the dreams of ordinary Germans collected between 1933 and 1939, Beradt shows the intrapsychic mechanisms whereby ordinary German people anticipated the Nazi terror, collaborating in their own control by it. The widespread inability of the dreamers to rebel, even in disguised form in their sleep, as Bruno Bettelheim pointed out in an accompanying essay, indicates that a totalitarian regime, by arrogating to itself the paternal role, takes on the omnipotence, the omniscience of the original authority, driving the subject back, unconsciously, to the helplessness of infancy.

These works were mostly essays and had less impact on political science than the monumental and more systematic *The Authoritarian Personality* (Adorno, Frenkel-Brunswik, Levinson, and Sanford 1950). Combining quantitative measures with psychoanalytically oriented interviews and experiments, the book delineated the authoritarian character structure and described its origins in psychodynamic terms. A rigid adherence to conventional morality and the proclivity for dividing the world into simply black and white categories was related to ethnocentrism and a tendency to project repressed characteristics onto outside groups. These traits, it was posited, are a form of armoring—a defensive mechanism aimed at holding together an otherwise vulnerable individual.

The impact of this work is evident in the wide commentary it inspired. By 1954 Christie and Jahoda's book evaluating *The Authoritarian Personality* had been published, and Frenkel-Brunswik had written an article for the *American Political Science Review* (1952) on the interaction between psychological and sociological factors. A guide to the published literature building on that work was published in 1958 (Christie and Cook), citing 230 published articles and books which referred to the work. And Frenkel-Brunswik was more frequently cited in the *Journal of Abnormal and Social Psychology* than any other researcher (Christie and Cook 1958, 1). *The Authoritarian Personality* had this impact, as Nathan Glazer (1954, 290) noted, because it "said something of importance about an important subject." But it also could not be ignored because, unlike some of the earlier work based on insights issuing from psychoanalytic practice, this was a scientific study. Indeed, the quantitative scales employed in the work could be used by others to see how high and low scorers on the various tests performed on scores of other tests. "A test to a social psychologist is like nectar to a bee," as Glazer suggested.

Several other works in the immediate postwar period focused on how the American military had motivated its soldiers for the recent war (Stouffer et al. 1945a; Hovland et al. 1949). But aside from *The Authoritarian Personality*, the works that would have the greatest long-term impact were those that explored the nature of the Communist threat of the day and the ways in which democracies were responding to that threat. Thus Gabriel Almond (1954), on the basis of interviews with former members of the American, British, French, and Italian Communist parties (supplemented by biographical data and psychoanalytic clinical case studies), concluded that the motivations for membership differed according to the political and cultural contexts in which the national parties operated and the roles the members played in the party. Those fully initiated into the party held to their faith in it as a force for good, even when deeply troubled by its actions. American Communists were the most likely to seek membership out of neurotic needs, the party providing a way of transferring their hostility toward parents to a safer target and a means for overcoming personal isolation. The widespread supposition that the political right and left were psychologically identical was not supported, however, by Almond's data, which showed that most party members did not turn to the extreme right or become religious converts after their defection from communism.

The reaction of the American public to what they perceived as the Communist threat, as Samuel Stouffer pointed out in another major study (1955), posed potential problems for civil liberties. A majority of Americans were willing to seek out information about Communists, even if innocent people were hurt in the process. The problems presented by these attitudes, however, Stouffer considered less serious than they might have been. Because fear of the Communists seemed to be based on bizarre misperceptions of what they were like and was related to low political information levels, and because the leaders of the community and the mass media were relatively tolerant, he felt that there was a real likelihood that mass opinion could be changed in a more tolerant direction.

The factors promoting democratic stability were explored in Almond and Verba's five-nation study, *Civic Culture* (1963). The polity that can best meet the demands of democracy and stability, Almond and Verba concluded, is one in which the citizens are sufficiently active politically to keep the political elite responsible, but sufficiently passive to enable them to govern. Stability was also a result of the fact that the most politically active and competent were supportive of the political system. Affect, too, the authors concluded, must be balanced between the poles of pragmatism and the passions. Loyalty to a system is necessary if that system is to remain stable. But if affect is too intense, it can limit the discretionary powers of the elite to deal with problems, raise the stakes of the game, and promote messianic movements that lead to democratic instability. The United States and the United Kingdom, they concluded, had achieved the most ideal balance between the participant and the subject modes.

At another level of analysis, several other studies suggested that wishful thinking and the need to avoid awareness of internal conflict played important roles in the electoral choices of American voters. Prominent among these studies were those done by Lazarsfeld et al. (1944), Berelson et al. (1954), Milbrath (1965), Greenstein (1965), and Campbell et al. (1960). Most of these studies relied on survey research, but Robert Lane (1962, 1969) attempted to get at the psychodynamic roots of voter choices through detailed case studies of blue-collar workers in "Eastport," U.S.A., and college students at Yale University.

Political participation, he concluded, serves emotional as well as instrumental needs, though no one-to-one relationship could be posited between the two. Political activity provides relief by taking one's mind off of one's inner tensions or by providing a socially acceptable channel for the expression of those tensions. Aggression, for example, may be externalized on political enemies. Dependency needs can be met by serving political leaders. Psychic tension, however, can also result in political apathy when the voter lacks political self-confidence and political activity seems futile.

The motivations of political leaders, too, was subjected to analysis. Harold Lasswell had called for studies along these lines as early as 1930, and by the 1950s and early 1960s several important biographical works along these lines were produced. Thus Alexander and Juliette George (1956) attributed Wilson's puzzling rigidity over the Senate vote on U.S. adherence to the League of Nations to an emotional defense, triggered off when important fatherlike figures attacked projects in which he had especially invested himself. Alex Gottfried (1962) showed how Anton Cermak's compulsive pursuit of power contributed to his creation of the first citywide political machine in Chicago. Kurt Schumacher's failure in his postwar political competition with Konrad Adenaur for political power in Germany, Edinger (1965) suggests, was due to adaptive mechanisms serving his personal needs that had been useful in the past but no longer fit the new situation. Charles Evan Hughes's intelligence, apparent self-confidence, and high levels of performance, as I showed in another biography (Glad 1966), enabled him to succeed in a variety of political roles. The tight self-control he had to exercise to avoid awareness of his personal vulnerabilities, however, limited his capacity for creative leadership at a time when the world was changing and could have used that kind of leadership.

A few studies went beyond single actors to explore the relationship of leaders to followers more generally. Thus Lane and Sears (1964), drawing from the earlier voting studies, suggested that the relationship of leaders to individual citizens can be understood in terms of dissonance theory. If a voter senses that a leader he likes has opinions which are discordant with his own, he can avoid stress through a variety of adaptations—for example, reevaluating his feelings about the leader, distorting the leader's position, or refusing to believe that the leader holds a discordant opinion. Several other studies raised questions about Lasswell's earlier suggestion that political leaders are motivated by the pursuit of power as compensation for feelings of personal weakness. These included McConahay's study of South Carolina legislators (1960); Hennessy's comparison of Arizona party activists to nonactivists (1959); and James David Barber's research on Connecticut legislators (1965). Indeed, Lester Milbrath (1963) found that highly social citizens were more likely to make contributions to political campaigns than nonsocial citizens.

THE YEARS OF NEGLECT

Despite these important and creative beginnings, the field of political psychology did not flourish as one might have expected. Some scholars worked in the byways, as we shall see below. But in the late sixties and seventies studies of whole political cultures were no longer in vogue and psychological analysis was not in the mainstream. Most studies of public opinion and participation relied on sociological rather than psychological variables. Leadership theory, despite the call to arms of Paige (1972) and the work being done in sociology (Gibb 1954), did not go beyond the studies of individual leaders to the building of general theory. The field of international relations, as a whole, remained relatively untouched by psychology. Freud and others had given psychological explanations of the sources of national identifications and wars. But the dominant schools of thought in the postwar period did not follow in these paths. Realists posited an objective national interest as the motive for national behavior (Morgenthau 1973), and the more "scientifically" oriented sought to correlate national behavior with objective characteristics such as size, capabilities, and alliances with others (Singer and Small 1968, 1972; Organski 1958).

The multidisciplinary work that was most popular during this period borrowed, not from psychology, but from economics and the pure rational-choice decision-making literature. The assumption was that one had only to know the utility function of the decision-maker and assume that his/her preference would be consistent over time. One did not have to know anything about how those values were derived, or even how he or she made probability estimates of uncertain events. Anthony Downs's *Economic Theory of Democracy* (1957) was one of the first works to employ this model in the analysis of political choices.

The bounded rationality approach, it is true, sought out more data about the decision-maker and his values, but the concern mostly was with information-processing and organizational variables. Thus Herbert Simon, in the second edition of *Administrative Behavior* (1957), argues that the organization defines the decision-maker's authority, structures the viable alternatives he can consider, and filters the information that he obtains (cf. Simon 1985, 295–96). Graham Allison (1971), in his work on the Cuban missile crisis, shows that foreign-policy choices can only be fully explained when one goes beyond rational choice theory to look at the interplay among bureaucratic interests, domestic political interests, and the skills and political access of the major players in the game.

Insofar as psychology was used in the decision-making literature, the emphasis was on the problems that human beings have in processing information. Drawing concepts and data from the field of cognitive psychology, Robert Jervis showed, in two path-breaking works, how decision-makers create images in an effort to influence others (1970) and how they selectively process new information through images they have of the world (1976). Images are necessary, he argued, in order to deal with a complex world. But the individual's need for cognitive consistency is apt to cause him to ignore or rationalize data that challenge these schema. The result is that decision-makers often apply lessons from the past to new situations which they do not fit.

The possible impact of affect and defense mechanisms on the decision-maker's choices, however, was mostly ignored or rejected. Allison, in his work on the Cuban missile crisis (1971), never directly addressed the impact of John Kennedy's personality and values on the flow of American deliberations. Robert Jervis, in his *Perception and Misperception in International Politics* (1976, 356–81), refuted the experimental literature suggesting that desires and fears, as manifested in wishful thinking, influence decision-making. Herbert Simon, in the introduction to the second edition of *Administrative Behavior* (1965, vii–x), explicitly rejected the idea that individuals make a difference in how organizations are run. Personality, as he saw it, "was a magical slogan to charm away the problems that our intellectual tools don't handle." Indeed, as late as 1985, Simon was still suggesting that emotions need not be directly considered. Though he was critical of the pure rational-choice approach to decision-making, he still thought that the instances in which a passion determines goals or results in the selective recall of facts were exceptions rather than the rule. Even in instances where the goals are determined by all-consuming passions, information-processing models may be successfully employed. "Hitler," for example, "was not just angry; he directed his hatred toward a particular group of people, Jews, and he made decisions that were arguably rational on the premise that the Jewish people were to be extirpated to satisfy that hatred." In these instances, Simon suggests, it may suffice to "postulate the overtly expressed values and goals without seeking their deeper roots in the unconscious" (301).

THE REASONS WHY

The reasons for this slighting of the field of political psychology were complex. Three kinds of factors will be considered here. First, the neglect of affect and defense mechanisms was rooted in certain broader intellectual trends in the social sciences. Psychoanalytic approaches, relying as they did on insight and soft data coming out of clinical practice, ran counter to broader trends in the discipline that emphasized systematic inquiry, hard data, and the search for general laws of the sort discovered in classical physics. Moreover, when the political scientists turned to academic psychology, they found that it was no longer concerned with motivation. A kind of neobehaviorism, as Sorrentino and Higgins have recently noted (in *The Handbook of Motivation and Cognition*, 1986), had taken over the field of cognitive psychology by the late 1960s. Information-processing models, it was assumed, could be used to explain human cognition, as well as the choice patterns in lower animals and machines. The concern was with how information is encoded and how diverse bits of information are integrated. Models were built to explain the process, but the inner processes, including the functioning of the brain, were mostly "blackboxed" (Crick 1988). The whole approach, as Simon (1985, 295) noted recently, was based on the assumption that cognition can be separated from the processes of sensation and emotion.

These trends were reinforced by a deeply ingrained attitude toward affect in Western culture. Ever since the Enlightenment, as George Marcus and Wendy Rahn (1990, 2–3) have noted, emotions have been viewed with distrust. From Spinoza through Descartes and Kant to Rawls, reason has been viewed as the source of good in political life. "To be rational," as they note, "is to be a good citizen and to be emotional is to be at best backward, childish and a bad citizen; at worst emotional responses to political life are seen as capricious, reactionary, and even dangerous." The extent to which this dichotomy influenced contemporary political scientists is evident in the assumptions of several key figures sympathetic to psychological approaches. Hans Morgenthau (1973, 5–7), for example, admitted the need to inquire into the psychological of group processes. But he saw that enterprise as investigating factors such as the "contingent elements of personality, prejudice and subjective preference, and . . . all the weaknesses of intellect and will which flesh is heir to"—factors that "deflect foreign policies from their rational course." Thus for him the goal of psychological inquiry was to develop a "counter theory of irrational politics."

A second reason for the retreat from political psychology was the desire to escape the methodological difficulties the pioneers in the field had experienced. The most important earlier applications of dynamic psychology had been embedded in ambitious attempts to explain cultural, political, or individual wholes and, as such, presented distinctive methodological problems. Inferential leaps, some of which were too simplistic, were made from the study of individuals to the functioning of whole political cultures. Adorno and his associates, for example, assumed that the widespread distribution of authoritarian personalities in a polity would increase the likelihood of authoritarian politics in that polity. That assumption, as Fred Greenstein (1965, 95) has noted, postulated too simple a link between personality type and political consequences: "Both personality and beliefs must be examined in situations in order to understand behavior." It is not possible to estimate the probability that fascism might come to the United States by simply studying the nature and distribution of the authoritarian personality structure, for there is not necessarily a relation between personality and policy (Greenstein 1965, 95, 91–93; Shibutani 1955).

Guided by their substantive concerns, these pioneers, too, sometimes settled for data which presented serious sampling problems. Almond, for example, was only able to interview *former* party members in his work *Appeals of Communism* and as a result wound up with an inherently biased sample. His suggestion that party membership in America was based on neurotic needs was founded on an even more problematic sample—namely, the reports of a few predominantly Freudian psychoanalysts willing to talk about party members who had sought out treatment.

Nor were these early endeavors value-free. *The Authoritarian Personality* was the product of German émigrés who had been influenced by Marx and Freud (Greenstein 1965, 90), and they saw some of the characteristics they noted as consequences of the class system (Adorno et al. 1950, 746–47). Other motives—for instance, the need to meet the Communist threat and sustain liberal values—explicitly motivated the work of Stouffer (1955, 13). Almond, too, was concerned about the Communist threat, noting in *Appeals of Communism* (1954, 370) that, despite its origins as a protest against the evils of the nineteenth century, it had become "the greatest evil of the twentieth." *The Civic Culture*, as Verba later noted (Almond and Verba 1980, 417), was influenced by the growing concerns pursuant to the fall of several countries to communism and the relevant question at the time of "why some democracies survive while others collapse."

The result of these value commitments were certain blind spots that influenced the work done. Adorno and his associates ignored the potential of a left-wing authoritarianism, as Franz Alexander pointed out in his review of *The Authoritarian Personality*. The "well-known fact that Communists can easily be converted into Fascists and vice versa," he argued, is an indication of how much alike the two totalitarian systems really are. But to ignore, "at this moment of human history existing threats to our still free society, appears strikingly out of date" (Alexander 1950, 79, 80). Edward Shils (Christie and Jahoda 1954) also argued that the work reflected the old liberal right-left polarity, ignoring the similarities between bolshevism and fascism.[1]

Verba and Almond, for their part, paid too little attention to class, regional, racial, religious, and sexual conflicts in the nations they studied. The underrepresentation in their samples of certain groups not fully integrated into their own polities—for example, of blacks in America and Communists in Italy—led the authors to an underestimation of the potential for conflict in those polities (Rokkan 1964, 77–678). Most importantly, their concern with stability led them to settle for a limited definition of democracy (Pateman, Almond and Verba 1980, 51–102). Ignoring definitions of democracy that emphasize the extent to which citizens share in decision-making and/or the distribution of economic and social benefits of the polity, they failed to anticipate the rise of the civil rights and women's movements in the United States. It was their concern with the survival of democratic society, Verba (Almond and Verba 1980, 399) later admitted, that led them to overlook subtler problems posed by social stratification and to miss the erosion of confidence in government that became evident shortly after their studies were published.

Third, the retreat from political psychology was no doubt a response to the critical responses that several of these early works elicited. Inquiry into important matters that raise questions about the fundamental values in one's own culture is a hazardous enterprise, and one likely to produce anxiety and resistance in others.[2] Depth psychology is especially apt to create special problems along these lines, suggesting as it does that some of the things we human beings do may be other than what they seem to be. It is not surprising, then, to find many people refusing to go down those paths.

The argument that opposition to the perspective of the depth psychologist is due to psychological resistance, it is true, can lead to an unfair form of intellectual warfare in which the views of the depth psychologists cannot be checked against any commonly agreed upon objective standards. Yet resistance is apparent in the reactions of certain critics—for instance, in their persistent slighting of hard data showing that personality influences political behavior, as well as in their often gross distortions of the arguments they reject.

In academic psychology this resistance was evident in the rejection of experimental data showing the existence of the unconscious. (For experimental works, see Erdelyli 1974; Nisbett and Wilson 1977; Fowler et al. 1981; cf. the subjective proofs of Machotka 1964). In political science it was most evident in the responses to the psychodynamics studies of political leaders. Works such as Alexander and Juliette George's *Woodrow Wilson and Colonel House*, now viewed as classics in the field, received mixed reviews when first published.[3] On several occasions, reviewers have simply ignored clear data indicating that a leader is emotionally disturbed. Arnold Rogow's biography of James Forrestal (1963, 4–5, 306–7, 344, 350), for example, provides overwhelming evidence that Forrestal was mentally ill near the end of his life and that influential people in Washington had difficulty accepting that fact.[4] Yet some reviewers, with all the hard evidence in front of them, still had difficulty in admitting that Forrestal had serious psychological problems. Thus L. Morton (1964, 1098) caricatured Rogow's work when he stated that Forrestal's political behavior could not be understood "in terms of a domineering mother, an indulgent father and feelings of guilt"; and he concluded that Rogow's interpretation, despite all the evidence he had given, "scarcely provides a convincing explanation of Forrestal's public career or private life." Another reviewer, G. M. Lyons (1964, 712), noted that "there are perfectly rational reasons for the stand Forrestal took on most important issues." According to him, what emerges from the facts Rogow gives "is a complex personality, but not necessarily a disturbed one."

The extent to which critics accuse psychobiographers of psychological reductionism when they clearly had not been guilty of that mistake is further evidence of resistance. James Q. Wilson (1962, 301), for example, in his review of Alex Gottfried's *Boss Cermak*, ignored Gottfried's detailed and sophisticated analysis of how Cermak acquired and maintained power as the boss of Chicago's Democratic organization, stating that it would "require more than a clinical look at the boss' bowels to understand how he did it." Other critics set up false polarities, insisting that one had to choose between political and psychological explanations—thereby loading the case in favor of political explanations. Thus Morton Kaplan (1964) questioned the whole use of psychological explanation in political science along these lines: "Did Churchill project his own hostility onto the Germans when he urged Britain to oppose Nazi aggression? To pose the question is to demonstrate that adequate analysis requires a political analysis of elements of Nazi policy. That is, one must know whether Germany was probably genuinely aggressive or Churchill probably genuinely hostile. And if one makes such [an] analysis, the policy consequences will generally be elucidated apart from psychological analysis."

THE COSTS OF NEGLECT

The neglect of psychology in the late 1960s and the 1970s meant that scientific explanation of some of the most important political phenomena of the time was simply not attempted. Public opinion studies were limited in their ability to explain dramatic shifts in public opinion because of their failure to probe the psyches of the voters in any depth. "Fascinated by the ideal of the self-reliant, independent individual," one of West Germany's leading pollsters, Elizabeth Noelle-Neumann, observed in 1980 (62–63), "scholars have hardly noticed the existence of the isolated individual, fearful of the opinion of his peers." Indeed, she suggests, "the fear of isolation" is a powerful factor, causing most people to heed the opinions of others.

The neglect of leadership theory and the widespread suspicion of psychobiography meant that the various ways in which personalities influence politics went relatively unexplored. The emphasis on structural factors in international relations limited the ability of political scientists to anticipate or explain the force and power of the new nationalism in both the developed and the developing countries. The emphasis on the national interest as the guiding force in policy left scholars at a loss to explain how great countries could become bogged down in enterprises such as the Vietnam and Afghanistan wars. (But cf. the later works of Lebow and Cohen 1986; Jentleson 1987; Glad and Taber 1990.) A key assumption in deterrence theory—that the reputation for using force is the key element in keeping others from aggression—was seldom subjected to critical tests, despite empirical studies suggesting that such a reputation is not a crucial variable in deterrence outcomes (Snyder and Diesing 1977). Indeed, the whole phenomenon of war was explained (7–8) without any consideration of the passion it evokes. "I think it is astounding," Robert Jervis (1987, 7–8) would later say, "that the political science literature on wars rarely mentions words like hatred."

Rational-choice decision-making studies assumed away some of the most important phenomena that political scientists should explore. The very definition of "self-interest," for example, is subject to a variety of interpretations, depending on the values of the individuals involved and the cultural context in which they operate. Thus Duverger's Law—that voters will not knowingly throw away their choice between two leading candidates for office and vote for a third alternative they are certain will lose—overlooks the possibility that some voters may see value in expressing their minority opinions as a means of building up the party for the future. (See Herbert Simon 1985, for this argument.) Nor is it so clearly in the self-interest of each member of the working class to become a free rider in the revolutionary movement, as Mancur Olsen has argued in his critique of Marx's theory of the revolution. The extent to which an individual is incorporated in a group and identifies with its goals will determine how that individual will view his individual interest when group leaders give the call for revolutionary action. (See Daniel Sabia 1981, for this argument.) Moreover, the long-term interest of individuals cannot be rationally defined without a look at the cultural context in which decisions are made. In prisoner dilemma games, as Anatol Rapoport points out (1990), the best solution occurs only when decision-makers resort to ethical norms or subjective factors. Deborah Larson (1986) has made a similar point in her study suggesting that whether or not nations cooperate in prisoner dilemma games depends on the social norms they recognize and the assessment they make of each other's motives.

Empirically, it is also clear that many decision-makers lack the ability to make value trade-offs, lack stability in the values they seek, and fail to search out the minimal information requisite to rational choice. Thus individuals confronted with multiple values that cannot be easily ranked or compared often settle on a single quantitative indicator in an effort to maintain feelings of certainty. Rapoport (1990) suggests that the arms race between the United States and the USSR, insofar as it equates strength with numerical superiority of arms, is one indication of this tendency. Several empirical studies suggest that voters make their electoral selections on the basis of very little information about the candidates. Moreover, they show little consistency in the various components of their value system, and there is little stability in those values over time (Campbell et al. 1960; Converse 1964, 1975; Schuman and Presser 1977; Erikson, Luttberg, and Tedin 1980; Kinder and Sears 1985; cf. Sniderman and Tetlock 1985; Nie, Verba, and Petrocik 1979).

Generally, as the experimental literature shows, individuals are not "good" statisticians. They show an aversion for risky choices, rejecting fair bets that could result in losses while accepting statistically identical bets on gains (Tversky and Kahneman 1981; Kahneman and Tversky 1984). They have difficulty in understanding that in any series of random events an extraordinary happening is apt to be followed by a more ordinary one. They make generalizations about the future based on a small sample of observed events. The probability of vivid, imagined events (such as accidents or murder as causes of death) are overestimated as opposed to the more common and less dramatic events (such as death due to strokes). They are even influenced by the words used in presenting alternatives to them, preferring choices that give the odds for survival over statistically identical options framed in terms of death rates (McKean 1985).

THE RENASCENCE OF POLITICAL PSYCHOLOGY

Despite these broader trends in the academy in the late sixties and seventies, some researchers persisted in the use of psychology to explain political phenomena. The relevant work in political cognition (Smith, Lane), socialization (Niemi), leadership (Katz), and personality theory (Knutson), as well as promising areas for inquiry in the future (Glad, McConahay, Knutson), were explored in Jeanne Knutson's *Handbook of*

Political Psychology, published in 1973. Shortly after that, the International Society for Political Psychology was formed and *Political Psychology*, the first journal to focus on the topic noted in its title, was launched. Students of the electoral process, as suggested above, engaged in lengthy discussions over the extent to which there were linkages between various issue areas in the minds of most voters. Ideological positions, too, were related to personality. Thus McClosky (1958,1967) and Wilson (1973) showed that political conservatives are likely to be anxious, rigid, and have problems relating to low self-esteem (see also Sniderman 1975; Stone 1980).

In the area of foreign-policy decision-making, Herbert Kellman (1965, 1968) looked at the nature of national identifications and the relevance of group behavior to foreign policy, Morton Deutsch and R. M. Krauss (1961) investigated the way in which threats influence interaction patterns, Charles Osgood (1962, 1969) studied the ways in which tensions might be deescalated, and Joseph de Rivera (1968) applied findings from social psychology to the foreign policy-making process. Irving Janis, in *Victims of Group Think* (1972), delineated the ways in which the desire for the maintenance of good feelings, esprit de corps in small groups, can lead to consensus-seeking behavior, with a consequent diminution in critical thinking. Robert Jervis (1976) argued that mind-sets formed relatively early in leaders' political careers are apt to lead them into selective misperceptions when they are called upon to make foreign-policy decisions in situations calling for new responses. In another study, Nomikos and North (1976) showed how misperceptions fed the counterproductive reactions of the leaders of the major European powers that contributed to the outbreak of World War I. In *Decision Making* (1977), Janis and Mann developed a broader theory of the decision-making process in terms of psychological variables. Consequential decisions (e.g., elite choices in crisis situations, they argued, may sometimes be characterized by vigilant information-processing, in which the individual engages in systematic searches for alternatives, remains open to discordant information, and engages in contingency planning. Certain kinds of situations (i.e., crises in which no satisfactory alternative is evident), however, are apt to lead to various forms of defensive avoidance in an attempt to minimize the psychological stress. These include procrastination, buck-passing, and the bolstering of preferred options.

By the early eighties, there were clear indications that this persistence was paying off, as political psychology once again entered the scientific mainstream. Studies of whole political cultures and of the ways in which individual citizens relate to the polity began to appear once again in major journals (e.g., Inglehart 1988). New topics, such as the composition of various environmental beliefs and values (Milbrath), the nature of public images of the presidency (Kinder and Fiske), the psychological bases of protest movements (Lederer) and political terrorism (Crenshaw), were explored in Margaret Hermann's *Political Psychology*, published in 1986. Students of the electoral process moved beyond the consistency debate to probe into the ideological and psychological roots of voter choices. Feldman (1982), for example, showed that Americans do not even vote on the basis of their economic self-interest, having internalized the liberal assumption that economic well-being is the result of personal rather than governmental initiatives. (See also Lusk and Judd 1988; Lodge, McGraw, and Stroh 1989.) William Kreml (1984) argued that the diverse political approaches are grounded in fundamentally different psychological and philosophic streams. Some researchers even suggested that cognitive consistency might not even be a virtue. Individuals with several values, aware of connections between those values, are apt to adopt policy approaches that are less simple and less predictable than the consistency models suggest (Sniderman et al. 1984.)

Fundamental topics explored by the pioneers in the field were once again tackled. Political tolerance was related to personality characteristics such as self-esteem and the perceived threat from groups disliked (Sullivan et al. 1982). Voting choices were linked to fundamental feelings evoked by the candidates—i.e., of mastery or threat (George Marcus, 1988). There does seem to be a linkage, as Altemeyer (1988) suggested, between submission to established authority, adherence to conventional values, and aggression against outgroups when that aggression is perceived to be sanctioned by established authorities. Moreover, experimental findings suggest that citizens in democratic societies (Altmeyer 1988, 308–9) have a greater potential for moving right than for moving left. Domestic crisis, whether created by a challenge from the left or the right, is apt to create a climate in which a people is predisposed to embrace traditional authority and the use of punishments to maintain order.

In the area of foreign-policy decision-making, Richard Ned Lebow (1981) contrasted the capacities of the motivational and cognitive models in explaining certain kinds of behavior. Defensive avoidance, for example, best explains the reasons for the procrastination of U.S. leaders during the Korean War in making a decision about how to meet the forthcoming Chinese intervention, as well as their subsequent scapegoating of MacArthur as the person responsible for not foreseeing that intervention. In another work, *Psychology and Deterrence*, Robert Jervis (1985) and several of his colleagues showed the role of motivated as well as unmotivated (i.e., cognitive) biases in several case studies of deterrence failures in the foreign-policy arena. National leaders, as Jervis and his colleagues show, often ignore deterrent threats because they are focused inward, paying attention to domestic political needs rather than to the external realities they face.

Shared emotions, too, have been shown to have had an impact on foreign-policy choices in crises. Fear, if it results in a very high level of stress, can lower the ability of decision-makers to respond rationally to threats, as Holsti has shown (1990). But a moderate amount of fear may have a positive impact in the handling of a crisis. During the Cuban missile crisis, Kennedy and several other key advisors backed off from the most confrontational stances recommended by other advisors because of their *fear* that war could occur inadvertently (Blight, Nye, and Welch 1987, 176). As Blight (1988) later noted, "the reason we did not have a war of some kind by the weekend of October 26–28 is the presence in many of the leaders on both sides of an overpowering fear of inadvertent nuclear war, a war arrived at by some process in which things get out of control and spiral into holocaust. . . . Both sides learned viscerally that they needed to know far more about the situation they were in than they could possibly know. So, they withdrew."

The kinds of emotions felt in such situations, as well as the response to those emotions, will vary, however, from individual to individual. During the Cuban missile crisis there were several American decision-makers who would have confronted the Soviet Union much more aggressively. Wedded to the classical rational-actor model of decision-making, they thought the United States could use its conventional and nuclear weapons superiority to cause the Soviet Union to back down. General Maxwell Taylor, for example, recalled his views along these lines (quoted from Blight, Nye, and Welch 1988, 174–75):

Neustadt: You have written in your retrospective in *The Washington Post* on October 5, '82, . . . that you don't recall any concern about the strategic balance, or any fear of nuclear exchange in this whole period. Now some of the civilians do recall worries about the time of that second Saturday; worries that really run to two or three steps up the ladder of escalation. The Soviets don't accept our demand; there follows an air strike; the Soviets then feel impelled to strike the missiles in Turkey; the Turks call on NATO for support; we feel we have to do something in Europe; the Soviets then launch a nuclear exchange—something like that was in their minds. I take it not in yours?

Taylor: They never expressed it to a military ear, I'll say that.

Neustadt: That's interesting.

Taylor: Not at all. It's the nature of some people [that] if they can't have a legitimate worry, they create them. Apparently they had some of that in the group you're speaking of.

Neustadt: In your mind, there was no legitimacy in this worry?

Taylor: Not the slightest.

Neustadt: Because Khrushchev could look up that ladder. . . .

Taylor: If he was rational. If he was irrational, I still expected his colleagues to look after him.

With a different president or under different circumstances, someone like Taylor might have prevailed. What would have been the result if they had? Would events have moved out of control as they had between the major nations on the eve of World War I (Snyder 1984)?

What this suggests, although Blight and his associates do not really explore this issue in any depth, is that the study of individual personality characteristics of key decision-makers is important to understanding the decision-making process. Personality factors, as Greenstein pointed out some time ago (1967), are most relevant for top political leaders acting in situations where their emotions and ego-defensive characteristics are apt to be triggered off because central values are at risk. Some of these relationships are evident in my own work on Jimmy Carter's handling of the Iranian hostage crisis (Glad 1989). Because Carter saw this crisis as a test of his presidency, and because his political interests were so clearly on the line, he personalized the drama in ways that were counterproductive both for himself and the country. Similarly, Reagan's difficulties in making choices between competing values, as well as his inability to confront directly people he likes, contributed to the difficulties he had in dealing with both Alexander Haig and Menachem Begin at the time of the Israeli invasion of Lebanon in 1982 (Glad 1988).

Other relevant questions have been touched upon by some investigators, but much remains to be done. What kinds of leaders are apt to be political risk-takers (Janis 1989; Glad 1969)? Creative leaders? Tyrants (Tucker 1973)? Do the aggressive needs of leaders influence their foreign-policy choices (Etheredge 1978)? Which kinds of leaders in which kinds of situations are apt to learn from previous mistakes? What impact does the group leader's personality have on group dynamics? What lessons have the leaders drawn from the vast array of possible lessons they could learn from history, and why and how did they apply those lessons to the cases at hand (Etheredge 1985; Glad and Taber 1990; Glad 1990)? How does he or she relate to political intimates and how do those relations influence policy (Marvick 1974, 1986; George and George 1956)? Eventually, as Janis (1989, chap. 9) has suggested, one may be able to develop a complex theory delineating the personality characteristics most likely to lead to good policy-making.

LOOKING TO THE FUTURE
Research Approaches

At this point, I would like to suggest three approaches to political psychological research that look especially promising. First, experimental work should be expanded. The specific experimental techniques which are likely to have high payoffs were delineated by McConahay some time ago (1973), and I shall not repeat them here.

The value of such work is that it allows one to get below surface phenomena to the underlying dynamics of group and individual behavior. The payoff, as a short review of several relevant works should suggest, are findings which are not all that obvious. Thus we know, as a result of experiments, that people are inclined, generally, to avoid high-risk choices (Tversky and Kahneman 1981); that they will follow "scientific" authorities, even when the behavior demanded of them involves apparent cruelty to research subjects (Milgram 1963, 1974); that they respond to threats by becoming more punitive (Deutsch and Krauss 1961); that threats are apt to lead to counterproductive social interactions, in which the fears and defensive reactions of each party are mutually reinforcing (Deutsch 1983). More recent studies suggest that people with some political expertise evaluate political candidates more extremely than do those who are less expert (Lusk and Judd 1988); that voters evaluate candidates not on the basis of specific memories about who they are and what they have done, but on the basis of impressions adjusted at the margin to take account of new data (Lodge, McGraw, and Stroh 1989; for an experimental study relating emotion to tolerance, see Marcus et al. 1989).

To make experimental findings such as these more directly relevant to the political process, a second approach is useful. One can test theories in the field where both leaders and followers have real values at stake. Several recent works in the foreign-policy arena suggest the ways in which we might proceed. Interactive interviews with decision-makers and key bureaucrats, as Steven Kull (1988) has shown in his study of nuclear strategists, can give us an idea of how strategic commitments relate to values and cognitive processes. The natural history experiment is another valuable approach. Thus one can relate decision-makers' images of foreign competitors to changing real-world events, as Holsti (1967) did for Secretary of State John Foster Dulles. Comparison of several key decision-makers employing evaluative assertion analysis techniques may be useful for delineating individual differences. One study comparing Kissinger, Kennedy, and Dulles (Stuart and Starr 1981–82) suggested that all three men had a tendency to attribute more cooperative behavior on the part of the USSR to weaknesses in their own foreign or domestic fronts, although this tendency was less evident for Kissinger and Kennedy than for Dulles. Cognitive processing theories may be tested through comparative case studies, as Deborah Larson (1985) has shown in her study of the responses of W. Averell Harriman, James F. Brynes, and Dean Acheson to the USSR in the early phases of the Cold War. Realist historians and economic revisionists, both, as she demonstrates, assumed a greater clarity in the decision-makers' minds about both means and ends in the definition of their containment policies than the documentary record supports.

Finally, psychobiographical studies can be utilized to a much greater extent than they have been to this point. Individual case histories, as I have argued elsewhere (Glad 1983), can be used to explore broader political phenomena. When a particular decision-maker is shown to be an exemplar of the official culture of his time, then one may explore through his life some of the complex connections between the dominant modes of thought of the time and the policy choices usually made. My work on Charles Evans Hughes (Glad 1966), for example, suggests that after World War I Americans coming from the well-educated eastern seaboard elite were ready to make only minor modifications in the traditional commitment to isolationism because of a widely shared mind-set that identified American institutions and interests with the *slow* evolution of the rule of reason throughout the world.

Comparative psychobiographies, however, are apt to be the most useful in refining and developing theories suggested in the social science laboratory. One approach is the cooperative endeavor among several experts in which they analyze the response of several national leaders to one important foreign-policy event. Barbara Kellerman's and Jeffrey Rubin's (1988) recent work on the responses of American, Soviet, and several Middle Eastern heads of state to the Israeli invasions of Lebanon in 1982 is an important endeavor along these lines. The complex interplay between the individual motivations, skills, and policy commitments of each leader relative to the opportunity structure in which he had to operate is admirably summarized by specialists in the bargaining process: Jeffrey Rubin, Saadia Touval, and Morton Deutsch.

Another approach to comparative biography is to hold the political role constant while looking at several individuals with different personality structures who have occupied that role. James David Barber's work on the effect of presidential character on role performance was a pioneering work along these lines. Although some scholars have questioned the utility of the personality theory he uses, his approach can provide guidelines for future researchers in the field. The distinctions he draws between character, style, and worldview, and the emphasis he places on the importance for the politician of his first successes in fixing his style, have already shown their utility in the works of several psychobiographers.

My work on the chairmen of the Senate Foreign Relations Committee is another endeavor along these lines. The comparison of Fulbright and Borah (1969), for example, led me to the conclusion that an ability to deal with a certain amount of cognitive dissonance over time and to experience stress while continuing to think and function is a condition of creative role performance. My analysis of Key Pittman (Glad 1986) suggests that persons with certain types of narcissistic vulnerabilities may be intelligent, perceptive, and politically astute, but fall apart in roles where the demands for outcomes are contradictory and/or ambiguous. Eventually, I shall compare all eight men who held the position of chairman of the committee from 1924 to 1974, in an effort to relate personality characteristics to adaptive, maladaptive, and creative role performances. For comparative work on revolutionary leaders, see Wolfenstein 1967; for charismatic leaders, see Willner 1984.

Clearing Away the Conceptual Underbrush

To facilitate work along the above lines, it would be useful, once again, to clear away some of the "conceptual underbrush" (to use Greenstein's, 1967, earlier phrase), that has impeded the use of psychological analysis in political science. Four kinds of considerations are useful here. First, one should note that new scientific images more congenial to the approaches utilized in the field of political psychology are gaining currency in the academy. Throughout the sixties and seventies, the social sciences, generally, were modeled on a physics model in which the goal was to find the broadest possible laws to explain the most behavior. Today, however, as the chaos theorists are showing, there are aspects of the physical world which are historical and/or indeterminate in nature (Gleick 1988). In the field of biology there is a growing realization that it is best not to search for grand abstractions.* Indeed, as Francis Crick (1988, 138–39) has recently noted, the elegance and deep simplicity that is often fruitful in physics can be very misleading in biology. Herbert Simon (1985) has addressed this problem as follows:

> We sometimes, perhaps, experience a mild malaise in that our research does not seem to be taking us in the direction of a few sweeping generalizations that encompass the whole of political behavior. A hope of finding our "three laws of motion" was probably a major part of the appeal of rational choice theory in its purer forms. But a more careful look at the natural sciences would show us that they, too, get only a little mileage from their general laws. Those laws have to be fleshed out

---

* Biologists may sometimes use natural history experiments to prove general theories. For a recent endeavor along these lines, see Gina Kolata, "A Breakthrough in Evolution as Guppies Change Behavior" (1990).

by a myriad of facts, all of which must be harvested by laborious empirical research. Perhaps our aspirations for lawfulness should be modeled upon the complexities of molecular biology—surely a successful science, but hardly a neat one—rather than upon the simplicities of classical mechanics.

In line with this new respect for complexity, certain leaders in the field of cognitive psychology are paying more attention to affect (e.g., Sorrento and Higgins 1986). The result is a richer literature in academic psychology from which observers of the political process can draw. As Brewster Smith and his colleagues (1956) noted some time ago, values often serve a value-maintenance function, helping the individual to maintain a basic equilibrium in a complex and potentially overwhelming world. In line with that earlier idea, researchers today are investigating the relationship of self-esteem and acceptance by others to perceptions and attitudes. Attributional theorists, for example, have shown that judgment of other human beings is characterized by systematic biases growing out of the need to protect and enhance one's own ego. People readily accept credit for their own successes but just as readily assign the blame for failure to others. The relevance of this theory for foreign policy-making is evident in Lebow and Cohen's (1986) analysis of U.S. perceptions of USSR motivations for the Afghanistan invasion in the winter of 1979–80.

A second and related idea we must confront is the one that idiosyncratic events are not important in political life and that inquiry into such matters somehow lacks legitimacy. After all, general laws are always evident in unique events, and one may be able to test and revise those general laws by referring to those unique events. But the study of particular natural and political constellations are a legitimate form of inquiry even if they are not used to build theories that apply across the board. The most important phenomena we wish to understand may not be static, repetitive, or even predictable.

In fact, some of the natural sciences are organized around such types of inquiry. In astrophysics, geology, and biology many scientists seek to explain how a particular constellation came into existence and how that existence shapes paths of future development. Thus the astronomer attempts to account for the evolution of the solar system; the geologist is concerned with the particular history and structure of the earth; and the biologist attempts to trace the evolution of various life forms. The patterns that emerge, as Crick (1988, 96) has noted, are the result of an interaction between certain process rules and accidental combinations. The genetic code, for example, could have had "almost *any* structure since its detail would depend on which amino acid went with which adaptor." Even the physical universe, as chaos theorists have pointed out, has an irregular side, marked by disorder, discontinuities, and unpredictabilities. Minor differences in input, as they have shown through various mathematical models, can quickly bring about over-whelming differences in output. Thus, as the so-called butterfly effect only "half-jokingly" suggests, the weather in New York can be trans-formed by a butterfly stirring the air in Peking (Gleick, 8).

Similarly, the political scientist may legitimately be concerned with how particular events have led to major changes in political forms. The actions of the Constitutional Convention at Philadelphia, for example, changed forever the direction America would take. What factors pro-duced that creative act? What was the importance of the leadership skills, the values, the personalities of George Washington, Benjamin Franklin, James Monroe, and John Adams to that outcome? Hitler's accession to power in Germany changed the course of world history in a more pathogenic direction. What political and sociopsychological fac-tors led to his rise to power in Germany and his subsequent acceptance by the German people? How did the personalities of Lenin, Stalin, and Gorbachev play on the evolution of political forms in the USSR? of Mao Tse-tung and Deng Xiaoping on the direction of political development in China?

The third kind of barrier we must overcome are those methodologi-cal critiques that have been used to question the very legitimacy of the psychological approach to politics. Is the whole field reductionist, as so many of its critics have suggested? Even scholars sympathetic to a cer-tain kind of political psychology have sometimes suggested that the field is plagued by such tendencies. Thus, Stanley Hoffman (1986a, 8–9) argues that radical political psychologists (i.e., those who envisage the possibility of a world transformed through the application of social-psychological findings) are inclined to ignore intractable political reali-ties. Ideologies, as he notes, are not just irrational constructs, but often rationally selected maps allowing individuals to cope with reality. Na-tional identifications are not simply "pathological appeals to a people's baser instincts, more aggressive impulses, or unsophisticated mental de-fenses." Nor is a nation's concern for survival in any way primitive. "Enemies are not mere projections of negative identities; they are often quite real."

This either/or approach, however, presents us with false alterna-tives. "Enemies," as Stein (1986, 247–48) points out, "are neither 'merely' projections, nor are they 'merely' real. Ideologies likewise are not 'just' irrational, nor are they altogether 'rationally' selected maps allowing individuals to cope with reality." No superorganism super-sedes "the influence of people thinking, feeling and acting together," as Stein argues. Thus, to understand war, one must look at a phenomenon noted by Hoffman—namely, the "reservoir of collective emotions and passion" that bursts forth on occasion. One will find, Stein suggests, that such "bursts" are inextricably tied to the mental images one has of oneself or of early caretaking figures. The phenomenon, in short, is rooted not only in specific political events but also in "what kind of animals we are."

Social structures, in short, are influenced by factors endemic to Homo sapiens, which shape and limit the variety of possible forms. To limit one's analysis to macropolitical structures and objective interests is to miss some of the most important underlying causes of those macropolitical structures and interests.[5] The problem with driving everything back to its origins, of course, is that one has to face the possibility of a kind of infinite regress. Unless one reaches the "most primitive original cause that initiated the sequence that led to the independent variable under study, one would always be able to find at least in principle an antecedent condition that really was responsible for the effect" (Hyman and Sheatsley 1954, 255–56).

The way out of this impasse is to recognize that new data are added at each level of analysis. One begins with a human nature that limits the variety of political forms one may find in the world. But within these limitations specific histories create divergent political and sociological forces, and these divergent forces shape personality, to some extent. But the intelligence, vitality, and intimate family experiences of each individual will also influence the ways in which those broader social factors impact on him or her. To equate particular institutional forms with a fixed human nature or to identify a particular individual with a particular sociological form is to lose information about the factors that make a particular political culture or a particular individual distinctive in important ways.

The appropriate response to this level of analysis problem, then, is to realize that breakthroughs in scientific knowledge may require one to move back and forth between the various levels of analysis, remaining fully aware of what one gains and loses by each of these moves. A close reading of the Hoffman (1986a) article cited above leads one to a position close to this. His real objection, despite the polarities he suggests at the beginning of his article, is that one cannot simply view the political structure as the individual writ large. Indeed, at the end of the article he suggests a research agenda upon which political scientists and psychologists can cooperate that does not differ much from the one offered in this essay.

Our objective, then, as Almond and Verba (1985, 402–7) have suggested, is not to force choices between the various levels of analysis, but to build bridges between them. In foreign-policy decision-making, as Deborah Larson (1985, 18–23) has noted, the two analyses can be integrated along the following lines. The international system describes the range of outcomes possible for a state in its dealings with others. But people vary in their interpretations of stimuli, and these interpretations do not simply reflect the objective properties of the situation. What this means is that to "increase the determinacy of the explanation, we must move to more specific levels of analysis—the domestic political context and the individual policy makers." To Larson's formulation, I would add that one must also know the underlying emotional and ego-defensive factors that influence both the perceptions of the situation and the values sought in the exchange.

The potentially biasing effect of values on research, moreover, should not be dealt with by attempting to make diverse political goals morally and psychologically equivalent. The problems one runs into when one drops the direction of political activity out of the analysis is evident, for example, in Barber's (1972, 58–95, 145–72) work on presidents. Wilson, Hoover, and Nixon, despite certain similarities that caused Barber to place them in his active-negative category, were very different in some very important matters of conscience and political goals which had important ramifications for the direction this polity would take. The same is true of George Washington, Calvin Coolidge, and Dwight D. Eisenhower, each of whom is placed in the passive-negative category. Endeavors to develop value-free tests of tolerance create similar problems. Rokeach's (1960) attempt to develop a value-free concept of authoritarianism led him to focus on cognitive processes, with a consequent loss of important information about the relevance of passions and defenses to the selection of one's particular enemies (Sanford 1973). Similar problems arise in the endeavor of Sullivan and his colleagues (1982) to develop a value-free test for tolerance. Certainly their finding that the perception of a group as threatening is related to intolerance is important (190–91). But when the definition of the threatening group is a subjective one, the researcher loses important information about the extent to which the subject's fear is based on a real threat to central values, in contrast to scapegoating based on ego-defensive responses to threats emanating from other sources.* One cannot distinguish between the black who would not let the Ku Klux Klan meet to pursue its political and social objectives and the white male who would not permit blacks or women to meet to promote their equality under the law. Reliance on the subjects' definitions of the nature of the threat posed does not permit one to make judgments about whether or

---

* Subjects in the Sullivan et al. study were asked to name the group or groups they disliked and then to define the extent of the threat emanating from those groups. The importance of taking into account the reality component of the threat perceived to come from a disliked group is evident in the recent rise of anti-Semitic statements in Poland. Trudy Rubin (in "Anti-Semitism on the Rise in Poland," *The State*, August 1, 1990), noting the miniscule number of Jews in Poland at the present time, quite appropriately sees both the state of the economy and the split in Solidarity as sources of a rising zenophobic nationalism.

not the subject *is* actually threatened by the group disliked, or simply *thinks* he is threatened. Considering the elimination of this central political fact, it is not surprising that Sullivan and his colleagues found blacks and Jews to be slightly less tolerant than non-Jewish whites.

There are alternatives to screening out values from social inquiry. One can frankly note the diverse political values and goals of one's subjects and directly address the implications of those goals and values for the broader political system. The researcher's own values should be made as explicit as possible, and he or she should be willing to submit detailed descriptions of his or her research procedures to possible critics, as a means of discovering potential blind spots induced by those values. The authors of *The Authoritarian Personality* and *The Civic Culture* both met these standards when they edited or in other ways collaborated with others on volumes containing critiques of their own work.

In policy debates it is especially important to make clear the extent to which differences are based on the ends deemed desirable, as contrasted to differing assessments of the appropriate means to accomplish agreed-upon ends. In James Blight's (1986, 1987a, 1988) critiques of certain social psychologists, these aspects of analysis have been intermingled in way that obscure the nature of the real issues. Thus Blight begins with the observation that many social psychologists are not listened to by policymakers because their messages are too far removed from the specific political and security concerns of the policymakers. But then he slips into the assumption that the decision-makers are in better contact with reality than social psychologists when they pursue policies which the latter oppose, such as an increase in the number and sophistication of nuclear weapons as a means of promoting the nation's security. What Blight inadequately addresses is the possibility that a policy-setting elite may fail to adapt to new realities, acting in ways that are detrimental to the national interest. Certainly policy elites have acted that way in the past, and whether or not they are doing so in any given historical epoch is a matter that can only be resolved by analyses he does not present. Certainly there is some indication, as Steven Kull's (1988) interviews suggest, that many strategic experts had not squarely faced several of the paradoxes presented by the sheer destructive power of nuclear weapons.

A final roadblock with which we must deal is the assumption that affect is so unpredictable it makes impossible a science which takes it into account. Cognitive psychologists, as Sorrentino and Higgins (1986, 13–15) have noted, have begun to to move away from this position, realizing that they lose predictive power when they ignore the impact of emotion or motivation on perception and attitudes. In political science, even scholars who earlier ignored or denied the importance of affect in political phenomena have realized that they now must study its impact. As Robert Jervis (1987, 3) has recently noted, emotions influence the establishment of values, the setting of goals, the perception of meaningful alternatives. Contemporary nationalism, he adds, cannot be understood without reference to pride and selective perception. Nor can war be comprehended without reference to hatred. Stanley Hoffman (1986, 11–21) has also admitted that interstate relations can be better understood if one looks at psychological factors such as shifts in mass moods, the psychological bent of leaders, the causes and consequences of group think. Even Herbert Simon (1985, 301), despite his insistence that models of information processing are adequate to explain decision-making, has admitted that emotional, or what he calls "hot," factors may play a role in what human beings actually do. Human behavior, he notes, must sometimes be "attributed to passion, to the capture of the decision process by powerful impulses that do not permit the mediation of thought."

I would go beyond these statements to suggest that the importance of unconscious motivations for political behavior should not be overlooked. One has to recognize that the value of questionnaire responses may be limited by the desire of ordinary people to hide their socially unacceptable attitudes. Polls in Germany in the early 1930s, for example, suggested that German workers were simple social democrats. The projective tests used by Max Horkheimer and his colleagues, however, revealed attitudes and values in the working class that suggested they would support Hitler (Sanford 1973, 140). Similarly, Simon's (1985) suggestion that Hitler's values could be taken as a given overlooks the possibility that some of his more fundamental goals were not always what they seemed to be. His overt objective was the conquest of Europe, but he pursued it in ways that suggest that he also had an unconscious desire for self-destruction. His failure to heed his generals and destroy British troops evacuating at Dunkirk, as Robert Waite (1990) has shown, can be understood in these terms. Even his frantic drive to kill all Jews in the later phases of the war can be understood as a form of self-sabotage. It was an enterprise that diverted men and resources from the front lines at a time when the whole war effort was in deep trouble.

This is not to suggest, as several of the above examples might indicate, that affect always has a negative impact on decision-making. Indeed, the very polarity between emotion and reason so endemic in our culture is one that should be addressed. It is based on a notion of reason, as Lewis Mumford (1963) has argued, that contradicts the fundamental message of Freud and Jung—namely, that human beings will be much clearer about what they are doing when their rationality is accompanied by an acceptance and understanding of their emotions, not a denial of them.[6] Creative thought, moreover, depends on keeping the lines of communication open between the passions and the mind. One cannot really have a new idea, as Lawrence Kubie (1961) suggests, when one is on guard, expending energy on the suppression of dangerous feelings and ideas. Preconscious processing is characteristic of all creative acts and can only occur when the impression barrier is not too rigid.

Indeed, certain kinds of emotions often have a positive impact on political behavior. Fear, as suggested above, may be an appropriate response to a crisis situation. When combined with empathic identification with the enemy and an ability to continue to search for realistic adaptations to that enemy's legitimate interests, it may provide a peaceful solution to a crisis that otherwise could escalate out of control. John F. Kennedy's extraordinary ability to put himself in the shoes of Soviet leaders during the Cuban missile crisis is informative along these lines. At the crucial EXCOM Committee meeting of October 27 (Bundy transcript, Blight 1987–88), Kennedy was the one who kept bringing the group back to the view that the Russians might really see a parallel between the U.S. missiles in Turkey and Soviet missiles in Cuba, that indeed they might not back down if the United States did not make some concessions to their feelings along those lines.

In certain circumstances, empathy may even lead to altruistic stances in which the individual risks his own basic self-interest in an effort to aid others. The Nazi experience has not only given us rich case material about regressive tendencies in masses of people, it has also shown us that some individuals were able to transcend their circumstances. Those individuals who went out of their way to rescue Jews and others in danger of being killed were characterized by a heightened empathy for others in pain and/or a strong sense of justice, of caring for others (Olliner and Olliner 1988; see also Adelson 1988). Their choices were based on enduring character traits, formed in households where parents lived up to the altruistic standards they preached—all the while loving their children and gently disciplining them. (See Moses, 1985, for a general discussion of the disadvantages and advantages of empathy for diverse types of political action.)

What all this suggests is that affect sometimes has a positive impact on the political process, and that if we concern ourselves more with affect, we will enhance our ability to explain and even predict political behavior, insofar as prediction is possible. The relevance of enduring character traits such as the capacity for empathy to both democratic theory and scientific prediction has been noted by Marcus and Rahn (1990). "Affective attachments and affective control," they suggest, "anchor enduring patterns of behavior." The most important item on the research agenda, as they note, may be to discover which specific affective patterns sustain democratic practice, and which ones undermine them.

NOTES

1. These critiques, however, did not mean that Adorno and his associates were not on to something. The bulk of the subsequent research, as Richard Christie has pointed out, indicated that there is indeed an authoritarian personality type, that it has its sources in emotional vulnerabilities and an earlier, harsh socialization process, and that such a personality type is predisposed to prejudice and political conservatism. Various studies of top Nazi leaders, some employing the Rorschach test, showed the authoritarian syndrome described in the original study (Christie and Jahoda 1954). Rokeach's (1960) later work, employing ideologically neutral tests, suggests that there were indeed characteristic differences between people in terms of their rigidity in problem solving, though the original F scale was a measure of right authoritarianism, not general authoritarianism (Christie and Cook 1958; Glazer 1954). Indeed, as Brown 1965, 489) reports in his subsequent review of the critical literature, one suspects intuitively that there is an authoritarian personality. "Do you know him—the authoritarian, the anti-democratic, the pre-Fascist: It seems to me I do."

2. The critical responses to *The Authoritarian Personality* were much more severe than the critiques of other major works produced at this time. Although the work received a great deal of attention, much of that attention, as Sanford later noted (1973, 161–63), consisted of research on the original work, rather than an adaptation of the analysis to new lines of inquiry. Stouffer's *The American Soldier* (1949), by way of of contrast, was very tamely dealt with in volumes designed to critique it (Glazer 1954, 291 n.). Almond and Verba's *The Civic Culture* was greeted as a great book by its first reviewers (Davis 1976). Though it was critiqued, it was seldom dismissed on the grounds that it was "wrong or irrelevant," as Verba later noted. Indeed, most scholars "responded with the most important kind of praise, . . . modifying, replicating, extending the scope of the study" (Almond and Verba 1980).

3. See, for example, Charles Jellison in the *American Historical Review* 62 (July 1957): 948; and H. H. Fockler, *Library Journal* 81 (December 15, 1985): 2947.

4. In the spring of 1947, while still secretary of defense, Forrestal was severely depressed, had paranoic fantasies, and engaged in bizarre behavior. After his resignation from office, he committed himself to a psychiatric unit at Bethesda Naval Hospital. He killed himself by jumping out of a window of his suite at the hospital.

5. Crick (1988, 161–63) has made a similar point for the fields of biology and psychology. The major advances in biology in the twentieth century have come through work done at the molecular level. Psychology, he argues, can only advance through detailed and imaginative work on the functioning of the brain.

6. Indeed, statesmen much admired for their self-control have broken down when subjected to emotional pressures they could not directly address. Harold Macmillan, for example, had a serious emotional breakdown in 1931 that was apparently triggered by the extramarital affair of his wife, Dorothy.

Although his wife's affair continued until her death in 1966, he never uttered a word about it. This extraordinary personal self-control won him the admiration of even his political opponents. Rab Butler, for example, saw his quiet suffering as a sign of his moral strength (Alistair Horne, 1989). I would suggest that he might have been better off had he been able to ventilate, at least to a few friends, the very complex feelings he must have had about that affair.

REFERENCES

Adelson, J. 1988. "The Psychology of Altruism." *Commentary*, November, 40–44.

Adorno, T. W., E. Frenkel-Brunswik, D. J. Levinson, and R. N. Sanford. 1950. *The Authoritarian Personality*. New York: Harper & Row.

Alexander, F. 1950. "Review of Adorno et al.'s *The Authoritarian Personality*." *Ethics* (1950): 76–81.

Allison, G. T. 1971. *Essence of Decision: Explaining the Cuban Missile Crisis*. Boston: Little, Brown.

Almond, G. A. 1954. *Appeals of Communism*. Princeton, N.J.: Princeton University Press.

———, and S. Verba. 1963. *The Civic Culture: Political Attitudes and Democracy in Five Nations*. Princeton, N.J.: Princeton University Press.

———. 1980. *The Civic Culture Revisited*. New York: Little, Brown.

Altemeyer, B. 1988. *Enemies of Freedom*. San Francisco: Jossey-Bass.

Barber, J. D. 1965. *The Lawmakers: Recruitment and Adaptation to Legislative Way of Life*. New Haven: Yale University Press.

———. 1972. *The Presidential Character: Predicting Performances in the White House*. Englewood Cliffs, N.J.: Prentice-Hall.

Beradt, C. 1968. *The Third Reich of Dreams*. Chicago: University of Chicago Press.

Berelson, B. R., P. F. Lazarsfeld, and W. N. McPhee. 1954. *Voting*. Chicago: University of Chicago Press.

Blight, J. G. 1986. "How Might Psychology Contribute to Reducing the Risk of Nuclear War?" *Political Psychology* 7, no. 4.

———. 1987. "Towards Policy-Relevant Psychology of Avoiding Nuclear War." *American Psychologist* 42(1):12–29.

———. 1988. "Must the Psychology of Avoiding Nuclear War Remain Free and Insignificant?" *American Psychologist* 43 (April 1988): 326–29.

———, ed. 1987–88. "October 27, 1962: Transcripts of the Meetings of the Excomm," McGeorge Bundy, transcriber. *International Security* 12 (Winter 1987–88).

———, J. S. Nye, and D. A. Welch. 1987. "The Cuban Missile Crisis Revisited." *Foreign Affairs* 66 (Fall 1987): 170–88.

Brady, H., and P. M. Sniderman. 1985. "Attitude Attribution: A Group Basis for Political Reasoning." *American Political Science Review*. 79:1061–78.

Brown, R. 1965. *Social Psychology*. New York: The Free Press.

Browning, R. P., and H. Jacob. 1964. "Power Motivation and the Political Personality." *Public Opinion Quarterly* 28(1):75–90.

Campbell, A., P. E. Converse, W. E. Miller, and D. E. Stokes. 1960. *The American Voter*. New York: Wiley.

———, G. Gurin, and W. Miller. 1954. *The Voter Decides*. Evanston, Ill.: Row, Peterson.

Christie, R., and P. Cook. 1958. "A Guide to the Published Literature Relating to the Authoritarian Personality through 1956." *Journal of Psychology* 45: 171–99.

———, and M. Jahoda, eds. 1954. *Studies in the Scope and Method of "The Authoritarian Personality."* Glencoe, Ill.: The Free Press.

Conover, P. J., and S. Feldman. 1981. "The Origins and Meanings of Liberal/Conservative Self-Identifications." *American Journal of Political Science* 25: 617–45.

Converse, P. E. 1964. "The Nature of Belief Systems in Mass Publics." In D. E. Apter, ed., *Ideology and Discontent*. New York: The Free Press.

———. 1975. "Public Opinion and Voting Behavior." In F. Greenstein and N. Polsby, eds., *Handbook of Political Science*, vol. 4. Reading, Mass.: Addison-Wesley.

Crenshaw, M. 1986. "The Psychology of Political Terrorism." In M. G. Hermann, ed., *Political Psychology*, 379–413. San Francisco: Jossey-Bass.

Crick, F. 1988. *What Mad Pursuit*. New York: Basic Books.

Davis, E. 1976. "The Impact of the Civic Culture." Unpublished paper. Stanford University.

De Rivera, J. 1968. *The Psychological Dimension of Foreign Policy*. Columbus, Ohio: Merrill.

Deutsch, M. 1983. "The Prevention of World War Three." *Political Psychology* 4(1):3–31.

———, and R. M. Krauss. 1961. "The Effect of Threat on Interpersonal Bargaining." *Journal of Abnormal and Social Psychology* 61:181–89.

Downs, A. 1957. *An Economic Theory of Democracy*. New York: Harper.

Edinger, D. J. 1965. *Kurt Schumacher: A Study in Personality and Political Behavior*. Stanford, Calif.: Stanford University Press.

Erdelyi, M. H. 1974. "A New Look at the New Look: Perceptual Defense and Vigilance." *Psychological Review* 81, no. 1.

Erikson, R. S., N. R. Luttbeg, and K. L. Tedin. 1980. *American Public Opinion: Its Origins, Content, and Impact*. 2d ed. New York: Wiley.

Etheridge, L. 1978. *A World of Men: The Private Sources of American Foreign Policy*. Cambridge, Mass.: MIT Press.

———. 1985. *Can Government Learn? American Foreign Policy and Central American Revolutions*. New York: Pergamon Press.

Feldman, S. 1982. "Economic Self-Interest and Political Behavior." *American Journal of Political Science* 26:446–65.

Fiske, S. T., and M. A. Pavlechak. 1986. "Category-Based versus Piecemeal-Based Affective Responses: Development in Schema-Triggered Affect." In R. M. Sorrentino and E. T. Higgins, eds., *Handbook of Motivation and Cognition: Foundations of Social Behavior*.

———, and D. R. Kinder. 1986. "Presidents in the Public Mind." In M. G. Hermann, ed., *Political Psychology*, 193–218. San Francisco: Jossey-Bass.

Fowler, C. A., R. Slade, L. Tassinary, and G. Wolford. 1981. "Lexical Access with and without Awareness." *Journal of Experimental Psychology* 110, no. 3.

Frenkel-Brunswick, E. 1952. "Interaction of Psychological and Sociological Factors in Political Behavior." *The American Political Science Review*, no. 1.

Freud, S. 1930. *Civilization and Its Discontents*. New York: Cape and Smith.

George, A. L., and J. L. George. 1956. *Woodrow Wilson and Colonel House: A Personality Study*. New York: J. Day Co.

———. 1982. "Woodrow Wilson and Colonel House: A Reply to Weinstein, Anderson and Link." *Political Science Quarterly* 96:641–66.

Gibb, C. A. 1954. "Leadership." In G. Lindzey, ed., *Handbook of Social Psychology*, 2:877–920. Cambridge, Mass.: Addison-Wesley.

Glad, B. 1966. *Charles Evans Hughes and the Illusions of Innocence*. Urbana: University of Illinois Press.

———. 1969. "The Significance of Personality for Role Performance as Chairman of the Senate Foreign Relations Committee: A Comparison of Borah and Fulbright." Paper presented at the annual meeting of the American Political Science Association, New York.

———. 1973. "Contributions of Psychobiography." In J. N. Knutson, ed., *Handbook of Political Psychology*, 296–321. San Francisco: Jossey-Bass.

———. 1983. "Black and White Thinking in Ronald Reagan's Approach to Foreign Policy." *Political Psychology* (Spring 1983): 33–76.

———. 1986. *Key Pittman: The Tragedy of a Senate Insider*. New York: Columbia University Press.

———. 1988. "Ronald Reagan's Response to the Israeli Invasion of Lebanon: Personality, Ideology, and Decision Making Processes." In B. Kellerman and J. Rubin, eds., *Leadership and Negotiation*. New York: Praeger.

———. 1989. "Jimmy Carter's Handling of the Hostage Crisis." *International Political Science Quarterly* (January 1989).

Glad, B., and C. Taber. 1990. "Images, Learning, and the Decision to Use Force: The Domino Theory of the United States." In B. Glad, ed., *Psychological Dimensions of War*. Newbury Park, Calif.: Sage Publications.

Glazer, N. 1954. "New Light on the Authoritarian Personality." *Commentary* 17:289–97.

Gleick, J. 1988. *Chaos: Making a New Science*. New York: Penguin Group.

Gottfried, A. 1962. *Boss Cermak of Chicago*. Seattle: University of Washington Press.

Greenstein, F. I. 1965. "Personality and Political Socialization: The Theories of Authoritarianism and Democratic Character." *The Annals of the American Academy of Political and Social Science* 361:81–95.

———. 1967. "The Impact of Personality on Politics: An Attempt to Clear Away the Underbrush." *American Political Science Review* 54:934–43.

Hennessy, B. 1959. "Politicals and Apoliticals: Some Measurements of Personality Traits." *Midwest Journal of Political Science* 3:336–55.

Hermann, M. G. 1986. "Ingredients of Leadership." In M. G. Hermann, ed., *Political Psychology*, 167–92. San Francisco: Jossey-Bass.

———, ed. 1986. *Political Psychology*. San Francisco: Jossey-Bass.

Hoffman, S. 1986a. "On the Political Psychology of Peace and War: A Critique and an Agenda." *Political Psychology* 7(1):1–21.

———. 1986b. "A Brief Reply to Critics." *Political Psychology* 7(2):255–57.

Holsti, O. 1967. In D. J. Finlay and others, *Enemies in Politics*. Chicago: Rand McNally.

———. 1990. "Crisis." In B. Glad, ed., *Psychological Dimensions of War*. Newbury Park, Calif: Sage Publications.

Horne, A. 1989. *Harold MacMillan*. Vol. 1, 1894–1956. New York: Viking Press.

Hovland, C. I., A. A. Lumsdaine, and F. D. Sheffield. 1949. *Experiments on Mass Communication*. Vol. 3 of *Studies in Social Psychology in World War II*. Princeton, N.J.: Princeton University Press.

Hyman, H. H., and P. B. Sheatsley. 1954. "The Authoritarian Personality—A Methodological Critique." In R. Christie and M. Jahoda, eds., *Studies in the Scope and Method of "The Authoritarian Personality."* Glencoe, Ill.: The Free Press.

Inglehart, R. 1988. "The Renaissance of Political Culture." *American Political Science Review* 82 (December 1988): 1203–30.

Janis, I. 1972. *Victims of Groupthink: A Psychological Study of Foreign Policy Decisions and Fiascos*. New York: Houghton Mifflin.

———. 1989. *Crucial Decisions: Leadership in Policymaking and Crisis Management*. New York: The Free Press.

———, and L. Mann. 1977. *Decision Making: A Psychological Analysis of Conflict, Choice, and Commitment*. New York: The Free Press.

Janowitz, M., and D. Marvick. 1956, 1964. *Competitive Pressure and Democratic Consent: An Interpretation of the 1952 Presidential Election*. 2d ed. Chicago: Quadrangle Books.

Jentleson, B. W. 1987. "American Commitments in the Third World: Theory vs. Practice." *International Organization*, no. 41.

Jervis, R. 1970. *The Logic of Images in International Relations*. Princeton, N.J.: Princeton University Press.

———. 1976. *Perception and Misperception in International Politics*. Princeton, N.J.: Princeton University Press.

———. 1987. "Notes on Cognition and Affect in International Politics." Manuscript, March 9.

———, R. N. Lebow, and J. G. Stein. 1985. *Psychology and Deterrence*. Baltimore: The Johns Hopkins University Press.

Judd, C. M., and J. A. Krosnick. 1989. "The Structural Bases of Consistency among Political Attitudes: Effects of Political Expertise and Attitude Importance." In A. R. Pratkanis, S. J. Breckler, and A. G. Greenwald, eds., *Attitude Structure and Function*. Hillsdale, N.J.: Erlbaum.

Kahneman, D., and A. Tversky. 1981. "The Framing of Decisions and the Psychology of Choice." *Science* 211:453–58.

———. 1984. "Choices, Values, and Frames." *American Psychologist* (April 1984): 341–49.

Kaplan, M. 1964. "Review of Klineberg's *The Human Dimension in International Relations*." *American Political Science Review* 58:682–83.

Katz, D. 1973. "Patterns of Leadership." In J. Knutson, ed., *Handbook of Political Psychology*, 203–33.

Kellerman, B., and J. Z. Rubin, eds. 1988. *Leadership and Negotiation in the Middle East*. New York: Praeger.

Kelman, H. C., ed. 1965. *International Behavior: A Social-Psychological Analysis*. New York: Holt.

Kennedy, P. 1987. *The Rise and Fall of the Great Powers: Economic Change and Military Conflict from 1500 to 2000*. New York: Random House.

Kinder, D. R., and D. O. Sears. 1985. "Public Opinion and Political Action." In Lindzey and E. Aronson, eds., *Handbook of Social Psychology*. 3d ed. Reading, Mass.: Addison-Wesley.

Knutson, J. N. 1973. *Handbook of Political Psychology*. San Francisco: Jossey-Bass.

———. 1973. "The New Frontier of Projective Techniques." In J. Knutson, ed., *Handbook of Political Psychology*. Washington, D.C.: Jossey-Bass.

———. 1973. "Personality in the Study of Politics." In J. Knutson, ed., *Handbook of Political Psychology*. Washington, D.C.: Jossey-Bass.

Kogan, N., and M. A. Wallach. 1964. *Risk Taking: A Study in Cognition and Personality*. New York: Holt, Rinehart, and Winston.

Kolata, G. 1990. "A Breakthrough in Evolution as Guppies Change Behavior." *New York Times*, July 26, A1.

Kreml, W. P. 1984. *Relativism and the Natural Left*. New York: New York University Press.

Kubie, L. S. 1961. *Neurotic Distortion of the Creative Process*. New York: Noonday.

Kull, S. 1988. *Minds at War: Nuclear Realities and the Inner Conflicts of Defense Policymakers*. New York: Basic Books.

Lane, R. E. 1959. *Political Life*. New York: The Free Press.

———. 1962. *Political Ideology: What the American Common Man Believes and What He Does*. New York: The Free Press.

———, and D. O. Sears. 1964. *Public Opinion*. Englewood Cliffs, N.J.: Prentice-Hall.

Larson, D. W. 1985. *Origins of Containment: A Psychological Explanation*. Princeton, N.J.: Princeton University Press.

———. 1986. "Game Theory and the Psychology of Reciprocity." Unpublished paper, October 29. Columbia University.

Laswell, H. 1930. *Psychopathology and Politics*. Chicago: University of Chicago Press.

Lazarsfeld, P. F., B. Berelson, and H. Gaudet. 1944. *The People's Choice*. New York: Columbia University Press.

Lebow, R. N. 1981. *Between Peace and War: The Nature of International Crisis*. Baltimore: The Johns Hopkins University Press.

———, and D. S. Cohen. 1986. "Afghanistan as Inkblot: The Carter Administration's Reaction to Soviet Intervention." Paper delivered at a meeting of the International Society of Political Psychology, June. Amsterdam.

Lederer, G. 1986. "Protest Movements as a Form of Political Action." In M. G. Hermann, ed., *Political Psychology*, 355–78. San Francisco: Jossey-Bass.

Lipset, S. M., et al. 1954. *The Psychology of Voting: An Analysis of Political Behavior*. 2:1124–75. In G. Lindzey, ed., *Handbook of Social Psychology*. Cambridge, Mass.: Addison-Wesley.

Lodge, M., K. M. McGraw, and P. Stroh. 1989. "An Impression-Driven Model of Candidate Evaluation." *American Political Science Review* (June).

Lusk, C. M., and C. M. Judd. 1988. "Political Expertise and the Structural Mediators of Candidate Evaluations." *Journal of Experimental Social Psychology* 24:105–26.

Lyons, G. M. 1964. "Review of Gottfried's *Boss Cermak*." *American Journal of Sociology* 68:375.

McClosky, H. 1958. "Conservatism and Personality." *American Political Science Review* 58:361–82.

———. 1967. "Personality and Attitude Correlates of Foreign Policy Orientations." In J. Rosenau, ed., *Domestic Sources of Foreign Policy*. New York: The Free Press.

McConahay, J. B. 1950. "Certain Personality Factors of State Legislators in South Carolina." *American Political Science Review* 44:897–903.

———. 1973. "Experimental Research." In J. Knutson, ed., *Handbook of Political Psychology*, 356–82. Washington, D.C.: Jossey-Bass.

McGraw, K. M., and N. Pinney. Forthcoming. "The Effects of General and Domain-Specific Expertise on Political Memory and Judgment." In *Social Cognition*.

Machotka, O. 1964. *The Unconscious in Social Relations*. New York: Philosophical Library.

McKean, K. 1985. "Decisions, Decisions, Decisions." *Discover* (June): 23–31.

McPhee, W. N. 1963. *Formal Theories of Mass Behavior*. New York: The Free Press.

———, and J. Ferguson. 1962. "Political Immunization." In McPhee and Glaser, eds., *Public Opinion and Congressional Elections*, 123–54. New York: The Free Press.

Marcus, G. E. 1988. "The Structure of Emotional Response: 1984 Presidential Candidates." *American Political Science Review* 82:737–62.

———, et al. 1989. "Reason and Passion in Political Life." Paper prepared for delivery at the Symposium on Democratic Theory, Williams College, Williamstown, Mass.

———, and W. Rahn. 1990. "Emotions and Democratic Politics." In S. Long, ed., *Research in Micropolitics*. New York: JAI Press.

Marvick, Elizabeth Wirth. 1981. "Favorites: A Recurrent Psychopolitical Role." Paper delivered at the annual meeting of the International Society for Political Psychology, Mannheim, West Germany.

———. 1986. *Louis XIII: The Making of a King*. New Haven: Yale University Press.

Milbrath, L. W. 1963. *Political Participation: How and Why Do People Get Involved in Politics?* Chicago: Rand McNally.

———. 1986. "Environmental Beliefs and Values." In M. G. Hermann, ed., *Political Psychology*, 97–138. San Francisco: Jossey-Bass.

Milgram, S. 1974. *Obedience to Authority: An Experimental View*. New York: Harper & Row.

Morgentau, H. 1973. *Politics among Nations: The Struggle for Power and Peace*. 5th ed. New York: Knopf.

Morton, L. 1964. "Review of Rogow's *James Forrestal*." In *American Historical Review* 69:1097.

Moses, R. 1985. "Empathy and Dis-Empathy in Political Conflict." *Political Psychology* 6(1):135–39.

Mumford, L. 1963. "The Revolt of the Demons." *The New Yorker* 23 (May 1963): 155–81.

Nie, N. H., S. Verba, and J. R. Petrocik. 1979. *The Changing American Voter*. Cambridge, Mass.: Harvard University Press.

Niemi, R. G. 1973. "Political Socialization." In J. Knutson, ed., *The Handbook of Political Psychology*, 117–38. San Francisco: Jossey-Bass.

Nisbett, R. E., and T. D. Wilson. 1977. "Telling More Than We Know: Verbal Reports on Mental Processes." *Psychological Review* 84, no. 3.

Noelle-Neuman, Elisabeth. 1986. *The Spiral of Silence: Public Opinion—Our Social Skin*. Chicago: University of Chicago Press.

Norikos, Eugenia V., and Robert C. North. 1976. *International Crisis: The Outbreak of World War I*. Montreal: McGill-Queens University Press.

Oliner, S. P., and P. M. Oliner. 1988. *The Altruistic Personality: Rescuers of Jews in Nazi Europe*. New York: The Free Press.

Organski, A. F. K. 1958. *World Politics*. New York: Knopf.

Osgood, C. E. 1962. *An Alternative to War or Surrender*. Urbana: University of Illinois Press.

———. 1969. "Calculated De-escalation as a Strategy." In D. G. Pruitt and J. Synder, eds., *Theory and Research on the Causes of War*. Englewood Cliffs, N.J.: Prentice-Hall.

Paige, G. D., ed. 1972. *Political Leadership: Readings for an Emerging Field*. New York: The Free Press.

Post, J. M. 1983. "Woodrow Wilson Re-examined: The Mind-Body Controversy Redux and Other Disputations." *Political Psychology* 4, no. 2.

Quattrone, G. A., and A. Tversky. 1988. "Contrasting Rational and Psychological Analyses of Political Choice." *American Political Science Review* 82, no. 3.

Rapoport, A. 1990. "The Problems with Gains Maximizing Strategies." In B. Glad, ed., *Psychological Dimensions of War*. Newbury Park, Calif: Sage Publications.

Rogow, A. A. 1963. *James Forrestal: A Study of Personality, Politics, and Policy*. New York: Macmillan.

———. 1968. "Review of V. Wolfenstein, *The Revolutionary Personality*." *American Political Science Review* 62:604–66.

Rokeach, M. 1960. *The Open and Closed Mind: Investigations into the Nature of Belief Systems and Personality Systems*. New York: Basic Books.

Rokkan, S., ed. 1964. "Review of Almond's and Verba's *The Civic Culture*." *American Political Science Review* 58 (September 1964): 676.

———. 1968. *Comparative Research Across Nations and Cultures*. The Hague: Mouton.

Sabia, D. 1988. "Rationality, Collective Action, and Karl Marx." *American Journal of Political Science* 32:50–71.

Sanford, N. 1973. "Authoritarian Personality in Contemporary Perspective." In J. Knutson, ed., *Handbook of Political Psychology*, 139–70. Washington, D.C.: Jossey-Bass.

Schuman, H., and S. Presser. 1977. "Public Opinion and Public Ignorance: The Fine Line between Attitude and Non-Attitude." *American Journal of Sociology* 85 (1977): 1214–25.

Sears, D. O., L. Huddy, and L. G. Schaffer. 1986. "A Schematic Variant of Symbolic Political Theory as Applied to Racial and Gender Equality." In R. R. Lau and D. O. Sears, eds., *Political Cognition: The 19th Annual Carnegie Symposium on Cognition*. Hillsdale, N.J.: Erlbaum.

Shibutani, T. 1955. "Review of Christie and Jahoda, eds., *Studies in the Scope and Method of "The Authoritarian Personality.*" *American Journal of Sociology* (1955): 92.

Shils, E. A., and M. Janowitz. 1948. "Cohesion and Disintegration in the Wehrmacht in World War Two." *Public Opinion Quarterly* 12(2):280–315.

Simon, H. A. 1957. *Administrative Behavior*. New York: The Free Press.

Snyder, G. H., and P. Diesing. 1977. *Conflict among Nations: Bargaining, Decision Making and System Structure in International Crisis*. Princeton, N.J.: Princeton University Press.

Sorrentino, R. M., and T. E. Higgins, eds. 1986. *Handbook of Motivation and Cognition: Foundations of Social Behavior*. New York: The Guilford Press.

Stanton, A. H., and S. E. Perry, eds. 1951. *Personality and Political Crisis*. Glencoe, Ill.:The Free Press.

Stein, H. F. 1986. "On Professional Allegiance in the Study of Political Psychology." *Political Psychology* 7(2):245–53.

Stevens, Jacqueline. 1989. "Empathy, the Self, and Politics." Paper delivered at the annual meeting of the American Political Science Association, Atlanta.

Stone, W. F. 1980. "The Myth of Left-Wing Authoritariansim." *Political Psychology* 2:3–20.

Stouffer, S. 1955. *Communism, Conformity, and Civil Liberties: A Cross-section of the Nation Speaks Its Mind*. Garden City, N.Y.: Doubleday.

———, A. A. Lumsdaine, M. H. Lumsdaine, R. M. Williams, Jr., M. B. Smith, I. L. Janis, S. A. Star, and Leonard S. Cottrell, Jr. 1949. *The American Soldier: Combat and Its Aftermath*. Vol. 2 of *Studies in Social Psychology in World War II*. Princeton, N.J.: Princeton University Press.

———, E. A. Suchman, L. C. De Vinney, S. A. Star, and R. M. Williams, Jr. 1949. *The American Soldier: Adjustment during Army Life*. Vol. 1 of *Studies in Social Psychology in World War II*. Princeton, N.J.: Princeton University Press.

———, et al. 1950. *Measurement and Prediction*. Vol. 4 of *Studies in Social Psychology in World War II*. Princeton, N.J.: Princeton University Press.

Stuart, D., and H. Starr. 1981–82. "The 'Inherent Bad Faith Model' Reconsidered: Dulles, Kennedy, and Kissinger." *Political Psychology* (Fall/Winter 1981–82): 1–32.

Sullivan, J. L., J. Pierson, and G. E. Marcus. 1982. *Political Tolerance and American Democracy*. Chicago: University of Chicago Press.

Synder, J. 1984. "Civil Military Relations and the Cult of the Offensive." *International Security* (Summer 1984): 108–46.

Tetlock, P. E. 1986. "A Value Pluralism Model of Ideological Reasoning." *Journal of Personality and Social Psychology* 50:819–27.

———, and C. McGuire. 1986. "Cognitive Perspectives on Foreign Policy." In R. White, ed., *Psychology and the Prevention of Nuclear War*. New York: New York University Press.

Tucker, Robert C. 1973. *Stalin as Revolutionary, 1879–1929: A Study in History and Personality*. New York: W. W. Norton.

———. 1987. *Political Culture and Leadership in Soviet Russia: From Lenin to Gorbachev*. New York: W. W. Norton.

Tversky, A., and D. Kahneman. 1981. "The Framing of Decisions and the Psychology of Choice." *Science* 221 (January 30, 1981): 453–58.

Volkan, V. D. 1988. *The Need to Have Enemies and Allies*. Northvale, N.J.: Jason Aronson.

Waite, R. 1990. "The Kaiser and the Führer." In B. Glad, ed., *Psychological Dimensions of War*. Newbury Park, Calif.: Sage Publications.

———. 1985. "Human Nature in Politics: The Dialogue of Psychology with Political Science." *American Political Science Review* 79(2):245–53.

Singer, J. D., and M. Small. 1968. "Alliance Aggression and the Onset of War, 1815–1945." In Singer, ed., *Quantitative International Politics: Insights and Evidence*, 247–86. New York: The Free Press.

———. 1972. *The Wages of War: 1816–1954: A Statistical Handbook*. New York: Wiley.

Smith, M. B. 1955. "Review of Stouffer's *Communism, Conformity, and Civil Liberties*." *American Sociological Review* 20 (December 1955): 750.

———. 1973. "Political Attitudes." In J. Knutson, ed., *Handbook of Political Psychology*. Washington, D.C.: Jossey-Bass.

———, J. Bruner, and R. White. 1956. *Opinions and Personality*. New York: Wiley.

Sniderman, P. M. 1975. *Personality and Democratic Politics*. Berkeley: University of California Press.

———, R. A. Brody, and J. H. Kuklinski. 1984. "Policy Reasoning in Political Issues: The Problem of Racial Equality." *American Journal of Political Science* 28:75–94.

———, and P. E. Tetlock. 1986. "Interrelationship of Political Ideology and Public Opinion." In M. G. Hermann, ed., *Political Psychology*, 62–96. San Francisco: Jossey-Bass.

Welch, D. A., and J. G. Blight. 1987–88. "The Eleventh Hour of the Cuban Missile Crisis: An Introduction to the ExComm Transcripts." *International Security* 12 (Winter 1987–88): 5–29.

Willner, R. A. 1984. *The Spellbinders: Charismatic Political Leadership*. New Haven: Yale University Press.

Wilson, G. D. 1973. *The Psychology of Conservatism*. Orlando, Fla.: Academic Press.

Wilson, J. Q. 1962. "Review of Gottfried's *Boss Cermak*." *American Journal of Sociology* 68:375.

Wolfenstein, E. V. 1967. *The Revolutionary Personality: Lenin, Trotsky, and Gandhi*. Princeton, N.J.: Princeton University Press.

———. 1969. *Personality and Politics*. Belmont, Calif.: Diskson.

Yinger, J. M. 1973. "Anomie, Alienation, and Political Behavior." In J. Knutson, ed., *Handbook of Political Psychology*, 171–202. Washington, D.C: Jossey-Bass.

7

Toward Cultural Theories of American Political Behavior: Religion, Ethnicity and Race, and Class Outlook

David C. Leege, Joel A. Lieske, and Kenneth D. Wald

INTRODUCTION

Our essay is based on the premise that culture counts. It argues that the field of voting behavior and American political behavior, generally, would be well served by research that includes sensitive cultural measures associated with the Columbia tradition of voting studies, alongside the attitudinal measures found so useful in the Michigan and Rochester schools. Our immediate objective is to recover a tradition first foreshadowed in the crude "index of political predisposition" of the 1940 study (Lazarsfeld, Berelson, and Gaudet 1944), better captured in the Social Processes section of the 1948 study (Berelson, Lazarsfeld, and McPhee 1954), nicely elaborated in the section on group-based political cognition in *The American Voter* (Campbell, Converse, Miller, and Stokes 1960, chaps. 12–17), and specifically focused on religion, ethnicity, and class life-style in the 1960 election (Converse 1966). If we do that effectively, we may move toward an alternate paradigm, a much more inclusive one, for understanding American political behavior.

The authors are listed alphabetically. They wish to thank the following panel members for their comments and evaluations: John C. Green, Richard Jensen, and Paul Kleppner.

What these early works have in common is a sensitivity to the role of cultural forces in providing identity and meaning, prescribing norms for responsible behavior, and establishing boundaries on legitimate institutional behavior (Dreitzel 1977; Wildavsky 1987). Empirically, cultural forces are indexed by religion, race, ethnic identification, class life-style, and other regional and subcultural attributes. Although not ignored in current voting studies, these factors have been assigned a peripheral role in understanding vote choice. The marginalization of group influences can be appreciated by examining the dominant paradigm that informs studies of voter decision-making.

This paradigm involves the "funnel of causality" argument elaborated in *The American Voter*. According to this metaphor, voting lies at the tip of a decisional funnel representing the convergence of factors that influence voter preferences. These include cultural values embedded in demographic characteristics such as race, ethnicity, religion, or region; social status characteristics such as class, occupation, and education; parental characteristics such as education, occupation, or partisanship; and finally, political attitudes toward the parties, candidates, and issues. What really matters are the durable effects of these personal and contextual variables on party identification. Party identification, in turn, affects and is affected by perceptions of candidates and issues, interest in the campaign, media use, and personal conversations. Productive research using this paradigm has enriched our understanding of political behavior from the mouth to the tip of the funnel.

As the assumptions, models, and estimating tools of economists entered the field of voting, first through Anthony Downs's influential *An Economic Theory of Democracy* (1957), and later through a host of works sired by the Rochester school, political scientists became increasingly attentive to models based on market assumptions and voter rationality, and on measures of economic well-being indexed by presidential approval ratings and personal net disposable income (Kramer 1971; Tufte 1978; Fiorina 1981). The influence of these approaches further intensified the belief that the action in voting research occurred near the tip of the funnel. Even journalists and pollsters now follow such work (Morin 1989), probably because it reduces a welter of confusing variables into something that makes practical sense to campaign organizations.

These models tend to assign an equilibrium term to the forces presumably operating near the mouth of the funnel—namely, the cultural factors that interest us here. If something were to happen, for example, that brought cultural forces directly to bear on a given election, the models would be of far less utility. The recent *Times-Mirror* study (Ornstein, Kohut, and McCarthy 1988) takes that possibility seriously and develops a typology of the electorate based on both cultural values and economic interests. While we do not yet know a great deal about the measurement properties of the typology, it does show some resonance with assumptions about both solid and swing voters and about the content and style of media appeals. Yet it is unusual among voting models precisely because it takes culture seriously.

We believe that most voting models adopt too short a time frame in seeking to understand the vote decision and accord too much influence to transient factors that operate at the tip of the funnel. More importantly, the dominant paradigm has given too little attention to the cultural forces that may shape the broad perceptions that voters bring with them to the campaign and that even affect their short-term calculations about the relative merits of candidates, parties, and economic issues. Along with Talcott Parsons (1959, 96), we contend that "the individual seems to vote, other things being equal, with the people whom he most directly feels to be his own kind, who are in social status and group memberships like, and hence like-minded with, himself. It may be said that the question is not so much on the level of psychological determination, for what he is voting, as it is with whom he has associated himself in voting."

To develop our argument: (1) we shall review a wide range of findings from comparative politics, American history, the sociology of religion, the measurement of ideology, and the study of racial/ethnic subcultures, all of which suggest a cultural agenda for expanding the understanding of voting and American political behavior; (2) we shall offer some theoretical considerations based on the notion that culture establishes identity, prescribes responsibility, and circumscribes boundaries, and that cultural values must be consulted to rationalize social structures and political hierarchies; and then we shall illustrate some areas of political behavior and political dynamics where a cultural interpretation would be beneficial; and (3) we shall discuss data needs and resources for reclaiming the cultural research tradition in voting and American political behavior.

SUGGESTIONS FROM RECENT RESEARCH

Once American political scientists began to collaborate with European scholars in comparative studies of voting behavior, they became increasingly aware of the significance of religion, ethnicity, language, and class culture (not class interest) as points of orientation for party mobilization and electoral choice. Initially this work was descriptive and involved statistical analyses across many nations (Rose and Urwin 1969; Lijphart 1979) or within a single country (Lijphart 1968). But in the effort to untangle the sequence of events that had made European polities so amenable to cultural differences, these scholars looked to the genesis of cleavages within national communities, and therefore to history (Lipset and Rokkan 1967, especially 33–50; Lipset 1964).

While *survey* scholars who confined their research to American voting behavior were slow to look at religion and other cultural factors, those who did *aggregate* analysis met a phalanx of historical studies that pointed to the politics, not of economic interests, but of religious and cultural differences (cf. Benson 1961; Silbey, Bogue, and Flanigan 1978; Hays 1980; McCormick 1986). Some American survey researchers were awakened to cultural interpretations emerging from the sociology of religion (cf. Lenski 1963;. Glock and Stark 1966). For example, in studying survey data on the American electorate from 1960 to 1968, Knoke (1974) discovered that religion had the largest net effect on party identification, followed by education, and then occupation and income. Further, Knoke found great variation among Protestant bodies. But it was not until the early 1980s, when Conover and Feldman (1981) revealed the symbolic and group-related referents of American liberalism and conservatism, and Carmines and Stimson (1980, 1982) demonstrated the renascence of the race issue, that survey researchers were forced to reconsider the reality of cultural influences on American voting. We shall now selectively review some of those milestones.

Religion and Other Cultural Forces in Cross-National Research

In one early study, Rose and Urwin (1969, 12) found that "religious divisions, not class are the main social basis of parties in the Western world today." Among eleven democracies, there were thirty-five credible (i.e., election-contesting) parties based on religion, thirty-three on class, and considerably smaller numbers based on urban-rural cleavages, regionalism, ethnic communalism, and language. Subsequent research has largely affirmed the primacy of culturally based electoral cleavages or their coincidence with socioeconomic divisions (Powell 1982).

Attempting to sort out hierarchies among the potential bases of electoral cleavage, Lijphart (1979) conducted an intensive study of voting patterns in four societies with multiple bases of stratification. He concluded that religion is the most potent basis of party alignment, followed by language/ethnicity, with social class no more than a subsidiary influence. Many scholars have been puzzled at these findings, because European societies are much less overtly religious and more culturally homogeneous than is the United States. Under such conditions one might have expected class divisions to be paramount.

Confronted with the staying power of cultural differences in a modern political world where economic interests were thought to predominate, political scientists could either plead American exceptionalism or consult historians to find out whether religious or other cultural differences are embedded in America's catch-all parties. Perhaps the fear of discovering nonbargainable conflicts rooted in cultural differences accounted for the preference for the former strategy. Had they consulted the historical record, students of voting would have learned that the United States is not immune to the tendencies toward cultural politics noted in cross-national research.

Religion and Other Cultural Forces in American History

Historical research also offers an impressive range of findings that bear on the enduring influence of religion and other cultural forces in American politics. Based on a review of this literature, Swierenga (1990, 146) contends that: "The most exciting development of American political history in the last twenty years is the recognition that religion is the key variable in voting behavior until at least the Great Depression. . . . By the 1970s this so-called ethnocultural (or ethnoreligious) interpretation of voting behavior had become the reigning orthodoxy, having supplanted the populist-progressive paradigm that 'economics explains the mostest,' to quote Charles Beard."

For years, historians had followed the lead of Charles Beard, James Bryce, and Frederick Jackson Turner in interpreting sectional rivalries and class conflicts as the stuff of American political history. But the early works of Benson (1961) and Hays (summary of works, 1980), and especially the recent quantitative works of Kleppner (1970, 1979), Jensen (1971), and Formisano (1971, 1983) have put economically oriented historians on the defensive. However, the ethnocultural historians do not deny that economic interests are important, asserting only that cultural preferences are more important. In Kleppner's (1982, 76) work, for example, religion is clearly important, but it is embedded in a network of socializing agents and contextual influences, including family, religion, education, and community.

The work of the quantitative historians, perhaps in design if not in substance, resonates with the political rhetoric of practicing politicians who argue that "all politics is local." For us, at a minimum, it suggests that political forces *both* before and after the Great Depression have registered the ebb and flow of diverse ethnocultural movements. Historically, these cultural conflicts can be seen in the Great Awakening; the abolition movement; the various forms of anti-Catholicism manifested in nativism, Prohibition, Progressive reforms to limit voting and the influence of big-city machines, the absence of child- or family-support policies, the arguments for nondenominational public schools; the doctrine of Manifest Destiny and American expansionism; the Social

Gospel and social Christianity; and the Ku Klux Klan. More recently, they can be seen in the civil rights movement; Theodore Sorenson's strategy for the Kennedys; the Peace Corps; the issues of abortion, school prayer, secular humanism, and nuclear disarmament; the growth of religious broadcasting networks; public controversies surrounding papal encyclicals and pastoral letters on social justice; anticommunist patriotism and "evil empire"; the absence early on of an AIDS policy; policies to stem the tide of new immigrants; protectionism targeted against Japanese (not English or German) imports and investments; and the ethnocultural appeals of both the Bush and Dukakis campaigns. Cultural politics is still a fixture on the American agenda, even in modern times.

Sociology of Religion: From Doctrine to Other Measures of Belief and Identity

To follow one strand of the historical studies, if "political choices were derived from beliefs about God, human nature, the family, and government" (Swierenga 1990, 150), where better to learn about such beliefs than in the sociology of religion literatures? Tocqueville, Weber, and Troeltsch all had characterized American Protestantism as a "doer's religion." Stressing right behavior in public, it often manifests itself in the moral crusades of American politics or as a basis for trust in a presumably self-regulating market. Its sect-type character, rooted in Calvinism, as opposed to a sacramental, otherworldly character, did not yield sharp dividing lines between religion and politics.

Early empirical studies by Glock and Stark (1965), Rokeach (1969), and others generally found relationships between "orthodox" doctrinal beliefs or the concern with salvation, and conservative political attitudes. Despite the measurement problems in such studies (cf. Wuthnow 1973), they document the propensity of those with articulated religious identities to make strict judgments about the behavior of others, an important consideration in any cultural theory of political activity or attitudes.

More recent studies have tried to capture religiosity in a variety of "more intense" ways, including foundational beliefs (Benson and Williams 1982; Leege and Welch, 1989; Leege 1989); imagery associated with God (Greeley 1984; Welch and Leege 1988); views of human nature (Wald and Lupfer 1985); self-identification with religious labels (Wilcox 1989); preferred devotional practices as extensions of beliefs (Welch and Leege 1988, 1991, for Catholics; Smidt 1984, 1989, for evangelicals, pentecostals, and fundamentalists; Kellstedt 1984); and even doctrinal cleavages within a single denomination (Turner and Guth 1989). Recent work has also suggested that denomination may capture a meaningful political reality if classification schemes are drawn with some sensitivity to religious tradition (Beatty and Walter 1984).

All of these studies show that the impact of religiosity on political attitudes and behavior depends on which aspect of religiosity is being measured. Further, the studies have often pointed to the heterogeneity of beliefs or devotional styles within the same denominational body, a problem not overlooked by Kleppner in his aggregate historical studies (see his discussion of the pietist-liturgical *continuum*, 1982, 186–88). Thus organized, religion may refer to (1) *ethnicity*, (2) a *religious style*, or a way of behaving publicly, (3) an *institution* with interests and motives for self-protection, or (4) a vehicle for political or social *mobilization* along moral or ethical lines.

Churches as Moral Communities and Agents of Political Mobilization

If a goodly share of politics is local, then perhaps a goodly share of religion belongs to local congregations, parishes, and religious communities. Moreover, as the 1948 voting study revealed, much local politics is really concerned with the political interaction of religious and other subcultural groups. Another insight drawn from the 1948 voting study (and the later communications study by Katz and Lazarsfeld 1955) is the important role that social context plays in structuring political conflict. Both results are derivative from cultural theory, since individual identity, norms for responsibility, and boundary evaluations are all socialized and mediated through social groups. But this is only a fragment of what we have learned from the politics of religion.

In addition, we are learning about the mechanisms that develop group consciousness and shared frames of reference linking religious beliefs to political action. Wald (1987, 24–27) argues that churches are quite likely to mingle in politics because of four key properties: (1) their creed; (2) their institutional composition as multipurpose agencies; (3) their composition as social groups with shared interactions, shared status (including stigma), and shared ways of life; and (4) their organizational capacity for mobilization.

We are also more confident that associational involvement in religious practices alone is of less political relevance than social identification with a reference community. Converse, for example, showed that church attendance explained less of the vote increment for Kennedy among Catholics than did identification with the Catholic community. Further, Converse found that where ethnic and religious identification reinforced each other—for example, in Irish Catholics rather than Italian or Polish Catholics—the support for Kennedy was further enhanced. Similarly, Fee (1976, 67) argued that "It is not the institutional, religiously devout Catholic who is a Democrat, but the social Catholic, the Catholic as an ethnic and as a minority member." Finally, Leege and Welch (1989) showed that party identification is a social structural variable among active Catholics rather than a creedal variable; it responds more to degree of ethnic assimilation and social class than to measures of religious belief or devotional life-style. Issue positions and ideology, on the other hand, are far more responsive to religious belief systems, political generations, and regional political climates.

In short, although religious communities do transmit political norms, the norms may come from different aspects of community life and thought. Although group identification may be more important for understanding political cues than group integration (see Conover 1984, 1985; Penning 1988), it remains unclear just what aspect of group identification—social community, perceived stigma, national versus local creedal attachment, or group membership—is sending the cues for each aspect of politics.

One recent study suggests that the transmission of political values may depend on the extent to which behavioral contagion operates in local churches (Wald, Owen, and Hill 1988). It shows that a congregational climate of theological conservatism is linked to political conservatism well beyond the linkage between the two within each individual member. Thus, in Durkheim's term, the congregation is a moral community, actively shaping values beyond those brought to congregations by individuals of similar social or psychological location.

This finding is of special relevance because, as Wald et al. point out, church congregations aggregated are the single largest bloc of voluntary organizations in the United States. Even if active participation is peripheral for a large number of members, the sheer numbers warrant political attention. However, the evidence suggests that religious commitment is not peripheral for a large proportion of the church members but constitutes a principal basis for social identity and a focal point for daily activity. Under such circumstances, the political capacity of religious congregations should not be underestimated.

For example, Leege (1988, 721–22, 728–33) has found that active, parish-connected Catholics are more willing to accord legitimacy to the social teachings of church leaders than are those who simply classify themselves as Catholics on national surveys. Leege and Gremillion (1986) have also found that consensus on both religious and social issues is higher among Catholics within the same parish than it is among Catholics with similar social characteristics in the national population. Thus, differences in the political views of American Catholics depend in part on the degree to which they defer to ecclesiastical authorities and the extent to which they interact within their local parishes.

Such findings are consistent with cultural interpretations of religious groups as "communities of memory" (Bellah, Marsden, Sullivan, Swidler, and Tipton 1985). In story theology, cultural identity, norms, and boundaries come from the retelling of local stories of triumph and tragedy, of vision and myopia, of dominance and persecution. The small-town German Catholic parish, for example, which switched its allegiance from the Democratic to the Republican banner because of shabby treatment by local Democratic officials who wanted to insure "patriotism" during World War I, leaves a legacy well beyond the lives of its members; the stories are told over and over "unto the third and fourth generation."

The role of local churches as agents of social and political mobilization has been demonstrated time and again in a wide variety of contexts and circumstances. The civil rights movement, perhaps the most impressive recent case of political self-assertion by a subordinate group, was centered in the mainstream churches of black America. In a meticulous reconstruction of the movement at the grass roots, Aldon Morris (1984) demonstrated how the churches provided the leadership, the networks of communication among elites and between elites and masses, the physical headquarters, the financial resources, planning, and coordination, and, no less important, the morale necessary to sustain a mass movement operating under extraordinarily adverse conditions.

Despite confident predictions that clerical leadership is an anachronism destined to recede with the incorporation of blacks into high-status occupations, the emerging black political elite remains strongly conditioned by the church, and the clergy retains a position of considerable political influence in the black community. The presidential candidacy of Jesse Jackson in both 1984 and 1988 was similarly rooted in black Christianity. Jackson's message, his rhetorical style, campaign organization, and fund-raising efforts all bore the strong imprint of the congregational milieu from which it emerged (Wald, forthcoming).

At the other end of the political spectrum, the political reawakening of conservative Protestantism in the 1970s was greatly facilitated by the access of conservative entrepreneurs to a ready-made network of congregations, parachurch organizations, ministerial associations, and religious broadcasting systems. These structures had emerged in the wake of a remarkable social transformation that brought traditionalist Protestants to urban areas and endowed them with sufficient resources to create impressive structures for worship, evangelism, social services, and charitable undertakings (Hunter 1987).

When threatened by outside forces, these same agencies could be turned to purposes of political countermobilization. Initially, the political reaction took the form of conservative opposition to the proposed Equal Rights Amendment, the teaching of evolution in public schools, and gay rights initiatives. All of these countermovements were tied into a supporting network of conservative church organization for funding, research, and expertise (Crawford 1980; Rainey 1981). When a funda- mentalist minister named Jerry Falwell attempted to harness social con- servatism as part of a larger right-wing alliance, he took advantage of ties to fellow ministers through an organization linking what were nom- inally independent Baptist congregations (Liebman 1983). Indeed, the leadership of the Moral Majority bore a striking resemblance to the mailing list of the Baptist Bible Fellowship.

Finally, it should be noted that the antiabortion movement, which developed following the *Roe v. Wade* decision in 1972, was formed from a nucleus of Catholic activists with a parish base. Because the pre- cise role of the Catholic church is currently the subject of litigation, it is important to stress that opposition to abortion was by no means the exclusive preserve of the church and that its precise role remains a mat- ter of dispute. Nonetheless, the church proved to be a critical element in the campaign to undo, by various means, what the Supreme Court had allowed in its decision. It has increasingly been joined in this effort by evangelical churches, which sponsor their own antiabortion efforts. It appears that church-based opposition to abortion, in particular, and feminism, in general, may be rooted in cultural images of female depen- dency, subordination, and confinement to the private sphere (Himmel- stein 1986, 10). To the extent that churches grant legitimacy to such sentiments, they also grant access to entrepreneurs who wish to recruit mass support for political organizations.

Religious Rite, Identity, and Political Ritual

The stories of "the particular" are not the sole techniques for identity development and value transmission. Rite and ritual are powerful com- munity builders. Searle and Leege (1986) and Raftery and Leege (1989) show that Catholic parishes that fail to celebrate inclusive, participatory liturgies are plagued by the lack of a sense of community and offer inef- fective catechetical programs. It is unclear which precedes which, but their conjoint presence or absence suggests that rites and ritual are forms of rehearsing community identity—that is, telling people who they are and what they ought to do. The hymn may be as powerful a medium of value transmission as is the sermon (Clark 1989). Certainly, "Onward Christian Soldiers" lent itself well not only to the revivalists but to the social reformers who were ushering in the Kingdom of God on earth during the Progressive period (for a description of the religious rationale for political reform, see Handy 1990).

These techniques for celebrating religious community may have di- rect application to the political campaign. In a fascinating reconstruc- tion of campaign styles in American political history, Jensen (1971) has argued that the revivalist tradition supplied the motif for campaign techniques at various points in the nineteenth century. Rather than regarding such enthusiasm as a quaint historical curiosity, it is worth noting that at least two candidates adopted it as recently as 1988. Jesse Jackson and Pat Robertson, Baptist ministers seeking the Democratic and Republican nominations, respectively, utilized biblical images and idioms in their quests (Wald, forthcoming). Jackson's rhetoric was replete with characterizations of his campaign as a crusade, his leadership role as Moses, and the goal as no less than the redemption of the United States. Constrained by popular doubts as to the political suitability of a former television evangelist, Robertson attempted to escape his roots in the world of pentecostalism. Nevertheless, his followers frequently converted campaign rallies into occasions for charismatic fervor.

Political Ideology: From Economic Orientations to Group Judgments

The singularly most significant piece for understanding the joint impact of cultural values and economic interests on voters' attitudes is a study of political ideology conducted by Conover and Feldman (1981). Recalling a substantial body of literature, the authors discuss the limited utility of measuring political ideology either as "level of conceptualization" or as "issue constraint." Working in particular with a self-identified measure of liberalism-conservatism, which is usually referenced with discussions of economic policy, and looking for consistent issue positions among a variety of governmental economic interventions, Conover and Feldman find instead that "liberal" and "conservative" are more likely to refer to positive or negative judgments toward groups. The strongest predictors of the symbolic meaning of "liberals" are change-oriented groups and only secondarily, economic issues. For the symbolic meaning of "conservatives," the group "capitalists" predicts well, but orientations toward social change and race are also in the picture.

One is again struck by the current (post-Depression) timeliness of Kleppner's observation (1979, 371), based on nineteenth-century historical data: "Attachments to ethnoreligious groups were relatively more important as determinants of nineteenth-century social group cohesiveness and party oppositions than were economic attributes or social status." Thus, even in the measurement of ideology, which in the post-Marx, -Beard, or -Turner worlds was to have had economic frames of reference, social groups—sometimes religious, sometimes life-style, sometimes racial—are likely to appear alongside economic concerns (see also Miller, Hildreth, and Wlezien 1988).

Even some degree of predictability on issue positions is estimated

from group labels. Brady and Sniderman (1985) coin the term "likabil-
ity heuristic" to describe this process. Because citizens have positive and
negative feelings toward political groups, they often attribute issue positions to members of the group without knowing precisely where either
the individual member or the group leadership actually stands on the
issue. The heuristic depends, first, on the individual's own position on
the issue and, second, on the individual's "feelings toward the pair of
opposing groups whose issue positions" are being estimated (1075). It
operates successfully, because in politics citizens tend to think in oppo-
sites—liberals versus conservatives, blacks versus whites, and so on. In
short, issue calculations are rooted in "us vs. them" cultural identities,
that is, in the boundary-maintaining function of cultural values.

To know a group in this shorthand is to know whose views you
approve or disapprove. Ideology becomes comprehensible, not as a set
of logically connected mental constructs or as a set of consistent issue
positions across the domestic policy spectrum, but as a way of drawing
lines between the views of people like "us" and people who are not like
"us."

Campaign Politics and Cultural Symbols

The popular press and scholars who comment for literate laypersons are
quite cognizant that both cultural values and economic interests are
central concerns of the American electorate. As mentioned previously,
the *Times-Mirror* study has built several measures of religious, racial,
and life-style values into its basic typology of the electorate and has
generated proximity ratings to several culturally symbolic groups and
individuals. Its November 1988 postelection report assessed the
relationship among campaign themes, the values held by typology
groups, and voter preferences. Campaign themes with patriotic, racial,
or life-style overtones were linked negatively to the term "liberal" and
resonated especially among swing sectors of the electorate (*Times-
Mirror*, November 1988, 22–42).

Political scientist-commentator William Schneider, in both his preelection and postelection articles for *The Atlantic*, has given wide lati-
tude to the value-based advantage that Republicans currently have over
Democrats. In the preelection piece, Schneider argued that recent history favored the Republican presidential candidates, not only because of
the change in demographics from city to suburb and Rust Belt to Sunbelt, or because of the electoral college phalanx of the South and the
West, but also because the Democratic party is perceived to be "ideologically extreme" (Schneider 1988). "Ideology" is referenced not simply
by government spending issues, but by who are the beneficiaries of
spending and symbolic policy legitimation: blacks, radical feminists,

the liberal media establishment, secular humanists, abortionists, and so on. In short, ideology is culturally defined.

In his postelection piece, Schneider focused attention on "the class of '74," the Watergate babies and those who were "Kennedy's children" (Schneider 1989), one of whom is Michael Dukakis. Their problem, in a nutshell, is that they are technocrats who, instead of cultivating value bases, thought that what the people wanted was competence in government. They have narrowed economic policy differences between neo-liberals and conservatives, but have abdicated racial, religious, and foreign-policy conservatism to the Republicans. As Schneider concluded: "In the past the Democrats offered protection against economic adversity to those who felt threatened or insecure. That they do so now is unclear. Meanwhile, the Republicans are offering strong defense, a tough stand on crime, traditional religion, and old-fashioned morality —what George Bush calls 'those values.' And low taxes besides" (57).

Scholars who also serve as publicists have pointed to some of the black-hats of contemporary cultural politics. A favorite target is an unrepresentative, secularized media elite (Lichter, Rothman, and Lichter 1986). In reaction, traditionalist counterelites use all of the techniques of contemporary society to mobilize their adherents (Hunter 1987). The result is a political war over cultural values.

Rather than constituting a uniquely American phenomenon, this conflict seems to be part of an emerging cleavage that has been noted in other advanced industrial societies. The most prominent expression of this thesis, Inglehart's 1971 work on postmaterialism, asserts that the relative affluence enjoyed by the post–World War II cohort has created a sizable new electoral bloc that approaches politics in terms of life-style concerns rather than economic security. This has generated a new cleavage between the traditionalists who remain attached to conventional values and the postmaterialists who embrace cultural relativism. Several commentators regard this dimension as the most potent explanation for the rise of cultural appeals in recent American politics (Ladd 1978; Shafer 1985; White 1988).

Subcultural Continuities and the Local Bases for Party Identification

Subcultural studies of the American electorate suggest that the bases for party identification are often local, and that both continuity and re-alignment in party identification are best understood by following the electoral history of subcultural groups operating within specific regions and locales. It has never been clear whether the respondent's frame of reference for the seven-point SRC/CPS measure of party identification is national, state, or local. Finkel and Scarrow (1985, 621) have demonstrated persuasively, however, that "party enrollment systems affect the way that some voters perceive of the nature of partisanship or at least the way they respond to the party identification question." And since these systems differ in the fifty states, and even in locales, it is quite simple for "national Democrats" to differ from Southern "States' Rights Democrats," or for individualistic "Sunbelt Republicans" to differ from communalistic "Frostbelt (i.e. Main Street) Republicans." Both Matthews and Prothro (1966) and Kolbe (1975) have shown decisively how party image and the local bases of partisan support differ widely from national images.

Although socialization theories of electoral realignment (cf. Beck 1979) point to the parties' responses to traumatic national events such as war or the Depression as the sources of realignment, historical studies of subcultural groups show that "critical" elections are happening with considerable regularity and that there is considerable fluidity hidden beneath "normal" national elections (Kleppner 1970; Kelley 1979). Flinn (1988) has argued that German-Americans gravitated into the Republican party, not during the critical elections of 1896 or 1932, but during the early decades of the twentieth century. Was this assimilation or a response to American entry into World War I? Erikson, Luttbeg, and Tedin (1988, 96) note that the New Deal realignment actually came in two separate stages, an urban-rural realignment in the 1920s over the Prohibition issue, and a class-based realignment in the 1930s over the role of the federal government in regulating the economy. Since the election of 1964, a debate has been raging over whether the American party system is undergoing another partisan realignment or whether it is nothing more than dealignment (compare Abramson, Aldrich, and Rohde 1985, with Carmines and Stimson 1989). While popular commentators would say the realignment came in 1980 with the Reagan revolution on the economy and government intervention, Carmines and Stimson locate one leg of the realignment in the mid-1960s on race, and Kellstedt (1989) places another in the early 1980s on social (moral) issues. Both, of course, involve cultural politics rather than the perpetuation of the New Deal economic agenda.

The impact of local cultural differences on both party loyalty and presidential choice may be seen clearly from two recent studies (Lieske 1988a, 1988b). Analyzing aggregate data for all three thousand U.S. counties, and addressing the relative effects of racial-ethnic ancestry, religious affiliation, socioeconomic structure, and regional culture (cf. Elazar 1970; Gastil 1975; and Garreau 1981), Lieske shows that (1) cultural and regional predictors account for most of the variation in party registration, and (2) an integrated cultural model, rather than a socioeconomic one, is more helpful in explaining variations in the presidential vote. Utilizing the Elazar classification of regional political cultures—a classification deeply rooted in the alternate worldviews of religious organizations—Lovrich, Daynes, and Ginger (1980) successfully predict the outcome of selected state referenda in Indiana. Thus, regardless of the political concern—continuity or change in party identification, candidate preference, or issues—subcultural differences remain apparent in the United States, and cultural models of politics appear more tractable than models indexing economic interests.

Race in American Politics

Few would dispute the profound influence of race in American history or the continuing legacy of racial divisions in American society (Myrdal 1944). As countless scholars have noted, racial divisions are paramount to understanding the partisan allegiances and candidate preferences of American voters. In the 1984 presidential election, for example, only 9 percent of all black voters reported casting a vote for Ronald Reagan (Erikson, Luttbeg, and Tedin 1988, 181). The overwhelming majority of black voters, of course, are registered Democrats, in part because of the long-term reversal in their party sympathies since the Great Depression, and in part because of their effective exclusion by dominant white groups in the Republican party today. From the Civil War until the New Deal era, it was natural for blacks to vote Republican because the GOP was the party of Lincoln and emancipation. But beginning with Franklin Roosevelt's presidency, the national Democratic party has clearly demonstrated a greater sympathy toward American blacks, first in regard to their economic condition, and then later in rectifying the systematic denial of their civil rights and liberties. However, the event that probably had the greatest impact in solidifying black support for the Democratic party was Lyndon Johnson's strong support of the 1964 Civil Rights Act and Barry Goldwater's equally vociferous opposition to it. This movement into the Democratic fold appears to have been further consolidated by the growing successes of the Republican party in pursuing a "Southern Strategy" in national and state politics (Phillips 1969).

But the real importance of race in American politics lies in its potential as a crystallizing issue for partisan realignment (Burnham 1970). The stage for Democratic dominance of the post-Depression Fifth party system was set when Roosevelt put together a grand coalition of all major "have-not" groups in American politics: white southerners, white ethnics, labor, liberals, and racial minorities. But the common ground they shared on most economic and social welfare issues has proven to be illusory when such race-related issues as desegregation, busing, and affirmative action are injected into the national agenda. These race-related issues, as well as the newly emergent "social" issues, appear to be driving cultural wedges between white southerners, white ethnics, and labor (largely white), on the one hand, and liberals and racial minorities, on the other. Since World War II there has been only one presidential election in which the Democratic candidate has been able to win a majority of the white vote (Erikson et al. 1988, 182). Conversely, though black voters will occasionally vote for Republican candidates who are more liberal on civil rights in state and local elections, the major determinant of voting for black (and white) voters in most local elections appears to be the racial background of the candidates themselves (Lieske and Hillard 1984).

Race has been such a critical factor in modern elections that several authors have found pronounced changes in the racial images of the two parties. These, in turn, appear to be linked not only to the civil rights voting records of Republican and Democratic members of Congress, but also to partisan racial attitudes in the electorate (Carmines, Renten, and Stimson 1984). In addition, Carmines and Stimson (1982) show that racial issues are also central to reported increases in the structuring of mass belief systems and in the changing connotations of "liberalism" and "conservatism." Moreover, the politics of racial polarization were being played out at the state and local levels throughout the 1960s and 1970s over such race-related issues as urban riots, urban crime, busing, and welfare.

In their analysis of the dramatic racial restructuring of American national politics during the past twenty-five years, Carmines and Stimson (1984, 1989) suggest that the electoral impact of racial concern derives from the ease with which voters can utilize racial schema in making electoral choices. Political scientists have normally searched for evidence of issue-based voting on public policies that demand considerable knowledge, interest, and information, and hence require more effort than most voters can muster. By contrast, racial voting is rooted in long-standing cultural identifications and social preferences that operate at the "gut" or visceral level. Requiring less political knowledge or effort, race has considerable potential as a source of issue-based voting. The qualities possessed by race and what Carmines and Stimson define as "easy" issues for voters—(1) "symbolic rather than technical," (2) "more likely (to) deal with policy ends than means," and (3) "long on the political agenda"—are the same traits we associate with cultural issues and identifications.

Class as a Cultural Variable

Although social class is often posed as an alternative basis of stratification to ethnic and religious conflict, it too can be understood as a form of cultural politics. The predominant treatment of class position as a function of economic interest has yielded only modest associations with many forms of political behavior (Hamilton 1972). Class has exhibited the greatest political potency when conceptualized as an all-encompassing style of life with its own symbols, institutions, and norms—its own culture, in other words. Marxists have long argued that class takes on analytical utility only when it is approached from such a perspective, a position that has gained increasing adherence among other researchers. These insights are supported by research demonstrating that political cohesiveness among economic groups is correlated with spatial concentration, organizational encapsulation, intense social interaction, and other variables that promote a perception of common fate (Hechter 1978; Huckfeldt 1986; Kahan et. al. 1966; Wald 1982). Only when it attains sufficient intensity to infuse perspectives—the status of a culture—does class identity seem capable of unifying individuals who share a common economic function or status but differ on other salient dimensions of social identity.

To extend the point, we would even suggest that seemingly narrow economic issues may themselves be culturally determined. While little research has apparently been conducted on this topic, it seems that certain economic issues may take on symbolic significance because of their relationship to widely held social values. For example, in considering a 1978 ballot proposition that would drastically reduce funding for public services, most California voters did not approach the issue with a substantial store of information or considered judgments rooted in broad ideological preferences. Rather than be guided by immediate calculations of self-interest, many voters tapped into preexisting images about the presumed beneficiaries of government spending. The authors of an intensive study of public opinion found that specifically racial attitudes were central determinants of support for the tax revolt (Sears and Citrin 1982, 169). Such cognitive ties between economic policy and social values may be the result of mobilization efforts by elites: the Reagan administration attempted to rally conservative support for its tax reform proposals by emphasizing that elimination of selected tax preferences would produce rate reductions that would encourage large families with traditional sex-role distinctions.

The point of this review is not to insist that class lacks social reality, but rather to recognize that economic differences achieve political relevance through the same process of cultural formation that characterizes religious groups, ethnic communities, races, and other social collectivities. Under these circumstances, the presence of class-based politics does not invalidate cultural interpretations and may even add evidence to the claim.

THE FUTURE OF MULTICULTURAL POLITICS

The preceding review of a wide range of literature serves as a warrant for continuing cultural analysis of American political behavior. That enterprise is sustained by the critical assumption that modernity (or postmodernity or whatever label is selected to represent the current social system) has not produced social homogeneity or diminished the significance of cultural communities. Far from losing its traditional mix of cultures, recent demographic studies show that the United States is becoming an increasingly diverse, multicultural society composed of racial, ethnic, religious, regional, and class subcultures. These group differences will provide a basis for cultural politics well into the future.

Racial and ethnic diversity—and the group consciousness that accompanies it—has accelerated rapidly in recent years. As recently as 1960, the United States was 88.6 percent white, 10.5 percent black, and less than 1 percent Asian and other. It was a sign of the times that the 1960 census did not distinguish Hispanics as a separate category. By 1985, the predominant population group, white Anglos, had dropped in population share by 10 percent, while blacks increased to 12 percent, Hispanics constituted 7 percent, and the residual category of Asians and others grew to 2.7 percent. By the year 2000, according to Census Bureau projections, whites will constitute less than 74 percent of the population, with blacks, Hispanics, and Asian/other at 13 percent, 9 percent, and almost 4 percent, respectively (Frolik 1988). These changes are attributable both to natural processes like differential childbearing rates and to governmental action. The 1985 immigration amendments, which overturned national origin quotas that favored large Western European nations, opened the portals to Third World nations. In fairly short order, the majority of legal immigrants originated from nations like Mexico, the Philippines, Korea, China, Vietnam, India, Jamaica, the Dominican Republic, and Cuba. Such patterns of immigration reinforce cultural heterogeneity by providing an infusion of new residents with traditions quite dissimilar to the now prevailing patterns (Fellows 1983).

Nor should it be assumed that the largest population group is immune to the pull of ethnic loyalties. In 1980, the United States Census Bureau also included a question on ethnic ancestry: "In addition to being American, what do you consider your main ethnic group or nationality group?" Based on responses to this question, Americans classified themselves into the following ancestral groups: (1) British (22.4 percent); (2) German (22.3 percent); (3) Irish (17.7 percent); (4) French (5.7 percent); (5) Italian (5.4 percent); (6) Slavic (3.8 percent); (7) Scandinavian (1.1 percent); (8) Russian (0.6 percent); (9) Hungarian (0.3 percent); (10) Portuguese (0.3 percent); (11) Greek (0.3 percent);

and (12) Other (19.4 percent). The classifications include both single and multiple ancestry figures. Over 118 million Americans (52.3 percent) classified themselves in a single ancestry group; some 69 million more (30.8 percent) designated a multiple ancestry group. Thus, of the 226 million Americans surveyed in the 1980 census, a surprising 83.1 percent identified with a nationality of origin in addition to being an American.

Contrary to the suppositions of some sociologists and futurists, religion continues to play a vital role in the life of the nation. Relative to other advanced industrial democracies, the United States stands out in the high proportion (58 percent versus middle teens to middle thirties for other countries) of its citizens who say that religion is still "very important" to them (Erikson, Luttbeg, and Tedin 1988). It also stands out in the high proportion of Americans who claim church membership (51 percent) and the large number of church denominations (some 111) to which they belong (Wald 1987; Glenmary Research Center 1982). The most recent estimate suggests that the American landscape is dotted by 294 thousand distinct congregations at the local level (Independent Sector 1988).

The complexity of the American religious landscape is evident from the lack of any majority faith beyond the heterogeneous Christian label. A 1980 survey based on church records revealed that the vast majority of church members were apportioned among fifteen major religious traditions, with only one grouping—Roman Catholics—claiming more than 10 percent of the population (Glenmary Research Center 1982). The process of religious group formation has further differentiated the religious community, as mergers among established denominations are offset by the rapid creation of new traditions and the extraordinary growth of smaller churches and sects (Kelley 1977; Stark and Bainbridge 1985). Although it has not yet progressed to the point that the mainline has become the sideline, the dynamism of the religious situation makes that outcome a distinct possibility.

Economic diversity, yet another pole of group identity in the modern world, continues to reign. Far from simplifying the class structure into two competing aggregates of workers and owners, as Marx is supposed to have predicted, advanced economic development seems instead to generate a variety of economic groups and occupational categories with distinctive interests and outlooks. The complexity of the contemporary class structure is evident from the plethora of stratification schemes devised by students of society. At a minimum, researchers have identified sectoral economic cleavages based on production, distribution, social organization, consumption, and labor-market segmentation. The persistence of multiple lines of cleavage within each of these broad sectors is illustrated by continuing disagreement among scholars about whether the principal divisions within the production sphere are based on ownership (the classic Marxist view) or on control and authority positions (Dahrendorf 1959). Even if some consensus should be obtained on how to distinguish one class from another, scholars continue to debate the relative weight that should be given to subjective consciousness versus objective structure in delineating class position.

These economic divisions have become intertwined with other dimensions of stratification, culminating in the increasing geographic segmentation of the American population by life-style choices. Utilizing a mixture of census and survey data, market researchers have identified forty basic types of neighborhoods that are inhabited by persons possessing common physical, economic, and social resources (Robbins 1989). The clusters are defined by measures of education and affluence, housing and urbanization, ethnic composition, mobility patterns, and stages of family life-cycle. Used primarily as a marketing tool, the neighborhood profiles nonetheless demarcate genuine communities with distinct boundaries, values, consumer habits, and political beliefs (Weiss 1988, xii). Such environments are fertile ground for the germination of cultural identities that may acquire relevance for political choice.

There are, in sum, multiple bases of group identity in contemporary American society and every indication that cultural pluralism will continue to withstand the homogenizing influences of mass society. If so, it behooves political scientists to take note of cultural values in the voting process. This suggests a need to return to the mouth of the funnel of causality to examine the social and cultural roots of political preferences. How would such an inquiry proceed? How would it relate to extant theories of political behavior? These are the subjects of the next section.

THEORIES OF AMERICAN POLITICAL BEHAVIOR

In the voting literature, it is possible to distinguish three competing models of electoral choice—the sociological, the psychological, and the economic. These three models are associated, respectively, with the Columbia, Michigan, and Rochester traditions. The Columbia school, the first to emerge in voting research, advanced a model that emphasized the primacy of group memberships (primary groups, larger interactive groups, and community residence) in electoral choice. The crucial elements in their theory—religion, occupational status, and residence—were combined in an index of political predisposition that predicted the eventual choices of voters with a high degree of accuracy. Finding little in the way of direct media effects in the 1940 presidential election for a panel sample of voters in Erie County, Ohio, the Columbia researchers concluded (1) that voters were brand buyers, i.e., bought by the party label; and (2) that voters' party preferences were largely fixed in the social structure (though it can be argued that at least two of their variables, religion and place of residence, were actually surrogates for cultural values).

The Michigan approach is known principally for positing party identification as the crucial mediating influence on voter choice, and it partakes to some degree of both the sociological and later economic models. Like the former, it emphasizes the contribution of social structure in the formation of political identity. It also resembles the economic model in its concern with the influence of short-term forces like candidates and issues. But the overriding emphasis of this model is on the stability and durability of party identification. Since voters are generally lacking in their knowledge and conceptualization of American politics, most must rely on the party loyalties they inherited from parents. And although group memberships are provided in the model, it is assumed they are largely rooted in calculations of economic self-interest. Finally, since the model is basically descriptive, and designed more to explain "normal" voting patterns, it is forced to rely on Burnham's 1970 theory of critical elections to supply the missing links of electoral change. Unfortunately, the integrated model can only describe or account for these changes in a post hoc fashion. And with the electorate's growing independence of the two major parties, the party identification model has become increasingly ineffective in explaining new patterns in presidential politics.

The Rochester school is known as the "public choice" approach to voting behavior. This approach assumes that voters employ a cost-benefit calculus and choose candidates who maximize their economic utility. Political preferences are generally treated as exogenous variables—that is, as given—and are conceived in terms of economic self-interest rather than values. This approach seems to hold the greatest promise for explaining short-term changes in political partisanship and presidential voting that can be linked to the performance of candidates and parties (Fiorina 1981). However, the model presumes a level of voter rationality and grasp of information that cannot be supported by decades of research on the American voter. In addition, it unrealistically assumes an electorate that is fundamentally atomized. Research, however, has demonstrated how voters are located in social networks (Huckfeldt and Sprague 1987, 1988).

As suggested by the typology in figure 1, we perceive the cultural approach as both an alternative to and an extension of traditional voter models. Voting models can be distinguished, first, by whether the source of political identity for citizens is the individual or the group. As we suggested previously, the Rochester and Columbia models begin

Figure 1
Typology of Voter Models

Source of Identity	Basis of Action	
	Interests	Values
Individual	Rochester	Columbia
Group	Michigan	Cultural

with the individual, while the Michigan tradition posits the voter primarily as a group member. The second dimension of voting theories encompasses the bases of action in either interests or values. We understand the Rochester and Michigan traditions to emphasize the former, while the Columbia approach stresses cultural norms. Thus conceived, a cultural approach shares with the Columbia tradition a sense that many voters are embedded in tightly bound subcommunities that help provide standards of political evaluation. Like the Michigan model, it contends that partisan preferences are relatively stable and enduring. Although the cultural approach appears to have the least in common with the Rochester model, it allows for the mediating influence of economic and social factors.

How is it that voters come to attach political meaning to cultural identity? How does culture change? How are new cultural groups created? While we cannot yet offer a comprehensive theory of culturally based politics, we can suggest some forces that drive such a process. Specifically, we offer some theoretical fragments that indicate how and why cultural values and groups become relevant to political competition.

Why Culture as a Political Force? Toward Theory

Definitions of culture have generally referred to the patterning of ideas, values, other symbols, and ways of doing things. Culture orders a way of life. Culture is social; it is created and transmitted by social groups. This definition captures the inherently abstract nature of culture (ideas, values, symbols) and reflects the scholarly consensus that culture is necessary to provide order, coherence, and stability to human collectivities (Geertz 1973). But it begs at least three important questions that bear on the political salience of culture: (1) What are the functions of political culture in modern societies? (2) Where do cultural identifications come from? and (3) How are cultural norms transmitted?

First, anthropological studies suggest that historically the primary function of cultures has been a civilizing one. According to this view, culture is a social creation designed to overcome the risks and uncertainties of nature (Douglas and Wildavsky 1983). In effect, a particular culture represents the differential adaptation of a group of people to their environment. As Lee Benson (1979, 189) argues, human life is a struggle to create a better world—"a world in which human beings realize their innate need and capacity to live in cooperative harmony with each other and with Nature and to function as free, creative, self-actualizing, communal individuals." Cultures, then, are ways of life that are created to satisfy human needs and provide individuals with the capacity to survive in a hostile world. Cultures allow adaptations to and transcendence of biological limitations.

The extent to which various cultures achieve the civilizing objective, however, depends on how well they perform three critical social functions: (1) provide individuals with a sense of identity and meaning (the "meaning" function); (2) establish norms for behavior (the "responsibility" function); and (3) institutionalize standards of social legitimacy (the "boundary maintenance" function). According to this view (Wildavsky 1987), each political culture represents a distinct "way of life" and system of shared values that legitimates a preferred set of social relationships. Conceptually, this approach is based on the idea that many of our most basic social and political preferences, including partisanship, are culturally derived.

Thus, cultural theory offers an expanded paradigm for understanding political behavior. The concerns addressed by such modern theorists as Lasswell, Easton, and Dahl have tended to focus on macrostructures. For them, the crucial questions in American politics are "Who gets what, where, when, how, and why?"; "How does the political system authoritatively allocate values?"; and "Who governs—a monolithic power elite or a pluralist elite?" A cultural theory builds up the macrosystem by raising the microquestions in the context of macroconcerns. It asks: (1) Who am I? (2) How should I behave? and (3) What is legitimate? (Dreitzel 1977; Wildavsky 1987). By helping individuals to locate their identity in a complex social matrix, culture provides a meaning to existence that may well take on political relevance. By establishing accepted social norms, culture guides individuals in the kinds of political behavior appropriate to members of a particular collectivity. Finally, when it supplies standards of social legitimacy, culture delimits the scope of individual choice, cements attachment to the group, and excludes unacceptable ways of life derived from other cultures. The boundary-maintenance function of culture thus helps to define the contours of political conflict in any given society.

Second, cultural theorists have located the sources of cultural identifications in the tribal divisions of society. According to such theory, cultural identifications are shaped, carried, and transmitted primarily by racial-ethnic and religious groups, and only secondarily by social classes (Elazar 1972, 1984; Banfield 1974). In the literature of political science, political culture has been treated both as a property of large groups such as the nation-state (Ladd 1978) and of smaller subcultural aggregates such as the various ethnic and racial groups that comprise a nation-state. The former approach, tracing to the national character tradition in comparative political studies, has focused on macrocultural regularities that operate at the level of national political systems (Almond and Verba 1963; Merelman 1984; Inglehart 1988). The second approach, which grew out of historical studies of American politics and comparative studies of state and local politics, has attempted to underscore the more subtle, yet at the same time more divisive, distinctions among different racial, ethnic, religious, and regional communities.

Finally, cultural theory argues that cultural norms are not innate but learned. That is, cultural norms are transmitted in a process that may be explicit and intentional, as in indoctrination, or implicit and accidental, as in learning by example (Bettelheim 1987). Describing the transmission of cultural traits as a process of socialization reflects the sense that the inculcation of social values and norms brings the learner into the community in a way that simply sharing ascriptive traits could not accomplish. The agents of cultural transmission range widely from primary groups, such as the family, to secondary and tertiary associations, such as the church, the school, the workplace, and the mass media. Recently, we have come to understand that such learning is lifelong and that socialization occurs at any age.

In political systems, cultural values rationalize the inherent inequalities of ruler-ruled relationships. Lasswell and Kaplan (1950, 72ff.) have offered illuminating discussions of four values of deference—power, respect, rectitude, and affection—and four welfare values—well-being, wealth, skill, and enlightenment—around which political systems have historically organized their cultural symbols. The terms of political discourse differ with the value around which rulership is organized. For example, where rectitude matters, the language of righteousness, appraisals of moral virtue, and the science of social ethics lace political discourse. Where wealth matters, on the other hand, the mechanisms of markets, the instruments of production and objectives of consumption, and the science of economics are paramount. It is difficult to mix the political discourse of alternate cultural systems. Thus, for "enterprisers" in the *Times-Mirror* typology (Ornstein et al., 1988), the criterion of rectitude in a president, so central to the "moralists," is an amusing, if not irrelevant, cultural artifact of another world. Who cares whether the candidate talks with God if he does not know how to meet a payroll? One of the ironies of the 1988 primary season was the Reverend Pat Robertson's addressing Main Street Republicans as a small businessman who had shown successful entrepreneurial talents rather than as a television evangelist. Thus he recognized the two dominant cultures of the Republican party.

If cultural theory is to be used more widely in studies of American political behavior, scholars must pay more attention to (1) the formation of subcultural communities, and (2) the processes by which subcultural communal identities take on political relevance. We shall not consciously address the former here but shall offer two applications of cultural theory to the latter, and in so doing, move cultural theory from static to dynamic analysis.

From Statics to Dynamics: Cultural Linkages and the Conditions of Influence

Assuming that subcultural differences are the lifeblood of American politics, how are the cultural preferences of Americans at the grass-roots level translated into political behavior at the state and national levels? The answer, we believe, is provided by the cultural images that are projected by political issues, candidates, interest groups, and parties. But if political behavior is fashioned primarily in response to salient cultural images, then two critical questions arise (Kleppner, 1970; McCormick 1974): (1) how do ethnocultural identifications become political ones? and (2) under what conditions are they most likely to influence political behavior?

To answer the first question, we propose three complementary linkages between the cultural and political identifications of Americans (McCormick 1974; Swierenga 1990). One is that negative (and/or positive) reference group feelings determine political behavior. This explanation argues that Americans take political sides in order to oppose those racial-ethnic and religious groups they dislike. For instance, it may be argued that since 1964, America's racial and ethnic groups have been coalescing into two partisan camps: a Republican camp composed of those groups who claim European ancestry or share a similar system of cultural values, versus a Democratic camp increasingly dependent on the support of racial minorities. According to this logic, Asians would be mostly independent because of their inability to identify with either racial coalition.

A second explanation (McCormick 1974, 359) contends that "political affiliations reflect differences in religious beliefs and worldviews." According to this interpretation, America's two major parties have been characterized as directing their moral appeals to two distinct clusters of religious groups. A Republican cluster has typically been characterized as puritan, evangelical, and pietistic. A Democratic cluster has been characterized as liturgical, nonevangelical, and ritualistic. However, it is becoming increasingly clear that although differences in church doctrine and practice within Christendom (and Judaism) are still important, these differences are reinforced by long-standing racial, ethnic, and sectional divisions, which American church denominations have historically reflected. In other words, most religious denominations seem to embody and preserve varying degrees of ethnocentrism and ethnocultural traditions. Thus members of predominantly northern and moralistic Protestant denominations have tended to register and vote Republican and/or Independent; while members of predominantly southern and traditionalistic Protestant denominations have tended to register and vote Democratic, at least in state and local elections (Lieske, 1988a). American Catholics, on the other hand, seem to be dividing their partisan loyalties because of emerging religious and social cross-pressures—namely, those that derive from tradition and religious orthodoxy versus those that are based on rising affluence and recent reforms in doctrine and liturgy that have helped to "protestantize" the American Catholic church (Welch and Leege 1991). Finally, more secular or unchurched groups have tended to register as Democrat and Independent and to cross party lines (Wald 1987).

A third explanation is cultural dominance. This interpretation contends that ethnocultural groups often pursue political means to extend their own cultural practices or protect them from attack. Issues of cultural dominance include, for example, bilingual education, illegal immigration, and cultural life-style issues such as urban crime, moral education, abortion, homosexual rights, and drug abuse. All other things being equal, it appears that moralistic groups and cultures have tended to register and vote Republican because of the Republican party's historical image as representing American nationalism and cultural orthodoxy (Lieske 1988a). Conversely, it is apparent that traditionalistic groups and cultures have tended to register and vote Democrat because of the Democratic party's historical image as the party of out-groups, minority rights, and cultural laissez-faire.

To answer the second question (i.e., the conditions that enhance cultural influences), we propose four conditions that Kleppner (1970) found to hold in his study of midwestern voting patterns. One condition concerns the extent of cultural heterogeneity versus homogeneity. As Kleppner (1970, 101) notes, cultural "perspectives are more likely to be politically salient in a culturally pluralistic society than in a homogeneous one." If true, this hypothesis may help to explain why the highest levels of white support for Jesse Jackson's candidacy in the 1988 Democratic primaries occurred in culturally homogeneous states like Minnesota (1.3 percent black) and Vermont (0.2 percent black). A second condition concerns the extent to which different cultural groups are committed to conflicting value systems. The presence of this condition on the abortion issue, for example, may help to explain why it reverberates not only among the pro-life Christian right but also the pro-choice secular left. Yet a third condition relates to the presence or absence of a commonly shared value, or a common negative referent, which could cut across divergent value systems. This condition may help to explain why the Italians in Boston and New York tend to vote Republican in state and local elections, while the Irish vote Democratic. It may also explain why both groups tend to vote Republican at the presidential level in New York (Lieske 1988b). A fourth and final condition concerns the role of political leaders, which we are about to address. Thus, Kleppner suggests that cultural conflicts attain political expression only when the involved groups perceive the relationship between them and the available political alternatives.

From Statics to Dynamics: Political Elites and the Manipulation of Cultural Symbols

Social differences and cultural norms do not happen to be bases for political action; rather, in the same way that public problems become political issues, latent group differences must be transformed into active political cleavages (Zelniker and Kahan 1976). This realization was at the heart of two major criticisms of the political culture studies conducted during the 1960s. *The Civic Culture* treated its object of inquiry, the citizenry's fundamental political outlook, as a relatively enduring orientation toward the political system. Though not immune to the forces of change, values acquired the status of cultural norms by the very fact that they were transmitted, learned, and widely shared over a substantial period of time (Devine 1972, 6). This conservative assumption became problematic as evidence accumulated that supposedly foundational political attitudes were highly responsive to the stimulus of political events. In addition to the problem of dynamics, cultural analyses have not adequately identified the mechanisms by which subcultural differences were politicized. As Giovanni Sartori (1969) observed in an acute critique of political sociology, most analysts were content to accept social group differences as independent influences on political behavior without specifying the origins of politicized group consciousness. Rather than explaining away these social conflicts as exogenous factors, he argued, the task of political scientists should include investigating the processes by which members of collectivities forged (or failed to forge) durable loyalties to parties and other political movements.

For culture to reclaim a large role in political behavior research, it will be necessary to address both the origins and the dynamics of politicized group differences. In our view, both processes are tied to the actions of elites who manipulate symbols and/or policies that encourage individuals to develop "us" versus "them" distinctions. By structuring consciousness in this manner, elites promote the formation of coalitions based on a positive sense of in-group identity and/or a reaction to a perceived threat from another group. Elites may select from a wide array of techniques used to heighten and politicize group awareness. The manipulation of symbols may stimulate consciousness, thus raising the salience of an issue or problem while simultaneously defining it in terms likely to appeal to a particular social group. The aspirations of cultural groups may also be attached to a party or movement when the latter bestows recognition through cooptation of activists for public office. Even more directly, government may stimulate political conflict by distributive and redistributive practices that benefit or impede selected cultural groups. Regardless of the technique, the intended goal is to instill a positive valence for the party among the target social group and thereby to induce group members to regard it as the natural political expression of their interests and values.

Cultural mobilization is commonly engaged to raise minority movements to political prominence. Perhaps the best recent example of such issue entrepreneurship was the sustained campaign by conservatives to replace the dominant New Deal alignment with a New Right majority. This movement had its roots in the Goldwater campaign of 1964. By staking out clear and extreme positions on a wide range of issues and positions, Goldwater hoped to crystallize what conservative strategists confidently assumed was a hidden Republican majority in the electorate. The attempt to forge a conservative electoral majority continued apace four years later with the third-party candidacy of George Wallace. Wallace rallied support around his platform by attacking war protesters, radical students, intellectuals, and government bureaucrats. A similar attack, aimed especially at radicals and the press, was part of the Nixon administration's attempt to drive the Silent Majority of decent, law-abiding, reverent Americans into the arms of the Republican party (Phillips 1969). Although derailed by the Watergate affair, the campaign to raise the Republicans to majority-party status resumed under different auspices during the Carter presidency. A handful of conservative activists set out to construct a New Right by blending militant anticommunism, free-market economics and cultural traditionalism into a popular conservatism that would dominate the national agenda (Crawford 1980; Blumenthal 1986). The election of Ronald Reagan to the presidency and the subsequent redefinition of the public interest are partial testaments to the success of these efforts. Some, political columnists and cartoonists among them, have suggested that the main reason the Moral Majority was disbanded is that President Bush's Republican party had taken over its agenda.

Cultural symbols may also be employed to purify or affirm a majority coalition rather than to defeat an ascendant alignment. This strategy is particularly likely in a complex multicultural society such as the United States where group loyalties may shift in response to decisive government actions. In his classic work *The Future of American Politics* (1952), Samuel Lubell compares group attachments to American parties to a political solar system. The minority moon, at that point the Republicans, shone in reflected brilliance to the heat generated in the majority sun, the Democrats. The political story of an age, then, is that of the group conflicts in the majority party and in the minority party's ability to catch those whose ways are most violently exploded by the dominant groups in the coalition.

The problem was given formal treatment in Luce and Rogow's (1956) seminal examination of unwieldy coalitions in legislative bodies. The further a majority party moves from a minimal majority toward a two-thirds majority, the more difficult it becomes to maintain party discipline on roll-call votes. Thus, part of the Democrats' problem in the late stages of the New Deal was that they won by such large margins that a "conservative coalition" with Republicans became, mathematically and psychologically, increasingly probable.

The problem was given practical treatment by the dilemmas of the Kennedy entourage (White 1961, 1969). The Democratic party of the 1950s constituted an unwieldy presidential coalition of urban ethnic Catholics, organized labor, intellectual liberals and Jews, southern Bourbon traditionalists, the Jeffersonian Democrats who constituted the traditional core of the party in many midwestern states, and a very few blacks. It was a massive majority, but it was so culturally diverse that it could not be held together. Southerners bolted first in 1948, and from then on many southern states regularly appeared in the Republican presidential column. The Jeffersonian Democrats were wary of the new power of labor and intellectuals, and had always been suspicious of big-city ethnic Catholics. The problem was not how to hold the coalition together but how to maintain a more culturally compatible but smaller winning coalition.

The key component, according to Theodore Sorenson's memo at the 1956 convention, was Catholic communal identity—a Kennedy on the ticket would mobilize sufficient numbers of Catholics in the key electoral college states to spell Democratic victory. When, in 1960, the strategy was put to its first test, the Democrats barely won—and only through a marriage of convenience with a southern branch of the party that was culturally repulsive to the Kennedy entourage. How to jettison that branch and mobilize new elements of a coalition that could be slightly more than a minimal majority? The embrace of both the "war on poverty," first a Kennedy creation, and the civil rights movement became a key element in the strategy for a svelte majority (cf. Lemann 1988, 1989, for other insights on the Kennedy and Johnson strategies). Ethnic Catholics would stay with a Kennedy and would drag labor along with them. Intellectual liberals created ideas but constituted little electoral strength in and of themselves. Blacks were there to be mobilized. And poor whites, whether in the hills of Appalachia or in their capital cities of Akron and Flint, were also there to be mobilized. The strategy, of course, assumed that a Kennedy would be on the ticket for the foreseeable future.

The contemporary Democratic party has gone in far different directions since the 1960s, of course, and is best understood under the symbols that attract those committed to cultural change and repel much of the party's Catholic base. Thus, Geraldine Ferraro and Mario Cuomo are both Italian Catholic neighbors yet poles apart culturally.

Elites may stimulate cultural conflicts for the express purpose of forestalling or preempting nascent coalitions that threaten established interests. Socialist pioneers in Britain commonly lamented the susceptibility of the British working class to ethnic and religious appeals—particularly those that painted Irish immigrants as job stealers—that undermined the electoral cohesion of the left's natural base. The exploitation of group differences in this way was also evident in the United States when the emergence of a biracial coalition between white tenant farmers and black sharecroppers threatened the hegemony of the Bourbon Democrats during the 1890s. As Schattschneider (1956, 201) noted in his recapitulation of this era, the southern Bourbons reacted to the Populist menace so strongly that they were willing to revive the tensions and animosities of the Civil War and Reconstruction in order to produce a noncompetitive, one-party, sectional southern political system that disenfranchised blacks and poor whites in nearly equal measure. Subsequent threats to southern solidarity were similarly derailed by race-baiting, an illustration of the use of politicized group differences to retard the emergence of alternative political movements.

We also note the phenomenon of inadvertent mobilization of cultural groups. The idea behind this concept recognizes that groups may acquire a sense of common political interest by diffusion or imitation. As an example, the ethnic revival among white nationality groups during the 1960s and 1970s is commonly credited to the black-consciousness movement. Whites observed the apparent success of blacks in gaining access to the national agenda and adopted similar tactics to justify their own claims. This group consciousness was fundamentally reactive and can be understood as a case of countermobilization (cf. Kotler 1969; Keller 1968). In the same terms, it has been hypothesized that the mobilization of white evangelicals during the 1970s followed directly upon the apparent success of liberals in changing government policy toward military spending, sexual morality, and other salient dimensions of public policy (Wuthnow 1983). Describing these efforts as reactive is not to denigrate them or to deny the efforts of entrepreneurs to stimulate a sense of collective grievance; the label simply recognizes that the success of countermobilization derives from a sense that the group had to organize because its enemies had already done so.

The enduring political potency of cultural appeals, however stimulated, seems to contradict the widely held assumption that modern politics involves appeals to economic self-interest rather than to preferences rooted in primordial social and cultural forces. Indeed, students of religion and politics repeatedly confront the notion that cultural politics is an anachronism destined to be swept away with rising levels of education, urbanization, industrialization, and other components of modernization. To counter this claim, we would argue that the conditions of modernity, rather than diminishing cultural identity, actually intensify it. The rootlessness characteristic of modern society appears to generate an intensified need for identity that is best served by cultural groups. When thrown into the maelstrom of urban existence after years of sheltering in traditional structures, the rural-to-urban migrant often turns to those traditional structures as a means to sustain body and spirit. This response seems universal, as true of the Iranian Moslems who fell back upon fundamentalist Islam as a base of countermobilization against the regime of the shah as it is of the uprooted American fundamentalists who rallied to their churches when modern social practices challenged their cherished values about appropriate behavior. It can even be seen in the movement toward the devolution of European nation-states—for instance, Belgium into Flanders, Wallonia, and Brussels, or the Scot and Welsh national parties in the U.K., or separatism in Spain—simultaneously with the emergence of European economic and political identities.

This response may be inherent in modernity. When he attempted to explain the low level of political consciousness among the American working class, Friedrich Engels observed that capitalist production itself engendered disunity. "What capitalism did," he recognized, "was to bring into close physical and symbolic proximity workers who imbibed radically different cultures with their mothers' milk" (Benson 1979, 205). Interaction with persons from different cultural systems intensified the sense of in-group identity, rendering a common political outlook unlikely. Compared to economic classes, which were artificial aggregates that had to be created as units of consciousness, cultural groups had a palpable reality that enabled them to provide the workers "with identity, communality, protection from hostile others, solidarity and strength in pursuit of material interest, a sense of worthiness, value-systems to help orient their lives, life-styles to practice, a living space in which they can try to escape from alienation and feel at home" (Benson 1979, 206).

The result is that cultural appeals are likely to be powerful bases for political action, overwhelming other forces competing for political loyalty. The 1988 presidential campaign illustrates the thesis. The Republican candidate entered the campaign facing substantial public doubts about his capacity to provide strong leadership and with little in the way of a policy agenda. The Republican campaign succeeded in neutralizing these weaknesses by diverting attention to salient cultural images. Instead of the budget deficit, we heard about Willie Horton's parole, Michael Dukakis's reluctance to mandate the Pledge of Allegiance and unwillingness to support military action abroad. The Democrats' efforts to portray Dukakis in a favorable light as an immigrant child who had made good by dint of intelligence and effort could not withstand the stronger cultural appeals so adroitly manipulated by Republican advertising. The alacrity with which many congressional Democrats have rallied around a proposed constitutional amendment protecting the flag suggests that the party does not wish to be caught out again on the patriotism issue.

DATA NEEDS AND RESOURCES

Much of the cultural literature, especially studies that focus on ethnicity and religion, has been written by quantitative historians or urbanists who work with aggregate census data. The methodological problems associated with aggregate analysis are well known, and we shall not discuss them here. Rather, we wish to call attention to the types of survey data and mixed survey-aggregate measures that could advance our cultural understanding of American political behavior. We shall use religious variables to illustrate the problems of generating appropriate survey data for cultural studies. However, similar examples could be drawn from the literatures on race, ethnicity, and class life-style.

Cultural approaches to the understanding of American political behavior have languished, in part, because of competition for scarce space on large-scale sample surveys. Generally, scholars have tried to use standard demographic items such as religious/denominational affiliation, race or ethnicity, sex, group memberships, objective or subjective social class, and even occupation (such as farmer) to tap cultural dispositions. While not subject to the ecological fallacy like the aggregate data studies, survey-based studies have not routinely established intensity of identification or consciousness, perception of group norms, and sense of we-they boundaries that might derive from a survey response locating one in a demographic classification. But two efforts of this kind are noteworthy (Verba and Nie 1972; Miller, Gurin, Gurin, and Malanchuk 1981) because they demonstrate the range of additional items, beyond group affiliation, needed to establish cultural effects.

Noting that blacks showed a higher level of political participation than standard socioeconomic models would have predicted, Verba and Nie explored the phenomenon of group consciousness as a political mobilizer. To measure black group identity, they developed a summated index based on the frequency of black respondents' references to race on open-ended items.

Notwithstanding several critiques of this early approach, Miller et al. argued that group consciousness is indeed politically relevant and that it is best conceived as a multidimensional variable with four components: (1) *group identification*, "a psychological feeling of belonging to a particular stratum" (496); (2) *polar affect*, in-group affinity and out-group hostility; (3) *polar power*, satisfaction or dissatisfaction with the in-group's current social location relative to the out-group; and (4) *individual vs. system blame*, the extent to which the previous disparity in social location is attributable to "individual failings or to inequalities in the social system" (497). Using data from the 1972 and 1976 national election studies, they showed that when the components interact with each other, turnout is enhanced considerably beyond the level predicted by socioeconomic characteristics alone. But the operationalization of each component required variables that are not routinely on the National Election Studies (NES) or the General Social Survey (GSS). Neither do these studies provide data on the intermediate link—group norms—between identity and politicized polarization. Further, such historically significant cultural groupings as religious bodies and ethnicity could not be included in the test.

Given the preponderance of religious variables in historical explanations of American voting behavior, it would seem desirable to increase the numbers of religious measures included in NES and GSS surveys. These might include more sensitive measures of: (1) religious group identity; (2) both doctrinal beliefs and religious worldviews; and (3) the susceptibility of different groups to political mobilization.

First, religious group identity is poorly identified by existing questions about religion—Protestant, Catholic, Jewish, something else, or none—and denomination. The NES denominational master code, for example, dates to the mid-1950s; instructions to interviewers do not capture the nuances of creedal and social differences among different denominations. Nor do the codes reflect the processes of religious accretion and segmentation that have taken place since that time. The GSS, on the other hand, reconstructed its Protestant denominational master code in 1984 and is making valiant efforts to advise users of its strengths and limitations (Smith 1986, 1989). Its improvements, however, are concentrated on the fundamentalist/nonfundamentalist dimensions and offer little insights for those who are interested in different types of Catholics, or who feel that the more cerebral doctrinal differences implicit in the fundamentalist dimension are of less significance to understanding the sacramental, liturgical, and ethnic churches. Even regarding fundamentalism, GSS offers a questionable classification of Mormons as fundamentalists and lumps all nondenominational Christians together. If a more precise breakdown were provided, analysts could develop their own classification schemes.

What is also needed are measures that respect differences between national denominations and local churches. For example, on the basis of pronouncements by their leaders, Missouri Synod Lutherans are thought to be closer to the fundamentalist end of the spectrum; yet many Missouri Synod churches are as liturgical as Episcopal churches, as inclusive as Catholic state-churches, and as activist on issues of social justice as urban black Protestant churches. The investigator, in short, must know the local church as well as the national denomination. Such a demand is impractical on national surveys such as the GSS or NES.

Another alternative is to ask the respondent for a self-classification measure—both for the local church and for herself/himself. Thus, for Protestants, the respondent could be asked to label her/his church as fundamentalist, evangelical, Spirit-filled or charismatic, conservative, or liberal. Or a Catholic could be asked to classify her/his parish as traditionalist in outlook, reflecting the reforms of Vatican II, ethnic, or charismatic. And because congregations, parishes, or synagogues are seldom homogeneous in outlook, it may be important to ascertain the respondent's self-classification of her/his own outlook. By collecting information on the labels each respondent attaches to her/his denomination, congregation, and self, it is possible to measure the extent to which identity is reinforced and clear norms can be promulgated.

The second set of important religious variables concerns doctrinal beliefs and religious worldviews. Studies that measure doctrinal beliefs (for example, Glock and Stark 1965; Rothenberg and Newport 1984) have proven especially valuable for understanding the conservative, evangelical, and fundamentalist ends of the Protestant spectrum. In particular, questions about Christology, biblical literalism, and being born again have displayed discriminatory power with political variables (Smidt 1984, 1989a, 1989b).

Such studies, in the critique of Yinger (1969), however, capture which components of a doctrinal code are *not* held, but they do not tell *how* a person is religious or offer a perspective on the operating religious-symbol system of people for whom the investigator's doctrinal code is less relevant. In recent years, Yinger's critique has stimulated research on *religious imagery* (Greeley 1984; Hoffman 1988; Benson and Williams

1982) and on *foundational beliefs* (Benson and Williams 1982; Leege and Welch 1989; Leege 1989). The former uses proximity to words or choice between word-pairs to capture how people think about God; configurations are developed through factor analysis. Appropriate data for studying religious imagery are now available on GSS but not NES, although the range of configurations and their utility have not been fully established by peer review. Foundational beliefs measures have been developed through content analysis of open-ended responses or through an instrument that orders elements of ideas. Although the strengths and limitations of a foundational beliefs measure that ranges from individualistic religiosity to communitarian religiosity have met peer-review standards (Leege and Welch 1989; Leege 1989), it requires paper-and-pencil treatment and cannot be used on telephone surveys. Thus, both efforts at characterizing religious worldviews are in the developmental stage and, we suspect, are not likely to appear soon on the NES.

The third concern—susceptibility to group mobilization for political purposes—has already shown promise and would benefit from some additional refinements. It usually appears on NES or GSS as a salience-of-religion measure. Religious practices such as frequency of attendance tell us something about association with fellow religionists, as well as, by projection, exposure to common values and exhortations. Media-habits variables that monitor exposure to television evangelists also permit projections of possible political mobilization. The missing link, however, is a direct measure of political salience. To date, NES and GSS have asked a general measure of the salience of religion in one's life, but not a measure of political salience.

There are two promising directions for NES to consider. One (see Roozen, McKinney, and Carroll 1984) shows that religion at the congregational level has political salience when it is this-worldly and encourages its members, either individually or corporately, to involve themselves in public issues; religion has little political salience when it is otherworldly and the goal of congregations is either to provide sanctuary from an evil world or to transform the hearts of people in preparation for the afterlife. Several question wordings can capture these dimensions, and can offer a single general political-salience item.

Probably a better direction is to measure the political salience of one's religious values on each of a variety of issues and candidates. Rothenberg and Newport (1984) show powerful relationships between religion and politics through such specific salience measures. We would argue for a branching scheme that would ask for the respondent's sense, first, that moral teaching on specific issues by religious leaders (through public statements, letters, sermons) is appropriate or inappropriate; second, that the leaders attempt to offer such advice and admonition; and third, that the individual feels her/his religious values affect her/his viewpoints on each of a series of issues. This type of scheme will pin down mobilization both as a corporate and as an individual property.

Such measures take scarce space on national surveys. If it can be shown through NES pilot studies that such approaches to religious variables yield a high payoff relative to economic interests, perhaps we shall achieve the more balanced explanations of vote choice that seem to be warranted by research of the last decade or two.[*]

Instrument space is such a critical problem that many of the breakthroughs on cultural symbols in campaign research have derived not from nationwide sample surveys but from focused interviewing. Already in the mid-1950s, Merton, Fiske, and Kendall (1956) argued that a problem could be better mapped by assembling a small target group with common characteristics, giving them a common topic or stimulus, maintaining group discussion of the topic, and then content analyzing the symbols by which the group got a handle on the topic. Immediately this approach lent itself well to consumer research, because a proposed piece of advertising could serve as the stimulus. Market researchers, however, recognized the method as a powerful tool for understanding changes in cultural norms (Yankelovich 1981) and for classifying different cultural life-styles (Mitchell 1983). Political advertisers and handlers quickly latched onto this method and test-marketed campaign appeals both for general themes and spot advertisements (Schneider 1989; Edsall 1989). Focused interviewing is powerful, cheap, and efficiently specifies market segmentation for later sample surveys and campaign monitoring.

With perhaps the exception of Lane's intensive interviewing (Lane 1962), mainstream voting-behavior specialists have been reluctant to take advantage of small, nonrandom sample interviews as a basis for scholarly research. Perhaps our attention to generalizability has limited our ability to adapt costly variables from outside the predominant paradigms to our basic instruments for research, such as NES or GSS. Recent work, however, continues to demonstrate the value of intensive

---

[*] Following the establishment of a Working Group on Religious Measures, the 1989 NES Pilot Study included a variety of new or modified measures of religiosity. The earliest reports regarding these measures (Leege, Kellstedt, and Wald 1990 a and b) show the benefits of improved probing and classification of denominations, the importance of screening for social desirability on both affiliation and attendance, the utility of measures of salience and private devotional practices, and the consequences of using a biblical inerrancy measure rather than an infallibility measure. Few political effects, however, can be traced to local church trait classifications or self-classifications, as worded. Recent analyses also assess the utility of a battery of issue-specific pastoral cue-giving items, an increasingly important concern in understanding political mobilization in religious groups (Welch, Kellstedt, Leege, and Wald 1990). The 1990 congressional election survey reflects many of the changes. We anticipate that a much wider range of scholars will find the modified measures of religiosity useful in understanding American political behavior, especially in testing hypotheses from cultural theory.

interviews of purposive samples (Botsch 1980; Hochschild 1981). The values that locate people in different groups, that separate subcultures, and that define different political objectives clearly emerge from such studies.

One approach that seeks to contextualize "atomistic" responses involves attaching group-level demographic data to individual respondents' survey files. Currently, scholars must take county or minor civil division locations for each respondent and merge them with census data, such as proportion in agricultural occupations, proportion black, proportion unemployed, proportion Catholic, proportion foreign-born, and so on. Such approaches assume that a "cultural climate" can be indexed by demographic data and that such climates have political consequences. Salisbury, Sprague, and Weiher (1984) have shown the utility of such data mergers in a study of the religious characteristics of counties. To date, the NES have added aggregate electoral statistics to the data files for each survey respondent, but have had insufficient funds to support the routine addition of contextual census data.

To conclude, we believe that survey researchers need to devote much more thought to measuring the cultural factors that condition American voting behavior. Although our illustrations have been largely drawn from the religion and politics literature, we believe that they are also applicable to the study of other types of ethnocultural influence. It has been said that a scientific field only advances to the extent that its practitioners are able to measure and analyze the variables used to explain physical or mental reality. While much progress is being made in the field of political behavior, much work still remains to be done.

REFERENCES

Abramson, Paul R., John H. Aldrich, and David W. Rohde. 1987. *Change and Continuity in the 1984 Elections*. Rev. ed. Washington, D.C.: Congressional Quarterly Press.

Almond, Gabriel A., and Sidney Verba. 1963. *The Civic Culture*. Princeton, N.J.: Princeton University Press.

Banfield, Edward. 1974. *The Unheavenly City Revisited*. Boston: Little, Brown.

Beatty, Kathleen, and Oliver S. Walter. 1984. "Religious Belief and Practice: Evaluating Their Impact on Political Tolerance." *Public Opinion Quarterly* 48:318–29.

Beck, Paul Allen. 1979. "The Electoral Cycle and Patterns of American Politics." *British Journal of Political Science* 9:129–56.

Bellah, Robert N., R. Marsden, W. Sullivan, A. Swidler, and S. Tipton. 1985. *Habits of the Heart: Individualism and Commitment in American Life*. Berkeley: University of California Press.

Benson, Lee. 1961. *The Concept of Jacksonian Democracy: New York as a Test Case*. Princeton, N.J.: Princeton University Press.

———. 1979. "Marx's General and Middle-Range Theories of Social Conflict." In *Qualitative and Quantitative Social Research*, ed. Robert K. Merton, James S. Coleman, and Peter H. Rossi, 189–209. New York: The Free Press.

Benson, Peter L., and Dorothy L. Williams. 1982. *Religion on Capitol Hill: Myths and Realities*. New York: Harper & Row.

Berelson, Bernard R., P. F. Lazarsfeld, and W. N. McPhee. 1954. *Voting*. Chicago: University of Chicago Press.

Bettelheim, Bruno. 1986. "The Importance of Play." *The Atlantic* 259 (March): 35–46.

Blumenthal, Sidney. 1986. *Rise of the Counter-Establishment: From Conservative Ideology to Political Power*. New York: Times Books.

Botsch, Robert E. 1980. *We Shall Not Overcome: Populism and Southern Blue-Collar Workers*. Chapel Hill: University of North Carolina Press.

Brady, Henry E., and Paul M. Sniderman. 1985. "Attitude Attribution: A Group Basis for Political Reasoning." *American Political Science Review* 79: 1061–78.

Burnham, Walter Dean. 1970. *Critical Elections and the Mainsprings of American Politics*. New York: Norton.

Campbell, Angus, P. Converse, W. Miller, and D. Stokes. 1960. *The American Voter*. New York: Wiley.

Carmines, Edward G., and James A. Stimson. 1980. "The Two Faces of Issue Voting." *American Political Science Review* 74:78–91.

———. 1982. "Racial Issues and the Structure of Mass Belief Systems." *Journal of Politics* 44:3–20.

———. 1989. *Issue Evolution: Race and the Transformation of American Politics*. Princeton, N.J.: Princeton University Press.

Carmines, Edward G., Steven H. Renten, and James A. Stimson. 1984. "Events and Alignments: The Party Image Link." In *Controversies in Voting Behavior*, 2d ed., ed. Richard G. Niemi and Herbert F. Weisberg. Washington, D.C.: Congressional Quarterly Press.

Clark, Linda. 1989. "Hymn-Singing: A Congregation Making Faith." Occasional paper, Boston University School of Divinity.

Conover, Pamela J. 1984. "The Influence of Group Identifications on Political Perceptions and Evaluations." *Journal of Politics* 46:760–85.

———. 1985. "The Impact of Group Economic Interests on Political Evaluations." *American Politics Quarterly* 13:139–66.

———, and Stanley Feldman. 1981. "The Origins and Meaning of Liberal/Conservative Self-Identifications." *American Journal of Political Science* 25: 617–45.

Converse, Philip E. 1966. "Religion and Politics: The 1960 Election." In *Elections and the Political Order*, ed. Angus Campbell et al. New York: Wiley.

Crawford, Alan. 1980. *Thunder on the Right: The New Right and the Politics of Resentment*. New York: Pantheon.

Dahrendorf, Ralf. 1959. *Class and Class Conflict in Industrial Society*. Stanford, Calif.: Stanford University Press.

Devine, Donald J. 1972. *The Political Culture of the United States*. Boston: Little, Brown.

Douglas, Mary, and Aaron Wildavsky. 1983. *Risk and Culture: An Essay on the Selection of Technical and Environmental Dangers*. Berkeley: University of California Press.

Downs, Anthony. 1957. *An Economic Theory of Democracy*. New York: Harper & Row.

Dreitzel, Hans Peter. 1977. "On the Political Meaning of Culture." In *Beyond the Crisis*, ed. Norman Birnbaum. London: Oxford University Press.

Edsall, Thomas. 1989. "GOP Honing Wedges for Next Campaign." *The Washington Post*, February 26, 1989, A6–A7.

Elazar, Daniel J. 1970. *Cities of the Prairie*. New York: Basic Books.

———. 1984. *American Federalism*. 3d ed. New York: Harper & Row.

Erikson, Robert S., Norman R. Luttbeg, and Kent L. Tedin. 1988. *American Public Opinion: Its Origins, Content and Impact*. New York: Macmillan.

Fee, Joan L. 1976. "Party Identification among American Catholics." *Ethnicity* 3:53–69.

Fellows, James. 1983. "The New Immigrants: How They Are Affecting Us." *The Atlantic* 257 (November): 45–103.

Finkel, Steven E., and Howard A. Scarrow. 1985."Party Identification and Party Enrollment: The Difference and the Consequence." *Journal of Politics* 47:620–42.

Fiorina, Morris P. 1981. *Retrospective Voting in American National Elections*. New Haven: Yale University Press.

Flinn, Thomas A. 1988. "Party Systems and Electoral Behavior." Paper delivered at the annual meeting of the Southwest Social Science Association, Houston, Texas.

Formisano, Ronald P. 1971. *The Birth of Mass Political Parties: Michigan, 1827–1861*. Princeton, N.J.: Princeton University Press.

———. 1983. *The Transformation of Political Culture: Massachusetts Parties, 1790s–1840s*. New York: Oxford University Press.

Frolik, Joseph. 1988. "Melting Pot Has Problems." *Cleveland Plain Dealer*, December 16, 21A.

Garreau, Joel. 1981. *The Nine Nations of North America*. Boston: Houghton Mifflin.

Gastil, Raymond D. 1975. *Cultural Regions of the United States*. Seattle: University of Washington Press.

Geertz, Clifford. 1973. *The Interpretation of Culture*. New York: Basic Books.

Glenmary Research Center. 1982. *Church and Church Membership in the United States, 1980*. Atlanta.

Glock, Charles Y., and Rodney Stark. 1965. *Religion and Society in Tension*. Chicago: Rand McNally.

———. 1966. *Christian Beliefs and Anti-Semitism*. New York: Harper & Row.

Greeley, Andrew M. 1984. "Religious Imagery as a Predictor Variable in the General Social Survey." Paper presented at the annual meeting of the Society for the Scientific Study of Religion, Chicago, October.

Hamilton, Richard F. 1972. *Class and Politics in the United States*. New York: Wiley.

Handy, Robert T. 1990. "Protestant Theological Tensions and Political Styles in the Progressive Period." In *Religion and American Politics: From the Colonial Period to the 1980s*, ed. Mark A. Noll. New York: Oxford University Press.

Hays, Samuel. 1980. *American Political History as Social Analysis*. Knoxville: University of Tennessee Press.

Hechter, Michael. 1978. "Group Formation and the Cultural Division of Labor." *American Journal of Sociology* 84:293–318.

Himmelstein, Jerome. 1986. "The Social Basis of Antifeminism: Religious Networks and Culture." *Journal for the Scientific Study of Religion* 25 (March): 1–15.

Hochschild, Jennifer. 1981. *What's Fair? American Beliefs About Distributive Justice*. Cambridge, Mass.: Harvard University Press.

Hoffman, Thomas J. 1988. "Religion and the New Cultural Analysis: Political Culture, Religious Imagery, and Sociopolitical Attitudes." Paper presented at the American Political Science Association annual meeting, Washington, D.C., September.

Huckfeldt, Robert. 1986. *Politics in Context: Assimilation and Conflict in Urban Neighborhoods*. New York: Agathon Press.

———, and John Sprague. 1987. "Networks in Context: The Social Flow of Political Information." *American Political Science Review* 81:1197–1216.

———. 1988. "Choice, Social Structure, and Political Information: The Informational Coercion of Minorities." *American Journal of Political Science* 32: 467–82.

Hunter, James D. 1987. *Evangelicalism: The Coming Generation*. Chicago: University of Chicago Press.

Independent Sector. 1988. *From Belief to Commitment: The Activities and Finances of Religious Congregations in the United States. Summary Report*. Washington, D.C.

Inglehart, Ronald. 1971. "The Silent Revolution in Europe: Intergenerational Change in Post-Industrial Societies." *American Political Science Review* 65: 991–1017.

———. 1988. "The Renaissance of Political Culture: Central Values, Political Economy, and Stable Democracy." Paper delivered at the annual meeting of the American Political Science Association, Chicago.

Jensen, Richard. 1971. *The Winning of the Midwest: Social and Political Conflict, 1888–96*. Princeton, N.J.: Princeton University Press.

Kahan, Michael, David Butler, and Donald Stokes. 1966. "On the Analytical Division of Social Class." *British Journal of Sociology* 17:122–32.

Katz, Elihu, and Paul F. Lazarsfeld. 1955. *Personal Influence*. Glencoe, Ill.: The Free Press.

Keller, Suzanne. 1968. *The Urban Neighborhood: A Sociological Perspective*. New York: Random House.

Kelley, Dean M. 1977. *Why Conservative Churches Are Growing*. 2d ed. New York: Harper & Row.

Kelley, Robert. 1979. *The Cultural Pattern in American Politics*. New York: Knopf.

Kellstedt, Lyman A. 1984. "Religion and Politics: The Measurement of Evangelicalism." Paper presented to the annual meeting of the American Political Science Association, Washington, D.C., August 30–September 2.

———. 1989. "Religion and Partisan Realignment." Paper presented at the annual meeting of the Midwest Political Science Association, Chicago, April.

Key, V. O., Jr. 1949. *Southern Politics in State and Nation*. New York: Knopf.

Kleppner, Paul. 1970. *The Cross of Culture: A Social Analysis of Midwestern Politics, 1850–1900*. New York: The Free Press.

———. 1979. *The Third Electoral System, 1853–1892: Parties, Voters, and Political Cultures*. Chapel Hill: University of North Carolina Press.

———. 1982. *Who Voted? The Dynamics of Electoral Turnover, 1870–1980*. New York: Praeger.

Knoke, David. 1974. "Religion, Stratification, and Politics: America in the 1960's." *American Journal of Political Science* 18:331–46.

Kolbe, Richard L. 1975. "Culture, Political Parties, and Voting Behavior." *Polity* 8:241–68.

Kotler, Milton. 1969. *Neighborhood Governments: The Local Foundation of Political Life*. Indianapolis: Bobbs-Merrill.

Kramer, Gerald H. 1971. "Short-Term Fluctuations in U.S. Voting Behavior, 1896–1964." *American Political Science Review* 65:131–43.

Ladd, Everett C. 1978. *Where Have All the Voters Gone?* New York: W. W. Norton.

Lane, Robert E. 1962. *Political Ideology*. New York: The Free Press.

Lasswell, Harold D., and Abraham Kaplan. 1950. *Power and Society: A Framework for Political Inquiry*. New Haven: Yale University Press.

Lazarsfeld, Paul F., B. R. Berelson, and H. Gaudet. *The People's Choice*. New York: Columbia University Press, 1944.

Leege, David C. 1988. "Catholics and the Civic Order: Parish Participation, Politics, and Civic Participation." *Review of Politics* 50:704–37.

———. 1989. "Toward a Mental Measure of Religiosity in Research on Religion and Politics." In *Religion and Political Behavior in the United States*, ed. Ted G. Jelen. New York: Praeger.

———, and Joseph Gremillion. 1986. "The People, Their Pastors, and the Church: Viewpoints on Church Policies and Positions." *Notre Dame Study of Catholic Parish Life Report No. 7*. Notre Dame, Ind.: University of Notre Dame.

———, and Michael R. Welch. 1989. "Religious Roots of Political Orientations: Variations among American Catholic Parishioners." *Journal of Politics* 51:137–62.

———, Lyman A. Kellstedt, and Kenneth D. Wald. 1990. "Religion and Politics: A Report on Measures of Religiosity in the 1989 NES Pilot Study." Paper delivered at the annual meeting of the Midwest Political Science Association, Chicago, April.

———. 1990. "Supplement to Religion and Politics." Paper delivered to 1990 Planning Committee, NES, Ann Arbor, Michigan, May.

Lemann, Nicholas. 1988. "Battleground: The Inside Story of the Wars Behind the War on Poverty." *The Atlantic* 262 (December): 37–56.

———. 1989. "The Unfinished War." *The Atlantic* 263 (January): 52–68.

Lenski, Gerhard. 1963. *The Religious Factor*. New York: Doubleday.

Lichter, S. R., S. Rothman, and L. Lichter. 1986. *The Media Elite: America's New Power Brokers*. Bethesda, Md.: Adler & Adler.

Liebman, Robert C. 1983. "Mobilizing the Moral Majority." In *The New Christian Right*, ed. Robert C. Liebman and Robert Wuthnow, 49–73. New York: Aldine.

Lieske, Joel. 1988a. "The Cultural Origins of Political Partisanship." Paper delivered at the annual meeting of the Western Political Science Association, San Francisco.

———. 1988b. "The Cultural Nexus in U.S. Presidential Elections." Paper delivered at the annual meeting of the American Political Science Association, Washington, D.C.

———, and Jan William Hillard. 1984. "The Racial Factor in Urban Elections." *Western Political Quarterly* 37:545–63.

Lijphart, Arend. 1968. *The Politics of Accommodation: Pluralism and Democracy in the Netherlands*. Berkeley: University of California Press.

———. 1979. "Religious vs. Linguistic vs. Class Voting." *American Political Science Review* 73:442–58.

Lipset, Seymour Martin. 1964. "Religion and Politics in the American Past and Present." In *Religion and Social Conflict*, ed. Robert Lee and Martin E. Marty. New York: Oxford University Press.

———, and Stein Rokkan, eds. 1967. *Party Systems and Voter Alignments*. New York: The Free Press.

Lovrich, Nicholas P., Jr., Byron W. Daynes, and Laura Ginger. 1980. "Public Policy and the Effects of Historical Cultural Phenomena: The Case of Indiana." *Publius* 10:111–25.

Lubell, Samuel. 1952. *The Future of American Politics*. New York: Harper Brothers.

Luce, R. Duncan, and Arnold A. Rogow. 1956. "A Game Theoretic Analysis of Congressional Power Distributions for a Stable Two-party System." *Behavioral Science* 1:83–95.

McCormick, Richard L. 1974. "Ethno-Cultural Interpretations of Nineteenth-Century American Voting Behavior." *Political Science Quarterly* 89: 351–77.

———. 1986. *The Party Period and Public Policy: American Politics from the Age of Jackson to the Progressive Era*. New York: Oxford University Press.

Matthews, Donald, and James Prothro. 1966. *Negroes and the New Southern Politics*. New York: Harcourt, Brace and World.

Merelman, Richard M. 1984. *Making Something of Ourselves: On Culture and Politics in the United States*. Berkeley: University of California Press.

Merton, Robert K., M. O. Fiske, and P. L. Kendall. 1956. *The Focused Interview*. New York: The Free Press.

Miller, Arthur H., Patricia Gurin, Gerald Gurin, and Oksana Malanchuk. 1981. "Group Consciousness and Political Participation." *American Journal of Political Science* 25:494–511.

Miller, Arthur H., Anne Hildreth, and Christopher Wlezien. 1988. "Social Group Dynamics of Political Evaluations." Paper presented to the annual meeting of the Midwest Political Science Association, Chicago, April 14–16.

Mitchell, Arnold. 1983. *The Nine American Lifestyles*. New York: Macmillan.

Morin, Richard. 1989. "The True Political Puppeteers: Pocketbooks and Partisan Ways." *The Washington Post National Weekly Edition*. February 20–26, 1989, 37.

Morris, Aldon. 1984. *The Origins of the Civil Rights Movement*. New York: The Free Press.

Myrdal, Gunnar. 1944. *An American Dilemma*. New York: Harper & Row.

Ornstein, Norman, A. Kohut, and L. McCarthy. 1988. *The People, the Press, and Politics*. Reading, Mass.: Addison-Wesley.

Parsons, Talcott. 1959. " 'Voting' and the Equilibrium of the American Political System." In *American Political Behavior*, ed. Eugene Burdick and Arthur Brodbeck, 80–120. Glencoe, Ill.: The Free Press.

Penning, James M. 1988. "The Political Behavior of American Catholics: An Assessment of the Impact of Group Integration vs. Group Identification." *Western Political Quarterly* 41:289–308.

Phillips, Kevin J. 1969. *The Emerging Republican Majority*. New York: Doubleday Anchor.

Powell, G. Bingham. 1982. *Contemporary Democracies: Participation, Stability, and Violence*. Cambridge, Mass.: Harvard University Press.

Raftery, Susan R., and David C. Leege. 1989. "Catechesis, Religious Education, and the Parish." *Notre Dame Study of Catholic Parish Life Report No. 14*. Notre Dame, Ind.: University of Notre Dame.

Rainey, Jane G. 1981. " 'Stand Up for Jesus': A Case Study of Confrontation and Cultural Encounter in the Educational Politics of the Christian Right." Paper presented to the annual meeting of the Southern Political Science Association, Memphis, Tenn., November 5–7.

Robbins, Jonathan. 1989. "Geodemographics: The New Magic." In *Campaigns and Elections*, ed. Larry Sabato, 106–25. Glenview, Ill.: Scott, Foresman.

Rokeach, Milton. 1969. "I. Value Systems in Religion." *Review of Religious Research* 11:3–23; "II. Religious Values and Social Compassion." *Review of Religious Research* 11:24–39.

Roozen, David A., W. McKinney, and J. W. Carroll. 1984. *Varieties of Religious Presence: Mission in Public Life*. New York: Pilgrim Press.

Rose, Richard, and Derek Urwin. "Social Cohesion, Political Parties, and Strains in Regimes." *Comparative Political Studies* 2:7–67.

Rothenberg, Stuart, and Frank Newport. 1984. *The Evangelical Voter*. Washington, D.C.: Free Congress Education and Research Foundation.

Salisbury, Robert, John Sprague, and Gregory Weiher. 1986. "Does Religious Pluralism Make a Difference? Interactions among Context, Attendance, and Political Behavior." Paper delivered at the annual meeting of the American Political Science Association, Washington, D.C.

Sartori, Giovanni. 1969. "From the Sociology of Politics to Political Sociology." In *Politics and the Social Sciences*, ed. Seymour Martin Lipset, 65–100. New York: Oxford University Press.

Schattschneider, E. E. 1956. "United States: The Functional Approach to Party Government." In *Modern Political Parties*, ed. Sigmund Neumann, 194–218. Chicago: University of Chicago Press.

Schneider, William. 1988. "An Insider's View of the Election." *The Atlantic* 262 (July): 29–57.

———. 1989. "JFK's Children: The Class of '74." *The Atlantic* 263 (March): 35–58.

Searle, Mark, and David C. Leege. 1985. "Of Piety and Planning: Liturgy, the Parishioners, and the Professionals." *Notre Dame Study of Catholic Parish Life Report No. 6*. Notre Dame, Ind.: University of Notre Dame.

Sears, David O., and Jack Citrin. 1982. *Tax Revolt: Something for Nothing in California*. Cambridge, Mass.: Harvard University Press.

Shafer, Byron E. 1985. "The New Cultural Politics." *PS* 18:221–31.

Silbey, Joel H., A. G. Bogue, and W. H. Flanigan, eds. 1978. *The History of American Electoral Behavior*. Princeton, N.J.: Princeton University Press.

Smidt, Corwin. 1984. "Evangelicals within Contemporary American Politics: Differentiating between Fundamentalist and Non-Fundamentalist Evangelicals." *Western Political Quarterly* 41:601–20.

———. 1989. " 'Praise the Lord' Politics: A Comparative Analysis of the Social Characteristics and Political Views of American Evangelical and Charismatic Christians." *Sociological Analysis* 50:53–72.

Smith, Tom W. 1986. "Classifying Protestant Denominations." GSS Technical Report No. 67, October. Chicago: National Opinion Research Center.

———. 1988. "Counting Flocks and Lost Sheep: Trends in Religious Preference since World War II." GSS Social Change Report No. 26, February. Chicago: National Opinion Research Center.

Stark, Rodney, and Williams S. Bainbridge. 1985. *The Future of Religion*. Berkeley: University of California Press.

Swierenga, Robert P. 1990. "Religion and Political Behavior in the Nineteenth Century: Voting, Values, Cultures." In *Religion and American Politics: From the Colonial Period to the 1980s*, ed. Mark A. Noll. New York: Oxford University Press.

Times-Mirror. 1988. "The People, the Press and Politics: Post Election Typology Survey." Unpublished report, November.

Tufte, Edward R. 1978. *Political Control of the Economy*. Princeton, N.J.: Princeton University Press.

Turner, Helen Lee, and James L. Guth. 1989. "The Politics of Armageddon." In *Religion and Political Behavior in the United States*, ed. Ted G. Jelen. New York: Praeger.

Verba, Sidney, and Norman H. Nie. 1972. *Participation in America*. New York: Harper & Row.

Wald, Kenneth D. 1982. "Stratification and Voting Behavior." *Comparative Political Studies* 15:57–83.

———. 1987. *Religion and Politics in the United States*. New York: St. Martin's Press.

———. Forthcoming. "Ministering to the Nation: The Campaigns of Jesse Jackson and Pat Robertson." In *Nominating the President 1988*, ed. Emmett H. Buell and Lee Sigelman. Knoxville: University of Tennessee Press.

———, and Michael B. Lupfer. 1987. " 'Human Nature' in Mass Political Thought." *Social Science Quarterly* 68:19–33.

———, D. E. Owen, and S. S. Hill. 1988. "Churches as Political Communities." *American Political Science Review* 82:531–48.

Weiss, Michael J. 1988. *The Clustering of America*. New York: Harper & Row.

Welch, Michael R., and David C. Leege. 1988. "Religious Predictors of Catholic Parishioners' Sociopolitical Attitudes: Devotional Style, Closeness to God, Imagery, and Agentic/Communal Religious Identity." *Journal for the Scientific Study of Religion* 27:536–52.

———. 1991. "Dual Reference Groups and Political Orientations: An Examination of Evangelically-Oriented Catholics. *American Journal of Political Science* 35:28–56.

———, Lyman A. Kellstedt, David C. Leege, and Kenneth D. Wald. 1990. "Are the Sheep Hearing the Shepherds?: Pastoral Cues, Congregational Responses, and Political Communication Processes." Unpublished paper, Notre Dame, Indiana.

White, John Kenneth. 1988. *The New Politics of Old Values.* Hanover, N.H.: University Press of New England.

White, Theodore H. 1961. *The Making of the President, 1960.* New York: Atheneum.

———. 1969. *The Making of the President, 1968.* New York: Atheneum.

Wilcox, Clyde. 1989. "The Fundamentalist Voter: Politicized Religious Identity and Political Attitudes and Behavior." *Review of Religious Research* 31: 54–67.

Wildavsky, Aaron. 1987. "Choosing Preferences by Constructing Institutions: A Cultural Theory of Preference Formation." *American Political Science Review* 81:3–21.

Wuthnow, Robert. 1973. "Religious Commitment and Conservatism: In Search of an Elusive Relationship." In *Religion in Sociological Perspective*, ed. Charles Y. Glock, 117–32. Belmont, Calif.: Wadsworth.

———. 1983. "The Political Rebirth of American Evangelicals." In *The New Christian Right*, ed. Robert C. Liebman and Robert Wuthnow, 167–85. New York: Aldine.

Yankelovich, Daniel. 1984. *New Rules: Searching for Self-Fulfillment in a World Turned Upside Down.* New York: Random House.

Yinger, Milton. 1969. "A Structural Examination of Religion." *Journal for the Scientific Study of Religion* 8:88–99.

Zelniker, Shimshon, and Michael Kahan. 1976. "Religion and Nascent Cleavages: The Case of Israel's National Religious Party." *Comparative Politics* 9 (October): 21–43.

Notes on Contributors

Pamela Johnston Conover teaches political science at the University of North Carolina at Chapel Hill. She received her Ph.D. from the University of Minnesota in 1979. She coauthored *Feminism and the New Right* and has published scholarly articles in a variety of social science journals.

M. Margaret Conway teaches political science at the University of Florida. She received her Ph.D. from Indiana University in 1965. She has written several books, including *Political Participation in the United States* (1985, 1991) and *American Political Parties: Stability and Change* (1984). She has also published scholarly articles in the *American Political Science Review* and other journals.

William Crotty is professor of political science at Northwestern University. He received his Ph.D. from the University of North Carolina at Chapel Hill in 1964. His areas of interest include political parties and election processes, policy-making, and American and comparative governing institutions. He has served as president of the Political Organizations and Parties Section of the American Political Science Organization, the Midwest Political Science Association, and the Policy Studies Organization. He is the author of a number of articles and books, including *Decision for the Democrats* (1978), *Party Reform* (1983), *The Party Game* (1985), *American Parties in Decline* (coauthor, 1980, 1984), *Presidential Primaries and Nominations* (coauthor, 1985), and *Political Parties in Local Areas* (coauthor, 1987). Professor Crotty has been the recipient of an American Political Science Association Fellowship to study the national political parties and he has served as a member of a number of commissions invited to observe elections and democratic processes in Latin America.

Jack Dennis teaches political science at the University of Wisconsin, Madison. He received his Ph.D. from the University of Chicago in 1962. He coauthored, with David Easton, *Children in the Political System* (1969) and edited *Socialization to Politics* (1973). In addition, he has published numerous scholarly articles in the *American Political Science Review* and other journals.

Betty Glad teaches political science at the University of South Carolina. She received her Ph.D. from the University of Chicago. She has written several books, including *The Psychological Dimensions of War* (editor and contributor, 1990), *Key Pittman: The Tragedy of a Senate Insider* (1986), *Jimmy Carter: In Search of the Great White House* (1980), and *Charles Evans Hughes and the Illusions Of Innocence: A Study in American Diplomacy* (1966). She has been a senior fellow of the National Endowment for the Humanities, president of the Presidency Research Group of the American Political Science Association, and vice president of the International Society for Political Psychology. At present she is cochair of the Psychopolitics Research Group of the International Political Science Association.

Doris A. Graber teaches political science at the University of Illinois, Chicago. She received her Ph.D. from Columbia University. She is the author of many books dealing with political communication, among them *Processing the News: How People Tame the Information Tide* (1988), *Verbal Behavior and Politics* (1976), and *Mass Media and American Politics* (1989). She is a founding member and chair of the political communications section of the American Political Science Association and is active in many other professional associations.

David C. Leege teaches political science and directs the Program for Research on Religion, Church, and Society at the University of Notre Dame. He received his Ph.D. from Indiana University in 1965. He has coauthored *Political Research: Design, Measurement, and Analysis* (1974), the fifteen-part *Report* series from the Notre Dame Study of Catholic Parish Life (1984-89), and numerous scholarly articles on religion and politics in the *Journal of Politics, American Journal of Political Science*, and *Journal for the Scientific Study of Religion*, among others. He currently chairs the Working Group on Religious Measures of the American National Election Studies and serves on NES's board of overseers.

Joel A. Lieske teaches political science at Cleveland State University. He received his Ph.D. from the University of North Carolina, Chapel Hill, in 1971. He has published numerous scholarly articles in the *American Political Science Review, Western Politics Quarterly, Political Methodology*, and *Public Opinion Quarterly*, among others.

Norman R. Luttbeg teaches political science at Texas A & M University. He received his Ph.D. from Michigan State University in 1965. He is the author or coauthor of several books, *American Public Opinion* (1988) and *American Electoral Behavior: 1952-1988* (1990) among them, was editor of *Public Opinion and Public Policy* (1981), and has written many scholarly articles.

Kenneth D. Wald is professor and chairman of the Department of Political Science at the University of Florida. Since receiving a Ph.D. from Washington University in 1976, he has concentrated on the role played by religion in mass political behavior. He is the author of *Crosses on the Ballot* (1983) and *Religion and Politics in the United States* (1987; 2d ed. 1991), and of numerous articles and book chapters. He has been the editor of *Religion & Politics*, the newsletter of the American Political Science Association's section of that name, and has served in the Working Group on Religious Measures of NES. He has held visiting teaching appointments at the University of Strathclyde in Glasgow and the Hebrew University of Jerusalem.